DISCOUNT TRAVEL HANDBOOK

Edited by Mary Lu Abbott

VACATION PUBLICATIONS
HOUSTON

DISCOUNT TRAVEL HANDBOOK

Edited by: Mary Lu Abbott

Art Direction and Cover Design: Fred W. Salzmann

Assistant Editor: Elizabeth Armstrong

Front cover photos by Mary Lu Abbott

Publisher's Note: This book contains information from many sources. Every effort has been made to verify the accuracy and authenticity of the information contained in this book. Although care and diligence have been used in preparation and review, the material is subject to change. It is published for general reference and the publisher does not guarantee the accuracy of the information.

Copyright© 1996 by Vacation Publications, Inc.

All rights reserved. No parts of this book may be reproduced without the written consent of Vacation Publications, Inc.

Published by Vacation Publications, Inc.
1502 Augusta Drive, Suite 415
Houston, TX 77057

Library of Congress Catalog Card Number: 95-62144
ISBN 0-9644216-3-1

Printed in the United States of America

VACATION PUBLICATIONS

The Contributors

Carol Barrington of Houston, TX, is a contributing editor of *Vacations* magazine and writes frequently for other national publications. She is a winner of the Lowell Thomas Travel Journalist of the Year award.

Carole Jacobs of Altadena, CA, is a contributing editor of *Vacations* magazine, writes for *Travel 50 & Beyond* and is travel editor at *Shape* magazine.

Joy Schaleben Lewis of Milwaukee, WI, is an award-winning writer who contributes frequently to national publications.

Sylvia McNair of Evanston, IL, is the author of a dozen books, including a series of children's travel publications and "Vacation Places Rated."

Stephen Morgan of Cambridge, MA, an editor at the *Boston Globe*, writes for national publications and received the Pacific Asia Travel Association Gold Award in 1991.

Everett Potter of Pelham, NY, a syndicated travel columnist, writes on consumer issues for *Vacations* magazine and other national publications. In 1993 and 1994, his service-oriented articles won Lowell Thomas Travel Journalism awards.

June Naylor Rodriguez of Fort Worth, TX, a features writer for the *Fort Worth Star-Telegram*, contributes frequently to *Vacations*, *Travel 50 & Beyond* and other national publications.

Lisa Rogak Shaw of Grafton, NH, who heads Williams Hill Publishing, is the author of "Moving to the Country Once and for All" and editor of "Sticks," a bimonthly newsletter for urbanites who want to move to the country.

Marcia Schnedler of Little Rock, AR, a syndicated senior travel columnist, is a contributing editor of *Travel 50 & Beyond* and the author of two books.

Judy Wade of Phoenix, AZ, is a contributing editor of *Travel 50 & Beyond*, writes frequently for other national publications and is a book author.

Table of Contents

Introduction 6

Fly There for Less
Chapter 1 11 Ways to Get the Lowest Airfares 8
Chapter 2 13 Questions to Ask Before You Book 12

Cutting the Cost of Lodging
Chapter 3 Checking Into Hotel Savings 18
Chapter 4 Slashing Hotel Costs 50 Percent 20
Chapter 5 The Boom in Low-Cost Lodging 24
Chapter 6 State Parks: Great Resorts, Great Prices 30

Deals on Wheels
Chapter 7 Curbing Car-Rental Costs 37

Getting the Lowest Cruise Rate
Chapter 8 Eight Ways to Sail for Less 42

Discount Travel Services
Chapter 9 Clubs Can Net Savings 49

Traveling Free — or Nearly So
Chapter 10 Be a Leader, a Host or a Speaker 52
Chapter 11 Tax-Deductible Volunteer Vacations 58

Seeing the USA for Free
Chapter 12 The Best Sightseeing From New York to Hawaii 65
Chapter 13 Getting Information: State Tourism Offices 74

Guide to Off-Season Discounts
Chapter 14 Sea Escapes 77
Chapter 15 City Getaways 86
Chapter 16 Mountain Highs 95
Chapter 17 Park Retreats 106
Chapter 18 Foreign Affairs 115
Chapter 19 Chart of U.S. and Foreign Travel Seasons 122

Bargain Hunter's Europe
Chapter 20 Cost-Cutting in Europe 125
Chapter 21 Beating the High Cost of Airfare 129
Chapter 22 Choosing a Tour 136
Chapter 23 Picking a Hotel 141
Chapter 24 Renting a Car 152
Chapter 25 Riding the Rails 158
Chapter 26 Boosting Your Buying Power 168
Chapter 27 Getting Around Town 174
Chapter 28 Seeing the Sights 179
Chapter 29 Dining Out for Less 182
Chapter 30 A Sampler of Dollar-Wise Travels: London,
  Paris and Switzerland 185
Chapter 31 Getting Information: European Tourist Offices 195

Savings for Singles
Chapter 32 How to Cut Surcharges When You Go Solo 198

Guide to Senior Discounts
Chapter 33 Senior Airline Discounts 202
Chapter 34 Senior Lodging Discounts 212
Chapter 35 Senior Car-Rental Discounts 217
Chapter 36 Senior Rail and Bus Discounts 220
Chapter 37 Senior City and State Discounts 224
Chapter 38 Senior Travel Clubs and Cards 226
Chapter 39 Low-Cost Learning Vacations 230
Chapter 40 Extended-Stay Vacations 234

Introduction

Frugality fuels the '90s. No one wants to pay full price for anything — and that goes for vacations, too. Everyone wants a bargain, a good deal, a discount of some kind.

Even in the spendthrift '80s, we at Vacation Publications were seeking value-oriented destinations, places where our readers' vacation dollars would go further. By the time the '90s dawned, we already were concentrating on money-saving travel, long before other travel publishers realized the mood of America had changed.

Over nearly a decade in our various travel publications — *Vacations*, *Travel 50 & Beyond* and *Cruises & Tours* — we have told readers how to save on airfares, hotels, rental cars, sightseeing, dining, tours and all other vacation components.

Now we have compiled all of our cost-cutting tips and advice into our first Money-Saving Guide, the "Discount Travel Handbook." In this one source, you will find everything you need to know to slash your travel costs, for vacation or business.

It takes a savvy traveler to ferret out the lowest prices these days, and you will become one using this book. Often the secret to finding bargains is simply knowing the right questions to ask, and we tell you, step by step.

The handbook is a savings guide to overall travel and to specific trips. For instance, you will learn how to get the best prices on airfares, hotel rooms and rental cars no matter where you go. Then, our Bargain Hunter's Europe section focuses on cutting costs of travel throughout the European countries.

Our Guide to Off-Season Discounts looks at the best seasons for savings at popular destinations around the world, and our Guide to Senior Discounts tells all the benefits you reap when you turn 50.

We even tell you how to travel for free — or as nearly so as possible.

Like all handbooks, this one is meant to be used repeatedly, to be your main resource in seeking out the best buys in travel. With the guidelines in this "Discount Travel Handbook," you'll never pay top dollar again for any trip.

— Mary Lu Abbott

P.S. Where applicable, we have given prices, often as examples of savings you can get by following our recommended action. We caution you that the specific prices quoted in this book are subject to change at any time. Use the prices as a planning guide and for comparisons, but before setting your travel budget, always check for updated costs.

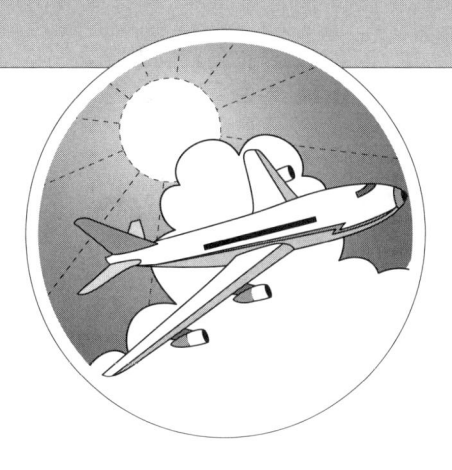

Fly There For Less

They say that getting there is half the fun, but this may not be the case if your airfare consumes half your travel budget. Approach your search for the lowest airfare with an open mind: The more flexible you are, the more money you'll save. The next two chapters will guide you to getting the lowest fare possible when you fly.

CHAPTER 1

11 Ways to Get The Lowest Airfares

With the increased number of special airfares and new airlines in the market, finding the lowest rate can be difficult and time-consuming.

The search is like a game: You want to get from Point A to Point B for the least amount of money as possible. Learn the following rules of the game and you'll reach your goal of finding the best bargains.

1. Travel midweek.

In general, the best days and times to travel are Tuesday-Thursday and late nights. In some markets, Saturdays are low-fare days. Check with your travel agent about specific peak times to your destination. You'll nearly always save by staying over a Saturday night.

2. Avoid peak seasons.

If you're going to Europe, airfares are highest in the summer and lowest in January and February. For the Caribbean and Mexico, fares are highest from Christmas to Easter. Domestic fares are not as season-driven; even for peak summer travel, you usually can find discounted fares at a savings.

3. Compare fares to area airports.

If your area of departure or arrival has more than one airport, the fares may differ. Check flights into all convenient airports. If all the low fares already are booked on flights into one airport, say Los Angeles International Airport, ask about low fares on flights into Long Beach, Orange County and Ontario airports. Also, you may discover a low-cost airline serving an alternative airport.

4. Be flexible about travel dates.

A promotional fare or a seasonal change may take effect a day or week after your planned departure, so always ask if there's a lower fare on another date close to when you want to travel. The more flexible you are about travel times, the greater the bargains you will find.

5. Plan ahead.

If you take advantage of advance-purchase fares, your savings can be dramatic. For example, on a weekday round trip between Chicago and Orlando, a full-fare ticket with no restrictions and no advance-purchase requirement cost $576 at this writing. The same ticket bought seven days in advance cost $308; a 21-day advance purchase with restrictions, including staying over Saturday night, was $248. The savings ranged from 47 percent to 57 percent.

6. Check special discounts.

Most airlines offer several lesser-known discount fares if you fit certain criteria. Among those eligible for specialty fares are: children (usually under age 12); youth (12-22, or 25 sometimes); seniors (usually 62 and up); military personnel; and travelers with a family emergency (may require the phone number of a hospital or funeral home, or presentation of an obituary).

7. Fly on holidays.

Planes often go empty on such major holidays as Thanksgiving Day and Christmas Day, even though the days before and after are some of the busiest for air travel. Depending on your destination, you may be able to fly on the holiday and still make dinner on time. The drawback is that you can't plan on these bargains. Promotional fares for these days normally are announced at the last minute, usually less than a week ahead; if flights are full, airlines won't offer the holiday fares.

8. Check low-cost carriers.

There's a growing number of new, small airlines that consistently undercut fares offered by the major carriers. Encouraged by the success of Southwest Airlines, most of these companies offer no-frills flights serving one region.

Their fares carry few to no restrictions (for example, none requires a Saturday-night stayover) and offer savings on one-way tickets and last-minute travel, which normally are expensive.

There are trade-offs. Few of these airlines serve meals, and most do not provide advance seating. Some may not be listed on travel agency computers, so you have to make the reservations yourself. Their service may be limited. They may not fly where you want to go — and if they do, they may fly there only on certain days of the week.

Still, if you can be flexible in your travel, the bargain fares are worth checking out. The following are some of the better-known low-cost airlines:

American Trans Air, based in Indianapolis, (800) 225-2995.
Carnival Air, based in Fort Lauderdale, FL, (800) 437-2110.
Frontier Airlines, based in Denver, (800) 432-1359.
Grand Airways, based in Las Vegas, (800) 634-6616.
Kiwi International Air Lines, based in Newark, NJ, (800) 538-5494.
Midway, based in Durham, NC, (800) 446-4392.
Reno Air, based in Reno, NV, (800) 736-6247.
Southwest Airlines, based in Dallas, (800) I-FLY-SWA.
Tower Air, based in New York, (800) 221-2500.
ValuJet, based in Atlanta, (800) 825-8538.
Vanguard, based in Kansas City, MO, (800) VANGUARD.
Western Pacific Airlines, based in Colorado Springs, CO, (800) 930-3030.

9. Consider consolidator tickets.

On international flights, consolidator tickets may be your best deal. Airlines calculate their excess seating capacity and sell those seats at deep discounts to consolidators, who add a markup but still sell the tickets at less than you can get from the airline.

For a full discussion of the pros and cons of consolidator tickets, see Chapter 21, "Beating the High Cost of Airfare," in Bargain Hunter's Europe section.

10. Check travel clubs and no-frills agencies.

These organizations give rebates to their customers, effectively giving you a savings even on discounted fares. But they are not full-service travel agencies. You do some of the work — finding your own flight at the best fare, sometimes even making the reservation. The travel club or no-frills agency writes your ticket and gives a rebate on the travel agent's commission. The rebate varies with the cost of the ticket, and some agencies set a required minimum price to qualify for a rebate. There may be an annual fee or service charge, so be sure your rebates will be worth the cost.

No-frills agencies include Travel Avenue, based in Chicago, (800) 333-3335, and Smart Traveller, based in Coconut Grove, FL, (800) 448-3338.

11. Look into charter flights and courier services.

When available, these two alternatives offer savings but carry numerous caveats. Charter flights are offered by wholesalers who lease planes from airlines; your arrangements are with the charter operator, not the airline. All tickets usually cost the same.

Charters often operate seasonally and target certain markets. For instance, you will find charters to Europe in the summer mainly from East Coast and West Coast cities. Charters go to the Caribbean in the winter, and sometimes year-round, from a variety of U.S. cities, but most notably in the North. And in ski season, you will find charters from major metropolitan areas to ski resorts in the Rocky Mountains and sometimes to Europe.

Disadvantages of charter flights include frequent delays, short-notice cancellations and the possibility that the charter operator will raise your fare as late as 10 days before you depart. You can book flights with charter operators, but it's best to go through a travel agent. For charters from your area, check newspaper travel sections or call a travel agent. Consolidators also sometimes have tickets for charter flights.

For a discussion about charters to Europe, see Chapter 21, "Beating the High Cost of Airfare."

Courier services operate to overseas destinations from main U.S. gateways, such as New York City and Los Angeles. The courier company provides you with

Take note!

☞ "Fly Rights: A Consumer Guide to Air Travel," published by the U.S. Department of Transportation, offers some "defensive flying" tips that will help your trip run smoother. For a copy, send $1.75 to Consumer Information Center, Department 133B, Pueblo, CO 81009.

a ticket at a deeply discounted price and uses your luggage allowance to transport materials to overseas clients quickly. To be a courier, you must be flexible about your travel time and be able to fly with carry-on luggage only. Also, you usually must return in one week.

To check out this option, look in the phone book under "Air Courier Services" for a firm in your area, or contact a broker such as Discount Travel International, (212) 362-8113, or Now Voyager, (212) 431-1616.

For a full discussion of this option, see Chapter 21, "Beating the High Cost of Airfare."

CHAPTER 2

13 Questions to Ask Before You Book

Securing the lowest possible fare and the most convenient service can require the talents of a Sherlock Holmes and the tenacity of Super Glue. You must persevere, stick to the task and use all manner of detective work to get the best deal aloft.

Unless you are totally flexible as to the day of the week that you travel, *and* plan to stay over a weekend, *and* don't mind the risk of cancellation penalties, *and* are booking 21 to 30 days in advance, you probably won't get the lowest possible fare. When the traveler's limitations come into play, that's when the task of getting a good deal becomes a real challenge.

To assist you through the maze of airline ticket purchasing, here are 13 pertinent questions to ask airline reservations agents before you book. Start your search with the major carrier in your market, but always check with competitors for a better fare or more convenient service at the same low fare.

1. What is the lowest fare for round-trip travel between Point A and Point B?

Don't be put off the track if the reservationist tries to pin you down to specific dates of travel before quoting a price. Tell her you are flexible on travel dates and that you can go when the fare is lowest.

The lowest fare offered for travel on a regularly scheduled airline is referred to as an APEX (advance-purchase excursion) or excursion fare. Special restrictions and limitations for these low fares will vary according to destination and carrier. Typically, you can expect restrictions such as an advance-purchase requirement of seven to 21 days, a minimum stay of seven days and maximum stay of 90 days.

Take note of the fare and all the restrictions.

2. Can I get a lower fare if...

Keep asking "what if" questions. Can I get a lower fare if I travel at a different time of day, if I go a different day of the week or if I extend my trip to include a Saturday night stayover? Is there a lower fare if I take a different itinerary? Are there alternate nearby airports with lower fares?

For those who don't mind some inconvenience, some airlines offer reduced fares on flights that make stops along a specific route generally dominated by non-stop flights. For example, travel from Point A on the West Coast to Point

B on the East Coast will cost a certain amount on non-stop flights, but flights involving stops or changes of planes may bring price breaks.

Traveling Mondays through Thursdays nearly always costs less than flying on weekends. Both days of the week and dates are important when checking for international flights because fares are tied to seasons. A difference of only one day can make the fare vary more than $100. If you can't be flexible on your travel dates, shop airlines that serve your destination. There's usually some variation in the dates that fares change from high season to what's called a shoulder season and then a low season.

These questions should lead you to a quote on the lowest, most restricted and least available fare in the market. Jot it down on your page of notes, along with all the booking and purchase requirements and cancellation penalties that it carries.

3. What's the lowest fare available on my preferred flight?

The hunt is on. You now know the airline's lowest fare, and your goal is to get as close to that as possible within the time frame you want to travel. Evaluate all the permutations of flight time, day of week, length of stay and cancellation penalties on the varying fares. Sift through the alternatives and select the one that's best for you.

Take note!

☞ **Mind your q's.** Airfares carry an alphabet soup of letter codes. Q fares usually are the lowest but are the hardest to get because only a limited number of seats on any given flight are sold at this fare. Y fares are the highest in coach cabin.

If the best available fare doesn't approach the lowest-fare-in-the-market quote already received, ask the reservations agent for the names of all airlines that fly the route you want. Before starting over with another carrier, it's wise to book the best deal you've found, as it may look more attractive when you've exhausted other possibilities. Don't give a credit card number at this stage — you may cancel if the price is right at another carrier. Reservations can be held at least 24 hours without payment of a fare.

When you've located the best available fare, know exactly what's covered so you can avoid surprises later. Nail down the specifics with more questions.

4. Are fees and taxes covered in the fare quoted?

You can talk to three different airlines serving the same route and get three different ticket prices for what will ultimately be the exact same fare. The discrepancy arises from whether an airline includes mandatory extra fees in its airfare quotations. Many airlines quote fares "plus taxes," so it's important to identify which taxes apply and how much they are.

At press time, international flights from the United States were subject to a minimum of about $20 in U.S. government fees and taxes. In many cases, you also will pay a U.S. airport facility charge and a security fee, and your destination airport may tack on charges. At press time, some round-trip fares to Europe carried fees of more than $50.

5. Does my flight require a change of planes?

Many travelers confuse flight terms used by airline reservationists. "Non-stop" means exactly that. "Direct" means that the plane will make one or more stops. "Change of plane" means what it says — and usually involves two flight numbers on your ticket. Some carriers dub change-of-plane flights as "direct" or "through" if the flight number remains the same, following a route of travel, not the specific plane.

Numerous carriers offer competitive service, so there's no need to deal with a time-consuming change of planes or even a stopover — unless such routing nets you a savings you want.

6. Are any of my flights on a commuter aircraft or a different carrier?

It is especially important to know your flight plan when making long-haul trips — transcontinental or trans-Pacific or trans-Atlantic — or when flying into smaller cities. If you will be changing planes, ask questions about your connecting service.

A number of major U.S. airlines today have affiliations with regional commuter carriers and international airlines allowing flight connections without a change in the carrier's name on your ticket. Under these "code-sharing" agreements, the carrier you book with may not operate all flight segments of your trip. For instance, when flying from New York City to Key West, FL, with American Airlines, you change to the smaller American Eagle commuter line in Miami. When flying from Houston to Rome with Continental Airlines, you go via Newark International Airport on a Continental flight operated by Alitalia Airlines.

Airlines are required to advise you when an itinerary will be changing carriers and/or using commuter aircraft. On commuter flights, which usually are in small planes, always ask about luggage restrictions. Small airplanes have less room for carry-on bags, and there may be weight limitations on luggage.

7. If there are any connections, how much time do I have between flights, and are there any later flights if I miss the first connection?

In the age of airline hub cities, connections are often inevitable. Avoid end-of-the-day flights, which can result in overnight layovers if you miss your connection.

With international travel, it is particularly important to watch connection times. Check carefully with the ticket agent or travel counselor for recommended international connection times for specific airports. It takes time to claim luggage, clear customs and immigration and make it to another flight, which often is in another terminal.

If you are changing carriers, a long hike or even a bus transit such as at New York's JFK International Airport may be required to move from one carrier to another.

Before you leave home, get a list of later flights and keep it handy in case you don't make that initial connection. This goes for travel either to your destination or on your return.

8. What happens if the fare goes up — or down — before my flight?

This is a most important question in today's volatile world of airfares. In most cases, if the fare goes up before the flight, the traveler will not be affected if he has already bought his ticket.

If a fare goes down — say a special promotion starts — airlines generally will reissue your ticket at the lower fare, giving a refund or credit for the difference that can be applied toward future flights. A service fee may be taken out of the refund. It's up to you to keep aware of promotions that beat your ticket price and call the airline.

9. When must I purchase the ticket?

Don't get caught as many people have by booking a seat at one rate only to find that it has increased anywhere from $10 to $200 by the time of purchase.

Most fares require that you purchase the ticket by a set deadline. Delaying purchase by even a day sometimes can result in your being subject to a higher fare. For the low-cost promotions, the deadline often is no later than 24 hours after making a reservation. The only way to positively lock in a certain fare is to make a purchase at the time of reservation.

If you have not paid by the deadline, your reservation may be automatically purged from the airline computers. To ensure that your reservation remains valid, always ask at the time you book how long you have before you must purchase the ticket or lose the reservation.

Take note!
☞ Did the airline lose your luggage or bump you from your flight, or did you encounter a less-than-helpful employee? Register your complaints with the Aviation Consumer Protection Division, C-75, U.S. Department of Transportation, 400 Seventh St. S.W., Washington, DC 20590.

If time allows between purchase of your ticket (via telephone with the use of a credit card) and your departure, airlines will mail the ticket to your home or office as requested. When time is short, you may have to pick up the ticket at the airport on departure. Or if working with a travel agent, the ticket may be issued and ready for you on the day of purchase.

10. Can I make my seat selection now?

Travelers can save time and hassle by getting a seat assignment at the time of ticket purchase. Many airlines allow seat selection within 30 days of flight departure. A few regional carriers and most commuters still don't offer advance seat selection.

11. Will a meal be served?

As airlines expand their cost-cutting maneuvers, meals aloft are changing.

You can expect sandwiches instead of hot meals at lunch and no meals on shorter flights. Find out the particulars of the in-flight meal service and eat on the ground accordingly, or pack a snack for midair hunger attacks. If you have particular dietary requirements, advise the booking agent and request a special meal. Most airlines offer a wide variety of special menus — low-fat, low-salt, kosher and vegetarian, for example. It's wise to reconfirm your meal request a few days before flying.

12. What documents will be required to enter or leave the countries on my itinerary?

Travel outside this country requires proof of your citizenship — not only as you enter another country but also when you return. Types of proof vary. For example, if you are traveling to Mexico, an original birth certificate or voter registration card is sufficient. If you are traveling to Western Europe, you will need a valid passport. And if Eastern European countries are on your itinerary, you may need a visa — a permit to enter granted by the country and stamped in your passport.

Check with your travel consultant for details on each country you will be visiting. Check with your air carrier if you will be overnighting along the route; you may need a transit visa.

The airlines are responsible for their passengers and normally check carefully for valid passports and visas when that is a requirement of the initial destination. You may arrive at the airport with a fully paid ticket, but if you don't have the proper documentation, you won't get on that flight.

13. Does this ticket entitle me to discounts on any other travel-related services?

International carriers regularly offer travel discounts to their passengers, but you may have to ask to get the information. These may be savings on hotels, rental cars and sightseeing.

Cutting the Cost Of Lodging

Whether you regard your hotel room as a mere place to sleep after a long day of sightseeing or a haven where you can retreat from the rest of the world, you needn't pay a lot for it. In this section, we offer tips on getting accommodations that fit your budget and your travel plans.

CHAPTER 3

Checking Into Hotel Savings

Before booking a room, think about your travel plans and the type of accommodations you're seeking. If you can be flexible about the time you travel, you'll save money. Consider these questions and tips for getting the best rates.

● Do you want affordability or amenities? If you're arriving late and leaving early and basically want a clean, safe place to overnight, why pay the high price of a full-service hotel? But if you're staying several days and want to play tennis, swim or work out, then you may get enough use from a full-service hotel or resort to pay the price.

● Is the location of the room within the hotel important? At resorts or large properties, rooms with less desirable locations offer a savings. "Less desirable" may mean no view or an inland view rather than an ocean view.

● Can you arrive a day earlier or stay a day later? Many hotels offer special discounted packages for weekends or midweek stays. Adjusting your travel time may save money.

● Are you flexible on the time of the year you travel? If you are visiting family or friends, consider going during the low season. Hotels usually offer greater savings during low-occupancy periods of the year. For instance, early to mid-December (before the holiday rush) in Las Vegas and September through mid-December (except Thanksgiving) in Orlando are slower periods.

The following is a checklist to finding the greatest savings and retaining them on your final bill:

● Always ask for the lowest rate available. You nearly always can get some kind of a savings over the standard rate. Ask about seasonal promotions, corporate and club memberships or weekend packages.

● Carry proof of a club or organization affiliation — military, clergy, AARP, AAA — to qualify for a discount you've booked or to get a last-minute discount.

● Query a chain's central reservations number first for the lowest room rate. Then check the individual hotels you want for possible specials that reservations agents at the toll-free number may not know.

● Make reservations early. Advance booking can save 25 to 50 percent off regular room rates.

● Use a credit card when making reservations to guarantee your room no matter what time you arrive.

● Always get a reservations or room confirmation number and the name of the reservations agent at booking. Note the date and time of your booking or any other transaction.

● Ask about the cancellation policy. If you wait too late to cancel, the hotel may charge for at least a one-night stay and sometimes longer. Many large hotels or resorts require cancellation up to 48 hours ahead.

● When canceling, remember to get a cancellation number and the name of the agent. This information can be important if you are mistakenly billed for the room.

● At check-in, verify the room rate to confirm your discount — and ask if a lower rate has become available since you booked. If discounts aren't confirmed during check-in, in most cases, the opportunity is lost when settling the bill.

CHAPTER 4

Slashing Hotel Costs 50 Percent

When you call a hotel to make reservations, is the rate quoted really the best you can get? Maybe not.

To get the best prices, there are two options to consider. Try a half-price hotel club, where a modest yearly fee can earn you 50 percent discounts at participating hotels. Or call a hotel reservations service, which costs nothing and offers discounts of 10 percent to 40 percent for booking through the service.

Hotel discounts exist for one simple reason: empty rooms. With hotel occupancy levels at about 60 percent nationwide and holding, hoteliers have to be creative to keep their rooms full.

Half-price hotel clubs and reservations services are probably the traveler's

Half-Price Hotel Clubs

Below are some of the major hotel discount clubs. Discounted rooms are available only when hotels expect vacancies; holidays and other dates may be blacked out. Savings are off the non-discounted room rate and may not apply to the

Club	Membership fee	Reservations number
America at 50% Discount	$19.95	(800) 248-2783
Encore	$49	(800) 638-8976
Entertainment National Dining & Hotel Directory	$42.95	(800) 445-4137
Great American Traveler	$49.95	(800) 548-2812
Hotel Express International	$49.95	(800) 634-6526
ITC 50	$36	(800) 342-0558
Quest International	$99	(800) 638-9819

best friends when it comes to locating discounts.

Half-Price Hotel Clubs

For a membership fee, typically $40 to $50 a year, travelers can join a hotel discount club that offers savings of 50 percent off the "rack rate" — the published price for the room you are booking. Many clubs also offer restaurant discounts and other travel-related bargains. You often can recoup the price of membership with a hotel stay of only one or two nights.

There are some restrictions, however. Discounts are subject to availability, and member hotels don't have to offer the lower price if they project an 80 percent occupancy rate for the dates you request. It's best to reserve as early as possible.

Many hotels require that you identify yourself as a discount-club member the minute you call about a room. If you don't, you may lose your chance at that special rate.

Don't expect to get the Ritz at Comfort Inn prices. Hotels that participate in these programs usually are in the budget- to medium-price range. The clubs negotiate discounts with individual hotels, not hotel chains, so the fact that one Marriott belongs doesn't mean they all do. Some hotels restrict the discounts to suites or superior rooms; others apply it to all rooms.

---

lowest-priced rooms. Some clubs also offer discounts off restaurant meals, car rentals and travel bookings. Membership fees indicated are assessed annually and are subject to change. Identification below is not an endorsement.

Notes

Offers 50 percent off rates for standard rooms at 1,100 hotels and resort condominiums in the United States and Canada.

Offers 50 percent off hotel rates and 20 percent to 50 percent off standard rates at bed-and breakfast inns. Has 4,000 hotels in the United States, Canada and Europe. (Discounts in Europe closer to 30 percent). Also offers 10 percent to 30 percent discounts at 2,500 Choice Hotels properties.

Offers 50 percent off rates at more than 3,500 hotels and resorts in the United States. Entertainment Publications also has individual directories for more than 130 U.S cities ($28-$48); Mexico ($42.45); and Europe ($48, see Chapter 23, "Picking a Hotel," in Bargain Hunter's Europe section).

Offers 50 percent off rates at 2,600 hotels in the United States, Mexico, Canada and Europe.

Offers 50 percent off rates at 4,000 hotels and resorts worldwide.

Offers 50 percent off rates at more than 3,000 hotels worldwide.

Offers 50 percent off rates at more than 2,100 hotels in the United States, Canada and Europe and on condominiums in North America.

How do you choose a club? There are three important considerations.
- Participating hotels. How many are there and where are they located? One club may have twice as many participating hotels as another club for the same membership price, but a smaller club may have more choices in the cities or towns you want to visit.
- Membership cost. What is the fee and what services do you get for it? Membership charges can vary substantially, so ask questions to clarify the differences.
- Additional discounts. How many restaurants are included in the program, and are other travel discounts offered? The more discounts available, the greater your overall travel savings.

Before joining any club, request a list of participating hotels and look at the ones in a city with which you are familiar. This will help you determine if the club has an inventory that suits your travel needs.

Hotel Reservations Services

Hotel reservations services work with large hotels in major American cities

Hotel Reservations Services

Below is a selection of hotel reservations services. These companies typically offer discounts at hotels in major cities; savings are applied to regular, non-discounted room rates. The reservations service is free.

Reservations service	Phone number	Notes
Capitol Reservations	(800) VISIT-DC	Discounts of 30 percent in spring and fall to 50 percent in summer at 60 Washington, DC, hotels.
Central Service Reservations	(800) 548-3311	Discounts of 10 percent to 40 percent at U.S. hotels, specializing in Miami, New York, Orlando, San Francisco and New Orleans.
Express Hotel Reservations	(800) 356-1123	Discounts up to 35 percent at about 40 hotels in New York and Los Angeles.
Hotel Network Reservations	(800) 96-HOTEL	Discounts at more than 400 properties in 23 U.S. cities and some European cities. New York is the biggest market, with 40 hotels.
Quikbook	(800) 789-9887	Discounts from 40 percent to 70 percent at 150 hotels in 24 U.S. cities.

where the 50 percent discounts often are impossible to find. These companies act as brokers for the hotels, which employ them to boost occupancy rates.

Customers call a toll-free number and tell the agent where they want to go and what they want to spend. The agent then lists the hotels the company represents in that city. Discounts typically range from 10 percent to 40 percent off rack rates. Some companies require prepayment by credit card, but there's no fee for the service.

These companies have one significant feature — they're free. They make their money on commissions from the hotels.

But there are disadvantages. They represent a limited number of hotels, usually only in big cities. Consumers may be steered to a particular hotel if the discounter is trying to fill it.

And, given the fluid nature of the hotel business, the rates that these companies offer may not be the lowest rates for a specific night. It's smart to compare by calling the hotel directly to find out what specials are available. Then you can book the best rate, either from the hotel or through the reservations service.

CHAPTER 5

The Boom in Low-Cost Lodging

Many cost-conscious travelers who are budgeting for a vacation regard lodging as one area where they can save some big bucks. Most of us can do without the room service, Jacuzzi and concierge if it means paying less.

We want something that meets our basic needs — a clean and comfortable room in a convenient location — and we don't want to pay a lot for it. To meet the growing demands, there has been a boom in new low-cost accommodations that will fill this order.

Those who haven't checked into low-cost lodging lately may still envision lonely roadside motels with shag carpeting, skimpy blankets and postage stamp-size towels. In truth, travelers will find modern, clean and comfortable no-frills spots at bottom-rung prices of $30-$35 a night, and for $50-$60 a night, you can buy rooms as nice as those found in many pricier hotels.

With more than 100 national and regional chains at the low-cost end of the lodging market, travelers have more choices than ever. So many selections, in fact, that those within the lodging industry have begun to subdivide the category. The following are the three basic classifications, although the categories may go by different terms since there are no standardized designations. Also, some hotels may fall into more than one category.

Low budget: Sometimes called budget or hard budget accommodations, these motels have room rates in the $25-$35 range. They stress value and comfort and typically have plain facades and interiors.

Economy: These are in the midrange of the lower cost lodgings, offering rooms for $35-$50. They have more curb appeal, including such amenities as landscaping, upgraded decor and perhaps a pool and restaurant.

> *Take note!*
> ☞ **Hotel safety.** For a free list of 10 hotel safety tips, send a stamped, self-addressed envelope to the American Hotel & Motel Association, Information Center, 1201 New York Ave. N.W., Washington, DC 20005.

Luxury economy: This is the upper end, motels with rooms in the $50-$65 range. They have the most curb appeal in the low-cost marketplace. Rooms often look similar to more expensive lodging, and you may find more amenities, even a continental breakfast included in the rate sometimes.

Low-cost motels also are known in the industry as limited-service lodging because you will find fewer amenities and less public space. Most don't have restaurants or coffee shops, for example, though some chains include self-serve continental breakfast. Low-cost lodging usually offers minimal recreational facilities or none at all, and guests won't find bellhops or valet parking. There's usually little, if any, meeting space.

The philosophy is to stick to the basics. All the resources are put into the guest rooms and a few recreation areas — maybe a swimming pool or small exercise room.

Since renting rooms is what makes money in the lodging business, shedding restaurants, ballrooms and bellhops — and the staff and management to operate these services — makes it easier for these chains to keep room rates down and profits up.

Low-Budget Lodging

Even at basics-only lodging, travelers are finding that the definition of "basics" has changed from the days when budget rooms were drab and featureless, without even a telephone or television.

At a minimum, all chains promise to give guests a clean, comfortable room with towels and a bar of soap, a telephone and television. Virtually every low-cost chain allows kids to stay in the same room with adults at no charge. Free local calls generally are included.

Motel 6, which vows to give customers the lowest prices of any national motel chain, provides a good example of what travelers can expect from low-budget accommodations. Its nationwide average single-room rate is around $30 for what it calls a "functional, not Spartan" room.

In addition to free local phone calls, there is no service charge on long-distance calls. While there's no clock-radio, the motel provides wake-up calls. The color television has HBO and ESPN. Non-smoking rooms are available upon request.

Motel 6 guest rooms are decorated with wallpaper (but no pictures) and shelves are being upgraded to dressers. Bedspreads are colorful and coordinate with the curtains. Furnishings include one or two double beds with a table and dining room-style chairs; the price is the same for either one or two double beds. Most bathrooms have showers rather than tubs, and extra towels are available. Children age 17 and under can stay free in the same room with adults, and one small pet is allowed at some properties.

Ninety-five percent of all Motel 6s have outdoor pools. Guests enter Motel 6 rooms from the parking lot and, for security reasons, they are asked to show identification when they check in — even when paying in cash. The company's reservations system can book a room at your next destination, locating the Motel 6 closest to a tourist attraction you might want to visit.

Take note!

☛ **Peaceful retreats.** For something different — and inexpensive — check out lodging in the "U.S. and Worldwide Guide to Retreat Center Guesthouses." The book lists more than 700 abbeys, priories, monasteries and other church-affiliated centers that welcome guests of any (or no) religious persuasion. Most rates are $30-$40 a night, including three meals a day. The guide is $15.95 from CTS Publications, P.O. Box 8355, Newport Beach, CA 92660, (714) 720-3729.

Motel 6 continues to grow and has more than held its own in recessionary times among the senior citizens, families and business travelers who make up most of its customers.

Economy, Luxury Economy Lodging

Middle- and upper-end low-cost chains charge more per room as they add amenities and services.

Low-Cost Lodging Chains

The following chart lists major limited-service/low-cost lodging chains in the United States. Rates shown are either average daily rates or the chain's published range of rates and are subject to change. When planning a trip, check prices at your chosen destination by calling the toll-free reservations numbers first. Then call individual motels directly to determine whether a price quoted by the central reservations operator is the best deal available.

National chains	Average daily rate	Reservations number
Budget Host Inns	$32	800-283-4678
Comfort Inns	$45-$65	800-228-5150
Country Inns & Suites by Carlson	$51	800-456-4000
Courtyard by Marriott	$64	800-321-2211
Days Inns of America	$45-$65	800-329-7466
Econo Lodge	$35-$45	800-55-ECONO
Fairfield Inn by Marriott	$44	800-228-2800
Friendship Inns	$35	800-453-4511
Hampton Inn	$53	800-426-7866
Hojo Inns	$47.83	800-I-GO-HOJO
Holiday Inn Express	$45-$55	800-465-4329
Knights Lodging	$34	800-843-5644
La Quinta Inns	$47	800-531-5900
Motel 6	$30	800-466-8356
Red Roof Inns	$30-$50	800-843-7663
Rodeway Inns	$40-$60	800-228-2000
Sleep Inns	$35-$45	800-62-SLEEP
Super 8 Motels	$35-$45	800-800-8000
Travelodge	$45	800-255-3050

Hampton Inn, one of the fastest-growing upper-end chains, has four styles of rooms, for example. These may include such upgraded furnishings as sleeper sofas and easy chairs.

Hampton Inn's lobbies are larger than those of low-end motels, often including several tables where guests can eat a self-serve continental breakfast that's included in the room rate. (Depending on the chain, self-serve continental breakfast can mean anything from thin coffee and gooey sweet rolls in

Regional chains	Average daily rate	Geographic region	Reservations number
Admiral Benbow Inns	$30-$50	Southeast	800-451-1986
AmericInn International	$47	Midwest, Southwest	800-634-3444
Best Inns of America	$42	Midwest, South	800-237-8466
Cricket Inns	$25-$39	Southeast, Mid-Atlantic	800-872-1808
Cross Country Inns	$30	Midwest, South	800-621-1429
Drury Inns	$49	Midwest, Rocky Mountains, South	800-325-8300
Exel Inns of America	$36-$50	Midwest, South	800-356-8013
E-Z 8 Motels	$30-$50	West	800-32-MOTEL
Family Inns	$40-$60	South, Southeast	800-332-9909
Innkeeper Motels	$39	East	800-822-9899
Inns of America	$30-$50	Southeast, West	800-826-0778
Lees Inns of America	$58	Midwest	800-733-5337
Masters Economy	$28	Midwest, South	800-633-3434
McIntosh Inns	$30-$50	Mid-Atlantic	800-444-2775
National 9 Inns	$34	South, Rocky Mountains, West	800-524-9999
Nendels Inns	$41	West	800-547-0106
Select Inns	$30-$50	Midwest	800-641-1000
Shilo Inns	$65	Southwest, West, Rocky Mountains	800-222-2244
Shoney's Inns	$30-$50	Southeast, Southwest, Midwest	800-222-2222
Signature Inns	$55-$60	Midwest	800-822-5252
Susse Chalet	$42	New England, Mid-Atlantic	800-258-1980
Travelers Inns	$35	Southwest, Rockies, West	800-633-8300
Vagabond Inns	$47.50	Southwest, West	800-522-1555
Wellesley Inns	$47	East, Southeast	800-444-8888
Wilson Inn	$35-$40	South, Southwest	800-945-7667

cellophane wrappers to a choice of muffins, bagels, cereals and juices.)

At Hampton Inn, three or four adults can share a room at the two-person rate. Each property has at least one room equipped for wheelchair-dependent guests. It is a company policy that guests are not expected to pay if they are not completely satisfied with their stay.

To attract business travelers with limited expense accounts, some Hampton Inns offer hospitality suites with conference tables, audiovisual capabilities and wet bars. Some provide free airport transportation. Many locations have indoor or outdoor pools, exercise rooms, whirlpools and saunas.

The Hampton Inn chain's national average room rate is $53 a night. Others in the high-end range are Comfort Inns, Signature Inns and Shilo Inns.

High-end economy chains with recently constructed or remodeled properties have been doing the best during recessionary times because they attract travelers from more expensive chains like Holiday Inn, Howard Johnson, Ramada and Marriott. In fact, those companies and others have moved into the upper-end economy market themselves by creating HoJo Inns, Holiday Inn Express, Fairfield Inn and Country Inns & Suites by Carlson, all less expensive than their big-name cousins.

> **Take note!**
>
> ☛ **The comforts of home.**
> To make a plain motel room seem more like a home away from home, pack a few personal items such as photographs of loved ones or a favorite pillow. Consider bringing your own alarm clock, too, so you don't waste time figuring out how to operate the one provided by the motel.

Company-Owned or Franchised?

From location to location, many low-cost motels vary in room and lobby sizes, amenities and services. These disparities are the result of "conversions" — a Best Western becoming a HoJo Inn, for example, or Motel 6 buying a Holiday Inn. This means that some motels in the chain have such amenities as swimming pools or lounges and others do not.

Travelers are likely to find the greatest motel-to-motel differences in chains that are franchise operations, compared to companies that own and manage their properties. For example, Motel 6 owns all of its lodgings while Hampton Inn is a franchise company. Some chains own some properties and franchise others.

Company-owned chains — including La Quinta Inns, Red Roof Inns, Drury Inns, Travelers Inns, E-Z 8 Motels, Vagabond Inns and others — have more control over the appearances, services and housekeeping standards. They also set rates at each property.

In the chains that franchise their names — including Days Inns of America, Comfort Inns, Super 8 Motels, Econo Lodge, HoJo Inns and Rodeway Inns — guests may find greater diversity in services, room size and quality of furnishings. With franchise operations, there's also likely to be more variation in prices.

Housekeeping standards can vary, too, depending partly on how often and thoroughly the franchising company inspects the motels. Super 8, for example, advertises that it inspects every motel every 90 days, more often than its major competitors.

Some of the newer franchise chains, such as Country Inns & Suites by Carlson, have more stringent building standards and guidelines so that the properties look more alike.

Even though there's more uniformity in ambiance among newer franchise chains like Country Inns, travelers find that some have restaurants while others do not but include a continental or full American breakfast in the price of the room. They'll find a lounge in one, an indoor pool in another. One Country Inn even has free barbecues.

Travelers who still are booking accommodations at full-service hotels and motels are finding that the limited-service competition benefits them, too. In order to keep customers and lure them back from low-cost chains, many more-expensive hotels and motels are offering discounts and package prices that make rack rates — full-price rates — all but obsolete.

For example, sometimes travelers can find a room at a hotel with a restaurant, lounge, pool and health club for only $5 or $10 more than rates at a low-cost motel in the same area. But travelers who find these deals should be sure to ask about service charges and other add-ons that can nickel-and-dime a travel budget to an early demise.

Needs vs. Wants

With such an array of lodging choices spread from chain to chain and coast to coast, how does the frugal traveler make a choice? The budget-conscious vacationer must first decide what services and ambiance he considers essential. Is a continental breakfast a necessity or not? Do the kids need a swimming pool to let off steam at the end of a long day on the road? Do you need a newspaper hanging from your doorknob in the morning? Will staying in a room with a remote-control television, armoire and thicker carpeting make it seem more like a real vacation?

None of the low-cost chains has as many types of rooms, suites and views — and corresponding rates — as a seaside resort, so they cannot maneuver as much in offering special deals. Especially among the low-end budget chains that charge less than $35 a night, you'll seldom find corporate rates, frequent-stay programs or discounts for seniors, students, AAA members or military personnel. The high-end luxury economy chains are more likely to have such programs. Nonetheless, it's a good idea to call the motel directly (rather than central reservations) to check whether a quoted price is the best deal available.

To be sure you're in a newer or recently spruced-up spot, ask when the motel was built, when it was last remodeled and whether it has changed owners.

Once you've defined the services, ambiance and price range you want, call for directories of chains strong in the areas you'll visit. By then you'll be able to choose the motels whose style and rates meet your needs.

CHAPTER 6

State Parks: Great Resorts, Great Prices

A vacation in a state park at one time meant roughing it — tramping through woods swarming with mosquitoes, sleeping in a tent or a drafty cabin and preparing meals over an open fire.

If you want rustic, you still can find it in many state parks, but that's not the whole story. Many of today's state parks have full resort facilities — championship golf courses, marinas and all kinds of water sports, gourmet dining rooms and more.

Most state parks have been built in regions of outstanding natural beauty, with a wealth of lakes, mountains, canyons, waterfalls, forests, caves or other natural attractions. Parks, by definition, are places where you can get away from the hubbub and turmoil of modern urban life. Vistas of quiet woods, fields and water give visitors places to stroll or sit and commune with nature.

All living creatures, humans included, suffer emotional damage from overcrowded conditions. In many state parks, it is possible to walk for miles without seeing another human — a rare experience for most Americans today. While these parks tend to be away from urban areas, most are not far from other natural and man-made attractions, which guests can take advantage of on side trips during their park stay.

Some parks also are nature preserves where the habitats of birds, animals and plant life are protected. They are among the few places left where people can watch wild creatures and find rare flowers in their native environments.

In addition to a variety of reasonably priced recreational facilities provided in state parks, many of them — especially resort parks — also offer educational programs and entertainment. Guided nature walks, crafts workshops, lectures and slide shows about nature and regional history are frequently on the schedule. Festivals and other special events — often with a unique regional flavor — are staged throughout the main visitor season.

State resort parks may have as much to offer as some of the finest private resorts, yet their prices are often much lower. Another plus for travelers on a limited budget is that most resort parks offer a range of accommodations. One may opt to stay in a campground, RV park or family-size housekeeping cabin and still have access to all the same recreational facilities.

The 10 resort parks described in this chapter are all in the South and

Southeast, where this type of lodging is especially popular and the parks stay open year-round.

Educational and recreational programs are more extensive during summer months, but winter vacations — when the crowds are smaller — can be a special pleasure, too. In addition to the facilities listed for each park, all have hiking trails, scenic drives and picnicking areas.

For complete lists of parks and lodges, write to the parks agencies in the states you intend to visit.

Prices are the minimum nightly rates during the summer. Lower rates generally apply off-season. Rates given for the lodges are for two people in a room. In most cases, rates for cabins are per night, making the cost per person cheaper than in the lodge. Tax is not included, except where noted.

Hickory Knob State Resort Park, South Carolina

South Carolina is noted for its numerous top-notch golf courses and resorts, and one of the finest is in a state park tucked among picturesque rolling hills on the western border of the state. Hickory Knob's 18-hole championship course stretches along the shore of Thurmond Lake.

Frequent nature and recreational programs are presented at Hickory Knob. Recreational activities include tennis, water sports, fishing, skeet, trap shooting and field archery. An unusual feature is the four-mile bird dog field trial area. Two other recreational state parks are nearby.

Take note!

☞ **Don't feed the animals.** It's not uncommon to see deer, chipmunks and squirrels in the parks, even near the lodges. Resist the urge to pet or feed any animal, no matter how tame it may seem. All animals in the parks are wild; feeding them teaches them to seek out humans for food and causes them to lose their ability to find sustenance on their own. If you are bitten by an animal, see a doctor immediately; small animals can carry diseases that are dangerous to humans.

Accommodations: The park has a 74-room lodge, 18 duplex cabins with phones and color televisions, 75 campsites, a store, restaurant and lounge. Lodge: $80. Cabins: $50, must rent for one-week minimum in summer. The rest of the year there is a two-night minimum during weekends.

Information: Hickory Knob State Resort Park, Route 1, Box 199-B, McCormick, SC 29835, (803) 391-2450.

Unicoi State Park, Georgia

Tucked into the north Georgia mountains, adjacent to Anna Ruby Falls, Unicoi State Park covers more than 1,000 acres of forest and includes a 53-acre mountain lake. A year-round schedule of special activities and programs focuses on regional culture and environmental matters at the preserve.

The park is only two miles from Helen, an alpine village and a popular tourist destination. Other area attractions include Brasstown Bald, the highest point in Georgia, and the town of Dahlonega, once the center of a short-lived gold rush. Sightseeing, swimming, boating, fishing, tennis and relaxing in the beautiful wilderness are the major activities.

Accommodations: The park has a 100-room lodge, a restaurant and crafts shop, 30 cottages and 96 tent and trailer sites. Other facilities include a camp store and interpretive center. Lodge: $118. Cottages: $65 for one-bedroom, $75 for two-bedroom, and $85 for three-bedroom.

Information: Unicoi State Park, P.O. Box 849, Helen, GA 30545, (706) 878-2201.

DeSoto State Park, Alabama

DeSoto State Park sits along the crest of Lookout Mountain, a long ridge in northeastern Alabama. A major feature of the park is Little River Canyon, the deepest gorge east of the Mississippi River. Wooded ridges, rocky bluffs and lacy waterfalls grace both sides of the 16-mile-long canyon. Five streams feed into Little River, creating side canyons.

Activities include tennis, rock climbing, water sports on the lake above DeSoto Falls and swimming and boating in the river. A trained park naturalist is at the Nature Center. The park is noted for its profusion of wildflowers and songbirds.

Take note!

☛ **Hiking hints.** If you plan to hike in a park, take a bottle of water to avoid dehydration, insect repellent, a rainproof jacket, sunscreen and perhaps a wide-brimmed hat to shade your face. If you're not an experienced hiker, don't overdo it; ask a park ranger which trails suit your skill level. Avoid hiking alone, if possible. Instead, consider one of the ranger-led group walks that highlight a park's most interesting features.

Accommodations: The park boasts a 25-room resort lodge with a restaurant and gift shop. All rooms have telephone and television and open onto a country porch. There also are 11 older, rustic cabins, 11 modern chalets and 78 campsites with hookups. Lodge: $46.20 for the first person, $5.25 each additional person. Cabins: $58.80-$69.30. Chalets: $71.40. Rates includes tax.

Information: DeSoto State Park, Route 1, Box 210, Fort Payne, AL 35967, (205) 845-0051 for the park, (205) 845-5380 or (800) 568-8840 for the lodge.

Ozark Folk Center, Arkansas

The Ozark Folk Center, in northern Arkansas, is a one-of-a-kind state park. It was opened in 1973 to preserve and honor the activities and traditions of the Ozark Mountains as they were practiced in the late 1800s and early 1900s.

More than 20 different demonstrations of crafts and other lifestyle interpretations are presented in the multibuilding outdoor museum. Special festivals, contests, workshops and exhibitions are on the calendar. Concerts feature traditional music performed on acoustical, usually string instruments, many of which were handmade in the region. Dance performances include square dancing, jigs, traditional waltzes and clogging.

The season of special programs and activities runs from mid-April to early November, offering live entertainment six nights a week. Additional musical performances and craft fairs celebrate the Thanksgiving and Christmas seasons.

Accommodations: A 60-room lodge is open all year, and there's a full-service restaurant with beautiful views of the wooded hilltop. The Folk Center Gift Shop features handmade toys, chairs, pottery, dolls, quilts, baskets, preserves and more. Lodge: $45 Sunday through Wednesday, $50 Thursday through Saturday. There are admission fees to the craft areas and music events.

Information: Ozark Folk Center, P.O. Box 500, Mountain View, AR 72560, (501) 269-3851 for the park, (501) 269-3871 for the lodge.

Lake Murray Resort, Oklahoma

Oklahoma's first state park, Lake Murray Resort, was built during the Great Depression of the 1930s. Federal emergency relief funds paid workers, including young men in the Civilian Conservation Corps, to create one of the largest man-made lakes west of the Mississippi and develop a recreation area around it. The 115-mile shoreline is completely wilderness — no private homes.

Diving, a sport most people associate with saltwater, has become popular in Oklahoma's clear, spring-fed lakes. Visibility in Lake Murray's waters averages about 15 feet year-round. Some divers go spearfishing for the bigger fish found at lower depths. Others prefer "noodling" — catching fish with their bare hands.

A marina and dive shop, lake cruises, paddleboat rentals and a beach make all kinds of water sports possible. In addition, the resort offers golf, tennis, miniature golf, bicycle rentals and stables. A museum and nature center are in a picturesque structure called Tucker Tower.

Special events during the year include a Mexican fiesta in the fall, a Pilgrim Thanksgiving dinner, country Christmas, western dances and heritage craft weekends that include classes in china painting, weaving, spinning and quilting.

Accommodations: Lake Murray Country Inn has 52 rooms and a restaurant. There also are 88 cottages, 236 campsites and a grocery. Reservations for summer or holiday stays should be made well in advance. Lodge: $58-$63. Cabins: $48 for two people, $73 for four and $120 for six.

Information: Lake Murray Resort, 3310 S. Lake Murray Drive, No. 12A, Ardmore, OK 73401, (800) 654-8240 or (405) 223-6600.

Barren River Lake State Resort Park, Kentucky

Kentucky's 15 state resort parks are among the finest in the nation. They represent all regions of the state and offer a range of scenery and activities. Barren River Lake Park is on the shore of a 10,000-acre lake in south central Kentucky and only a short drive from a major cave system.

Resort facilities are extensive, including an 18-hole golf course with pro shop and a marina with 140 slips, a launching ramp and boat rentals. Outdoor attractions also include horseback riding, bicycle rentals, tennis, basketball, shuffleboard and volleyball. There's a pool and lake-side beach for swimmers.

Accommodations: Facilities include a 51-room lodge, 22 cottages each sleeping up to six adults, 99 campsites, a dining room and gift shop. Lodge: $65.72. Cottages: $131.44, or $163.24 in one of 10 newer cottages. Rates include tax.

Information: Barren River Lake State Resort Park, 1149 State Park Road, Lucas, KY 42156, (502) 646-2151.

Cumberland Falls State Resort Park, Kentucky

Deep in southern Kentucky's Daniel Boone National Forest near the small town of Corbin, this treasure of a state park on the Cumberland River sports the "Niagara of the South," the second-largest waterfall east of the Mississippi River.

On most nights, you can observe a rare rainbow phenomenon called a "moonbow."

Rafting trips on the Cumberland River start below the falls, which are 125 feet wide and 60 feet high. There are 17 miles of hiking trails, plus fishing, horseback riding, a swimming pool, museum and nature center. Plan additional days for exploring the surrounding mountains.

Both the Big South Fork National River and Recreation Area and the Levi Jackson Wilderness Road State Park are short drives away. The latter encloses portions of two historic trails and includes a working gristmill and pioneer life museum.

Accommodations: The 1,657-acre resort park has a 52-room lodge, 20 duplex cottages with bedroom and bath only, 26 fully equipped housekeeping cottages (most with fireplaces) and excellent, inexpensive dining facilities. There are 50 campsites. Lodge and duplex cottages: $67.70. Housekeeping cottages: $69.88. Rates include tax.

Information: Cumberland Falls State Resort Park, 7351 Highway 90, Corbin, KY 40701, (800) 325-0063.

Take note!

☛ **Pack picnic supplies.** Park settings invite picnicking to take advantage of the scenic outdoors. All parks have picnic facilities, and many have camp stores where you can buy sandwich makings, snacks, drinks and even more extensive foodstuffs. Some parks also have outdoor grills. Plan ahead to take some utensils — such as plastic plates, cups, tableware, napkins, a paring knife, bottle opener and even a corkscrew — so that you don't have to buy the basics.

Paris Landing State Park, Tennessee

Road maps show a large green area stretching across the Tennessee-Kentucky border northwest of Nashville. Called Land Between the Lakes, it is one of the most extensive recreation areas in the eastern United States.

Authorized by President Kennedy in 1963, the recreation area nestles between two large lakes: Kentucky Lake, created by damming the Tennessee River, and Lake Barkley, formed similarly from the Cumberland River.

The lakes make possible nearly every water sport imaginable, and numerous trails invite visitors to explore on horseback, bicycle, off-road recreational vehicle or foot.

Paris Landing State Resort Park, on the west side of Kentucky Lake, is an excellent headquarters from which to enjoy all the area has to offer. Just south of the park, U.S. 79 crosses the lake into the Land Between the Lakes. Within Paris Landing Resort Park are an 18-hole championship golf course and pro shop, a full-service marina with boat rentals, lighted tennis courts and pool.

Accommodations: All 100 rooms at the lodge have balconies overlooking Kentucky Lake. The park also has a dining room, store, gift shop and 61 campsites. Lodge: $63.42 Sunday through Thursday, $65.69 Friday and Saturday. Rates include tax.

Information: Paris Landing State Resort Park, 16055 Highway 79 N., Buchanan, TN 38222-4109, (901) 642-4311.

Cacapon Resort State Park, West Virginia

Cacapon Park is a long, narrow preserve of 6,000 acres that stretches most of the way between the Virginia and Maryland borders of West Virginia. A mountain resort, it offers golf, tennis, volleyball, fishing, horseback riding and cross-country skiing in season.

Just north of the park is Berkeley Springs, the oldest spa in the nation. George Washington and his family vacationed here many times, and he is credited with popularizing the spot and the special mineral waters that are piped throughout the town.

Accommodations: The park has a 49-room lodge, an 11-room inn, 30 housekeeping cabins, a restaurant, recreation room and gift shop. There is no camping. Lodge: $58. Inn: $33-$36. Cabins: From $330 weekly for two people to $621 for eight.

Information: Cacapon Resort State Park, Route 1, Box 304, Berkeley Springs, WV 25411, (304) 258-1022.

Davis Mountains State Park, Fort Davis, Texas

In mile-high Limpia Creek Valley, the historic pueblo-style Indian Lodge commands a sweeping view of the surrounding Davis Mountains of West Texas. About three hours southeast of El Paso, Davis Mountains State Park with its lodge and campgrounds is a favorite family getaway year-round.

Part of the white adobe lodge was constructed in the Depression era, and additional rooms and a swimming pool were added in 1967. Original rooms have open beam-and-cane ceilings and rustic handcrafted furniture. Hiking trails are accessible from the lodge, and a park road winds up the mountains for a spectacular panoramic view of flatlands and peaks rising above 7,000 feet.

Visitors can join stargazing parties on Tuesday, Friday and Saturday nights at nearby McDonald Observatory. About four miles from the park, the Fort Davis National Historic Site shows life in the 1850s when soldiers established a fort to protect the settlers moving west.

Accommodations: The park has a 39-room lodge with swimming pool, restaurant and gift shop. There are 94 campsites. Lodge: $55-$85, including breakfast. Add a 10 percent tax. Early reservations are advised; lodge closes for two weeks in mid-January.

Information: Davis Mountains State Park, P.O. Box 1458, Fort Davis, TX 79734, (915) 426-3337 for the park, (915) 426-3254 for the lodge.

Deals
On Wheels

When it comes to getting around on vacation, nothing is more convenient than having a car. Finding a good deal, however, can prove a challenging game as car-rental firms continue to add extra charges. This chapter will steer you to the lowest prices for your next car rental.

CHAPTER 7

Curbing Car-Rental Costs

Before you start checking car-rental rates, know the rules of the road for getting the lowest price. The following basic guideline will speed your search for the best price to suit your individual trip needs.

1. Rent on weekends or by the week.
Weekend and weekly rates offer savings over the basic per-day rates. Weekend prices generally apply Thursday-Monday. Companies usually cut rates then because they have a surplus of cars returned by business travelers, whose peak demand is during the week.

Check the weekly rate even if you need a car only five days; that's usually the minimum rental time required to qualify for a lower weekly rate.

Take note! ☛ **Avoid cars labeled with rental firm logos.** Tourists often are seen as prime crime targets in large cities, and a car-rental sticker makes you easy to spot. Check with the agency before booking to see if it puts logos on its cars.

2. Be flexible on travel days.
January to mid-March, April to late May and Labor Day to Dec. 15 are the best times to rent. Also, sometimes adjusting your vacation by a day or two may qualify you for lower rates. Always ask whether a better rate is available by changing your travel schedule.

3. Look for package promotions.
Some of the best car-rental deals are part of a travel package, such as to a ski resort in Colorado, a tour to Disney World or a trip to Hawaii. Some frequent-flier programs include discounts on car rentals. Many airlines offer fly/drive promotions, and hotels, particularly those in Hawaii, frequently package rooms with a free car rental.

4. Check for membership discounts.
Belonging to an organization such as the American Automobile Association, American Association of Retired Persons, a professional organization or even a college alumni group can earn you discounts. When shopping for rental rates, let the agent know what memberships you have, to see if one qualifies you for a discount. Terms of group discounts vary; find out if a discount applies only to the regular rate, or if it is also good for any special promotions. You usually can

beat the group discount with a special, but the group rate can help at peak times when no other discount is available.

5. Compare car sizes, costs.

Rental firms offer late-model cars in many sizes, usually categorized as subcompact, compact, midsize, full-size, premium, luxury, minivans, station wagons and four-wheel-drive vehicles. Ask for examples of the specific cars that a rental firm offers in the categories that interest you. While the smallest cars are usually the least expensive, the price difference between categories often is minimal. So, for a few dollars more, you may get a much roomier car with more horsepower. Recently, renting a compact car through Avis in St. Louis cost only $1 more per day than renting a subcompact. Check a couple of different sizes to see if the price difference is significant.

6. Ask about special promotions.

Sometimes companies promote rentals of larger, more expensive cars, making them cheaper than a small car you might have been booking because you thought it would be the least expensive.

7. Reserve early for holidays and summer rentals.

These usually are peak cost periods, but you may get a price break by booking several weeks ahead. Rates are constantly changing — usually rising — and by booking in advance you usually can obtain a lower rate. Find out how long the rate is guaranteed; when you pick up the car, verify that your rate is still the lowest price available.

8. Keep a clean driving record.

Many car-rental companies are now checking the driving records of prospective renters from specified states and may refuse to rent to those with questionable driving histories. For instance, Hertz will decline to rent to anyone whose license has expired or has been suspended or anyone with three or more convictions for moving violations within the past 24 months, including seatbelt violations and convictions for speeding more than 15 mph above the posted limit. More serious violations also are included in the criteria. While car-rental firms usually will advise you at booking if your state records will be checked, the actual checking isn't done until you're at the counter — and then you can be turned down on the spot. If you have had some tickets, clarify a car-rental firm's policy for declining rentals when booking so you won't be left without wheels.

9. Check the taxes.

Several taxes may apply to car rentals, adding up to an unexpected wallop on the wallet when you return the car. Many states and cities charge both a sales tax and a car rental tax, which may be a percentage of the rental fee or a set amount. These additional car-rental taxes range from 30 cents per rental in Massachusetts to $2.05 per day up to 30 days in Florida.

The Taxing Situation

Here's a sampling of the total tax impact on car rentals in a few popular tourist cities.

City	Surcharge
Las Vegas	13%
New York City	13.25%
Miami	6.5% plus $2.05 per day
Los Angeles	8.25%
Seattle	15.1%

10. Compare prices.

Don't think all the big car-rental companies charge the same; there's often a large variance in rates among the top firms. Also, check to see if there's a price difference between renting at the airport vs. in the city. For instance, travelers who rent a car at Denver International Airport are assessed a "facility user fee" of $2.98 per day, applied to all who fly in and rent a car at the airport within 24 hours of arrival. That fee does not apply to cars rented in the city.

If you decide to rent from a city location, ask about return policy. If you return it to the airport on your way out of town, you may be charged extra. If you decide to return it to a city location, check what its business hours are and if the agency will provide transportation to the airport, either free or for a fee.

11. Don't overinsure yourself.

Before you rent, check your auto insurance policy to see if it provides coverage if your rental car is damaged in an accident, stolen or vandalized. Also, check the coverage offered by your credit cards; many provide supplementary coverage to your primary car insurance. If you're already covered, there's no need to purchase the car rental firm's insurance, called Loss Damage Waiver (LDW) or Collision Damage Waiver (CDW) and Personal Accident Insurance. Insurance from a car-rental firm can cost $5 per day to $18 per day, depending on location and type of car.

12. Check extra charges.

● Drop-off fee.

If you don't return the car to the original rental site, you may pay a higher rate. Some firms charge a drop-off fee, while others assess an "intercity rate" or a flat rate that varies with destinations. At Hertz, for example, a midsize car rented in New York City and returned to the same place will cost $430 for a week. If you were to drop off that car in Boston, the rate would be $462. The gap in fees gets larger the farther you go. A midsize car rented and returned in

Car Rental Agencies

Company	Reservations number
Advantage	800-777-5500
Alamo	800-327-9633
Avis	800-331-1212
Budget	800-527-0700
Dollar	800-800-4000
Enterprise	800-325-8007
Hertz	800-654-3131
National	800-227-7368
Payless	800-729-5377
Thrifty	800-367-2277
Value	800-468-2583

Denver would cost $172 for a week, but the cost would jump to a whopping $420 for the week if you rent it in Denver and return it in Los Angeles.

Some car-rental companies don't allow you to drop the car off in a different city, so be sure to check before you rent.

● Extra driver fee.

If you plan to share the driving duties with someone, you may have to pay an extra fee for each additional driver. For example, Avis charges $25 per additional driver for the entire length of the rental. At some firms, charges vary from city to city; for example, in Denver, National Interrent charges $4 per day for each additional driver but assesses no extra fee in Los Angeles.

● Airport access fee.

Check for this "hidden" cost, often charged by car-rental firms located "off-site," adjacent to the airport rather than inside an airport terminal. Off-site companies usually must pay the airport to run their shuttles to the terminals, and they pass these costs to the consumer in the form of airport access fees. These can be either a flat rate or a percentage of the total rental charge.

Getting the Lowest Cruise Rate

If you like the idea of taking a cruise but balk at paying full price, don't worry — you can find a deal. It's a buyer's market as more ships come on line, eager to fill their berths. Use the following chapter to chart your course to savings.

CHAPTER 8

Eight Ways to Sail For Less

Cruise brochure rates these days are only starting guidelines for true cruise fares. Savvy travelers rarely need to pay the full rate, unless they are locked into vacationing at a particular time that's already heavily booked or want to sail on holidays. Even for holiday sailings, though, there are ways to save.

Those who are flexible on sailing dates reap the best discounts, but don't worry about having to pack for a departure tomorrow. The best discounts normally are available six weeks to three months ahead of sailing.

Before shopping for a cruise, think about what kind of vacation you want and identify your budget. While many ships do similar itineraries, both their prices and personalities vary. Some ships are small and intimate, while others are 2,500-passenger, glitzy megaships. Some are known for their entertainment, while others emphasize sports, dining or shore excursions and lectures. Some ships draw younger passengers, some older.

If your idea of a good time is enjoying peace and quiet while lounging on deck, you may not enjoy a ship known for its wild parties. If you're single, you don't want to sail on a small ship that draws all couples.

Having a general idea about the type of cruise you want and a budget in mind will help you more quickly find the right ship.

Follow these tips, and you will set sail at the best rate.

Take note!

☞ **Deck plan.** Save money on the new superliners by booking a cabin on a lower deck. Most cabins have the same amenities and square footage, but you pay a higher amount each deck you rise.

1. Use a cruise specialist.

Cruise specialists usually know the cruise lines and ships well, can guide you to the ship that best suits you and your budget and can get you discounts.

Cruise lines, like airlines, track bookings and project their excess space. The lines then discount that space and make it available to cruise/travel agencies that do a high volume of cruise bookings. The agencies sell the cruises at a discount. The more cruises the company sells, the better your discounts will be.

The best discounts usually are through large cruise-specialist agencies that serve a nationwide audience through an 800 number. If you live in a metropolitan area or near cruise ship ports, you also may find a local agency that can get you discounts.

Discount Cruise Agencies

The following agencies/organizations are among the many that offer cruises at a discount. Bookings can be made through the phone numbers given. There may be cruise specialists in your area also.

Agency/ organization	Location	Phone number
Cruise Co. of California[1]	Huntington Beach, CA	800-872-7847
Cruise Fairs of America	Los Angeles, CA	800-456-4386
Cruise Holidays	San Diego, CA	800-866-7245
Cruise Marketplace	San Carlos, CA	800-826-4343
Cruise Pro[2]	Thousand Oaks, CA	800-222-7447
Cruise Shoppe Operations	N. Miami Beach	800-338-9051
Cruise Stars	Woodland Hills, CA	800-732-7287
Cruise Time	San Francisco, CA	800-338-0818
	Fairfax, VA	800-627-6131
Cruises by Brennco	Kansas City, MO	800-955-1909
Cruises Inc.	E. Syracuse, NY	800-854-0500
Cruises of Distinction	Livingston, NJ	800-634-3445
Cruises Only	Orlando, FL	800-683-7447
Cruises Worldwide	Irvine, CA	800-627-8473
CSAA Travel Agency[3]	San Francisco, CA	800-228-6339
Golden Bear Travel	Novato, CA	800-551-1000
Just Cruises and Tours	Las Vegas, NV	800-551-7447
Kelly Cruises	Oak Brook, IL	800-837-7447
South Florida Cruises	Fort Lauderdale, FL	800-327-7447
Spur of the Moment Cruises[4]	San Pedro, CA	800-343-1991
Time to Travel	San Francisco, CA	800-524-3300
Travel Advisors	San Rafael, CA	800-423-8271
The Travel Company	Atherton, CA	800-367-6090
Vacations To Go	Houston, TX	800-338-4962
Village Travel Cruise Club	San Pedro, CA	310-519-1717
White Travel Service	West Hartford, CT	800-547-4790
World Wide Cruises[5]	Fort Lauderdale, FL	800-882-9000

[1]In CA: 800-992-7847. [2]In CA: 800-258-7447. [3]AAA affiliate; 38 branch offices. [4]Hot line with cruise specials: 310-521-1060. [5]In FL: 305-720-9000.

Discount Cruise Clubs

Club	Location	Phone number	Yearly fee
TravLtips[1]	Flushing, NY	800-872-8584	$20
Worldwide Discount Travel Club	Miami Beach, FL	800-783-2642	$50

[1]Focuses on freighters

For the best savings, contact an agency three to four months ahead of your desired time to travel. For Alaska cruises, call in late fall or early winter — by Feb. 1 — for the biggest discounts.

Ask what the best specials are around the date you want to sail. For instance, a cruise line may be offering a special one particular week because its bookings are lower at that time.

For a list of some of the larger national cruise discounters and cruise-only agencies, see the accompanying chart. You also can contact the National Association of Cruise-Only Agencies, which will mail a free list of its members in any states you request. Contact NACOA, 3191 Coral Way, Suite 630, Miami, FL 33145, (305) 446-7732.

Caveat: Some agencies may push a particular cruise line because they have a preferred relationship with that line, allowing them to give bigger discounts. If you want another cruise line and the agency doesn't have a good discount on it, check with another agency.

> *Take note!*
>
> ☞ **Make an impression.** To ensure the best possible service from your cabin steward, provide a gratuity upfront. Nothing makes a better first impression than a $10 or $20 bill presented as the ship sails.

2. Check for 'last-minute' deals.

When available, last-minute discounts offer the greatest savings in the cruise industry, up to 65 percent off the brochure rate at times. If you can be flexible about your sailing date, these deals are your best bet.

Fortunately, in the cruise business short notice normally means 45 to 90 days before sailing. Some last-minute specials also crop up within 30 days of sailing.

Vacations To Go is a discount cruise agency that has specialized in finding and booking last-minute bargains since 1984. The company works with every major cruise line worldwide. Call for current specials or send a request to be added to its mailing list. Contact Vacations To Go, 1502 Augusta Drive, Suite 415, Houston, TX 77057, (800) 338-4962.

Some last-minute deals, particularly those within 30 days of sailing, do not include airfare. Your savings could be reduced or even negated if you have to book airfare at a premium. But if you have frequent flier mileage, can take advantage of sudden airfare wars or can drive to the port, these are very good deals — sometimes $100 or less per person per day for a seven-day Caribbean cruise on a high quality ship with normal prices twice that amount or higher.

3. Cruise in the low season.

You can save by sailing at off periods, which vary according to the cruise region. In the Caribbean, fall and early winter are bargain times. Rates usually are lowest from early September to mid-November and the first three weeks of December, or until just before Christmas. Winter generally is the highest season, and summer is only slightly less expensive. Within those periods, though, lines may offer promotional rates for specific times when advance bookings are light.

In Alaska, the lowest prices are for the early and late sailings of the season. These are from May into early June and in late August or September, depending on a ship's schedule.

In Europe, where the season extends from spring through fall, the earliest and latest sailings are the lowest priced.

Of course, the tradeoff for sailing in the low season is that the weather is more changeable. The Caribbean stays warm year-round, but in the fall you're likely to encounter more rain and you're in the hurricane season. Weather in Alaska will be cooler in May and September than in the summer. Early spring and late fall are pleasant in Europe, though cool on Atlantic ports. Most Northern Europe sailings are in the summer only.

The most expensive time to cruise is Christmas and New Year's; some lines charge a supplement then, but you may get an early-booking discount for holidays.

4. Ask about regional discounts.

When cruise lines see that particular sailing dates are not filled, they may promote special discounts targeted to particular regions or specific states, say Texas and Oklahoma, for example. The bargains, good only for residents in the defined state(s), usually are restricted to specified departure dates and may be limited to certain categories of cabins. The savings can be substantial — but may not include airfare.

An example of a regional discount: At press time, Royal Caribbean Cruise Line was offering seven-day Caribbean sailings as low as $849 per person, double occupancy, from Houston, TX, with airfare included. Similar regional specials were available for varying prices from different gateways.

The drawback of regional discounts, of course, is that passengers can't count on them becoming available and must be willing to take potluck on itineraries, dates and cabins. To find out about regional discounts, scan the travel section of local newspapers on Sundays, or ask a cruise specialty agent if any deals are available for travelers from your area.

5. Book early.

If you want a particular ship, itinerary or class of cabin or if you are locked into a certain vacation time, then your best discount may be through booking early.

Faced with rampant discounting in the market, most major cruise lines have started pushing their own early-booking discount programs. With a number of lines, the earlier you book the greater your discount off the brochure price. The amount of the discount lessens — or ends

Take note!

☞ **Clean sweep.** Check the sanitary ratings by the Centers for Disease Control for ships that interest you. Free twice-monthly reports, scoring vessels on a 100-point scale, are available from the Vessel Sanitation Program, 1015 N. America Way, Room 107, Miami, FL 33132.

— as the sailing date draws closer, but the discounts and the deadlines can change depending on how quickly the ship is filling.

Early-booking discounts can trim substantial amounts off the price.

Ships sailing to Alaska traditionally offer early-booking discounts with specified deadlines. For instance, for its latest Alaska sailings, Princess Cruises was offering discounts of $1,100 to $1,500 per couple on its seven-day cruises and up to $2,400 per couple off 10- and 12-day cruises if you booked by mid-February. Also in Alaska, Holland America Line was offering 25 percent discounts until late February and then 15 percent discounts, all on a limited-availability basis.

In the Caribbean, Holland America Line offered savings of 15 percent to 45 percent, or $298 to $1,615 per person, double occupancy, on a limited-availability basis.

> **Take note!**
> ☞ **Going ashore.** Before booking shore excursions, determine if they're worth the time and money. If it's a small island, the best bet may be a self-guided walking tour, a do-it-yourself driving tour or a taxi ride to the nearest beach.

High-volume cruise specialists usually can sweeten these discounts by 3 percent to 10 percent, depending on the ship.

Caveat: When booking early, be sure you do get the best deal offered. Ask your agent if the line guarantees you will get a lower rate if one becomes available. Many cruise lines will guarantee that if the prices do go lower than the lowest early-booking rate, earlier purchasers will be refunded the difference. Check with your travel agent periodically to see if any lower rates have become available.

6. Look for repositioning cruises.

When a ship changes its itinerary, the cruise line sometimes offers trips at deep discounts — up to 65 percent or even more off normal daily rates. Look for the best sailings on repositioning cruises from the Caribbean to Europe in the spring and from Europe to the Caribbean in late fall.

These cruises are for those who enjoy lazy days at sea because there are fewer ports of call. These also are usually longer cruises. They are one-way sailings and may not include airfare.

7. Sail with one line repeatedly.

Cruise lines offer special discounts and on-board credits to past passengers. But before accepting the cruise line offer, check to see if a better discount is available from a cruise specialist.

8. Pay early.

Some lines give an extra discount if you pay for the cruise in full early. For example, Royal Cruise Line takes 7 percent off its already discounted fare if you pay in full nine months in advance, or 5 percent off for payments six months ahead.

Many cruise lines offer early-payment (and early-booking) discounts on holiday cruises, for which there usually are no other discounts available. Holiday cruises also fill fast.

Caveat: Always read the fine print. Substantial deposits may be required to hold space on a cruise and heavy cancellation fees are a norm. Depending on the cost of the cruise, you might think about investing in trip-cancellation insurance. This would protect you in the event of an emergency cancellation or natural disaster, which the cruise line can't cover.

Discount Travel Services

For those who like one-stop shopping for vacation deals, discount travel clubs are an option. The following chapter gives you a sampling of the savings these groups offer.

CHAPTER 9

Clubs Can Net Savings

Discount travel clubs can give you access to a number of savings through one source. Generally, club members receive mailed notices or can call a hot-line number to learn the latest discounts — sometimes up to 65 percent — off cruises and travel packages.

Members also may qualify for discounts at hotels and rebates on scheduled airfares, saving an additional amount on already discounted tickets. Rebates may be a set dollar amount or a percentage of the ticket price; in both cases, the higher the ticket price, the greater the rebate. Some clubs may require that a ticket be a minimum price to qualify for a rebate.

The number of discount travel clubs has declined in recent years. When the clubs first started, travel bargains were less common and required the expertise of an insider to ferret out. Most clubs charged fees for membership. As discounts became readily available in the marketplace, clubs often reduced or eliminated fees, and some began specializing in one travel segment. With the cruise industry leading growth in travel, many clubs have become cruise clearinghouses, matching passengers with bargains that have developed in cruises with the advent of many new, larger ships. Other clubs have tapped into the growing field of half-price hotel rooms.

It's not necessary today to join a club or pay a fee to find travel discounts, but you may want to look into some clubs to see if any would net you additional savings. If a club does have a fee, determine if your savings through the club will equal or exceed the yearly charge. If you book several flights a year, for instance, a 5 percent rebate given by a club on your airline tickets can amount to a good savings you couldn't get elsewhere.

Clubs work best for those who travel frequently, are flexible enough about vacation times to get the best deals or who can go on short notice.

Here is a sample of nationwide discount travel clubs with fees. For more cruise discounters, see Getting the Lowest Cruise Rate section of this book, and for hotel discounters, see Chapter 4, "Slashing Hotel Costs 50 Percent," in Cutting

> *Take note!*
> ☞ **Check out a company.** Call the Better Business Bureau in the town where a club or agency is based. Some complaints against a company, however, shouldn't cause alarm, especially if they were resolved. Ask the BBB for the number of unresolved complaints against an agency.

the Cost of Lodging section. Also check in the travel section of a Sunday metropolitan newspaper for discount agencies that specialize in regional departures.

Moment's Notice Discount Travel Club, 7301 New Utrecht Ave., Brooklyn, NY 11204, (718) 234-6295. Annual fee: $25 per family. Members have access to a hot line that offers discounts of 20 percent to 60 percent off tours and cruises. The company also acts as a consolidator, selling international flights at discounts. Has 10 percent to 50 percent discounts at a few hotels.

Preferred Travelers Club, 4501 Forbes Blvd., Lanham, MD 20706, (800) 444-9800. Annual fee: $69. Has discounts on cruises, airfares, car rentals and one- and two-night "escape" packages. Also offers 50 percent discounts at certain hotels, motels and resorts.

> **Take note!**
> ☛ **Look for experience.** Ask how long the club has been in business. The longer they've been in the travel industry, the better.

Travelers Advantage, 40 Oakview Drive, Trumbull, CT 06611, (800) 548-1116. Annual fee: $49 per family. Full-service travel agency offering 5 percent to 25 percent off cruises, vacation packages, condominium rentals and car rentals. Members get 50 percent off the published room rates at more than 2,500 hotels listed in the club's directory. Offers a 5 percent rebate on all purchases made through their agents, including air travel. (Rebate is not offered on half-price hotel room rates.)

Vacations To Go, 1502 Augusta Drive, Suite 415, Houston, TX 77057, (800) 338-4962. Annual fee: $5.95. Discounts up to 65 percent off cruises. Fee covers twice-monthly mailings of cruise specials, including deeply discounted last-minute bargains. Cruises may be booked without paying the fee.

Worldwide Discount Travel Club, 1674 Meridian Ave., Suite 206, Miami Beach, FL 33139, (305) 534-2082. Annual fee: $50 per family, $40 per single person. Discounts average 30 percent to 40 percent off cruises and tours. Sends monthly mailings about current trips.

Traveling Free — Or Nearly So

It's true — you can travel for free or close to it sometimes. Turn the page and learn the different ways, but be prepared: You may be "paying" with your time and talents.

CHAPTER 10

Be a Leader, a Host Or a Speaker

It sounds like the best vacation deal of all — the chance to travel free. Simply get together a group of 15 or so people who all want to go on the same tour or cruise, and you go with them free.

If you're a single male age 50 and beyond and can ballroom dance well, you can waltz around the world on a cruise ship — free.

Or if you can counsel others on how to deal with stress, lecture about rain forests or teach the techniques of tai-chi, you may be the expert some tour operator or cruise line is seeking as a guest lecturer — again going for free.

Yes, the offers are legitimate, but there's never any truly free lunch.

Whatever the free trip, you can count on some personal "costs" or requirements, such as these:

- a hefty commitment of time, both prior to the trip and during it.
- a love of people — and patience with their foibles.
- an unflappable nature and sense of humor.

Here's a look at some of the popular forms of free travel and how you can qualify.

Be a 'Pied Piper'

If you can convince enough people to sign up for a tour or cruise, travel agents and tour operators will allow you to go along free. The group size required to earn that free trip averages 15, but it may be as low as six or eight or as high as 20 or 25.

But it's not as easy as choosing that dream tour of China or luxury Panama Canal cruise, then merely spending an hour or two on the phone convincing 15 friends to join you — despite the blandishments of "How You Can Travel Free as a Group Tour Organizer," a 40-page paperback guide on the market at one time.

Successful group organizers — also called Pied Pipers after that mythical figure who led the children out of the town of Hamelin — must have certain types of contacts and skills and a willingness to work hard.

A Pied Piper is outgoing and likes to take charge. He or she is a catalyst within an organization or among friends and family and acts in a professional manner.

Take note!

☞ **Assess your personality.** A tour group organizer must wear many hats — problem-solver, travel agent, marketer, salesperson and whatever else is called for. Above all, you need to truly enjoy working with people — all day. If this doesn't sound like you, then leading a tour may not be your calling.

Sometimes spouses work together; both may qualify for free travel but sometimes one must pay.

Some people become group tour organizers unintentionally, when they volunteer, or are appointed, to head a club's travel committee. Others go into tour organizing as a business, independently developing travel programs and drawing participants from neighbors, friends and clubs in which they are members.

A beginner Pied Piper must first find a market for recruiting travelers. One of the biggest markets is seniors, who have both the time and money to do more traveling and enjoy the group camaraderie of a tour. Senior clubs and organizations often have active travel programs.

Other Pied Pipers create groups from their workplace or from their social, professional or religious organizations. For instance, teachers frequently lead student tours. Country clubs, tennis clubs or other athletic organizations are markets for sports-oriented trips.

> *Take note!*
> ☞ **Be entertaining.** If you have some expertise that you can share with fellow cruise passengers, remember that the cruise lines seek lecturers who can present their material in a fun and engaging way. They want enthusiasm and originality, not someone who's dull and lifeless.

Special-interest tours draw participants from local historical societies, museum auxiliaries, theater groups, wine-tasting societies and clubs for those interested in gardening, photography, square dancing or other hobbies.

Your own family and friends may want a reunion, or an ethnic organization may be interested in a heritage and genealogy tour.

A group leader's responsibilities are numerous. Work begins six months or even a year ahead. Here are some responsibilities, plus tips on being a group leader:

● Pick a destination or type of trip.

Get ideas from the group on several trip options for you to investigate. Remember, your own dream trip may not be what the group wants and you may have to foster enthusiasm for destinations not on your must-see list.

● Know the group's budget.

Does the group want low-cost or upscale travel? What's an approximate per-person cost that most participants can afford? How long a trip is desired? It's important to have parameters for money and time before even looking at tours.

Group members usually expect a leader to seek out tours and cruises that are the greatest value — often crucial to convincing people to join the trip.

● Take your idea to a travel agent, tour operator or cruise line.

A group leader doesn't have to bother with the fine points of an itinerary, make reservations, rent a bus or act as a tour manager. Instead, group leaders act as the liaison with the tour operator, cruise line or travel agent who supplies the packaged trip.

● Promote the trip.

A leader must develop a marketing plan, which may include public notices, promotional mailings and programs to discuss the trip, show videos and distribute brochures. Any marketing costs involved must be built into the price or come out of the organizer's pocket.

● Supply information, handle bookings.

The group organizer answers travelers' questions, — at whatever hour they call — assists in filling out forms and may have to collect deposits and final payments.

The organizer does a pre-trip briefing, giving participants information about travel arrangements, climate, sightseeing, shopping, extra expenses and other basics.

Sometimes the organizer receives all the tickets and travel documents and must check them for accuracy and distribute them to group members.

Almost inevitably, one or more people will drop out at the last minute. A wise organizer signs up more than the minimum number required for the group trip and may even start a waiting list.

● Act as spokesperson — and nursemaid — on the trip.

Most tours will have a professional manager or guide, supplied by the tour operator, who is responsible for all air, land, hotel and sightseeing arrangements when the group travels. The tour leader acts as a liaison between the group and the tour guide. If the tour doesn't go smoothly, the tour organizer hears about it from members — and must soothe ruffled feathers of his/her group as well as work with the tour manager to solve problems.

Successful Pied Pipers work hard to earn their free trips. Max and Sara Zeman of Pittsburgh, PA, have organized trips for their local chapter of the American Association of Retired Persons for several years.

"It's nice when it's all over. Everybody is kissing you instead of swearing at you," Max said.

"We took it over without much training and found out all the pitfalls that first year. Sid Caesar was our worst problem — we had 86 people going on a theater trip, and Sid Caesar (the star) canceled (at the last minute). We had to call all 86; half of them canceled and we had to give them a refund," he said.

Sara added, "One of the nice things about these trips is the single people — especially older ladies in their 80s — who wouldn't go anywhere without having the group. They're chipper and have so much fun."

In some areas, group organizers can take advantage of short trade shows that feature discussions on developing group travel and exhibits by tour operators, cruise lines, hotels, destinations, attractions and others in the travel industry. These offer a good opportunity to see the wide variety of tours available.

The large group-leader organizations are:

● Group Leaders of America, with a membership of 50,000 nationwide, publishes a monthly newspaper with information on destinations, tours and cruises, plus ideas and tips from organizers. It sponsors trade shows and offers a video explaining the association. For information, contact Group Leaders of America, P.O. Box 129, Salem, OH 44460, (800) 628-0993. No membership dues.

●National Association of Senior Travel Planners (NASTP), with a membership of about 35,000, is focused primarily on the East-Central and Atlantic Seaboard states. Besides sponsoring trade shows, it publishes newsletters and directories. Contact National Association of Senior Travel Planners, 44 Cushing St., Hingham, MA 02043, (617) 740-1185. Dues are $10 a year, usually paid by the organization the travel planner represents.

• Senior Travel and Recreation Activities Council (STRAC) focuses on travel in California and has about 3,000 group organizers as members. It holds free trade shows and publishes a newsletter. Contact Senior Travel and Recreation Activities Council, P.O. Box 2055, Palm Desert, CA 92261, (800) 566-3466. No membership dues for group organizers.

• Senior Travel Tips serves 14 Western states and Western Canada and has a membership of about 10,000. It publishes a newsletter bimonthly. Senior Travel Tips, 5281 Scotts Valley Drive, Scotts Valley, CA 95066, (408) 438-6085. No membership dues for qualified travel leaders.

Dance the Night Away

If you're a debonair gentleman age 50 or older with the stamina to exude charm 16 hours a day and dance until the orchestra stops, you might be a social host aboard cruise ships.

In exchange for socializing, you'll receive free passage, usually including airfare, shore excursions, gratuities and some bar credits.

Royal Cruise Line is known for its host program, introduced in the early 1980s after the line noted that the ratio of single women to unattached men ran as high as 100 to 1 on some cruises. Many passengers were single women 50 and beyond, often widows who had been accustomed to an active social whirl but now had no partner.

Royal Cruise Line began recruiting sophisticated, single older men to be partners, to dine with a table of single women, dance, join in daytime activities aboard ship and escort groups on tours. American Hawaii Cruises, Crystal Cruises, Cunard, Delta Queen Steamboat Co. and Holland America Line have host programs. Other lines may have extra single men on some sailings.

Most hosts are retired or semiretired from professional fields. They're carefully screened for general congeniality, conversational skills, respectability, travel experience and enthusiasm. The two major rules for hosts are: treat all single women passengers equally, showing no favoritism such as dancing with one woman all evening, and always act in a gentlemanly manner — no hanky-panky allowed.

The hosts function as part of the cruise staff, though not paid. They provide their own wardrobes and usually share a cabin with another host.

"The most difficult part is getting enough sleep," said Ted Armstrong, 73, of

> *Take note!*
> ☞ **Be light on your feet.** If you want to be a gentleman host on a cruise ship, brush up your dancing skills. You don't need to be Fred Astaire, but you do want to be graceful enough not to step on any toes. You may be asked to do more sophisticated dances, such as the tango, but cruise lines often will give dance lessons for hosts.

Pasadena, CA. "Sometimes we dance five to six hours — that's a marathon day."

"I always bring eight to 10 pairs of shoes," said Earl Arthurs, 79, of Charlotte, NC.

Most cruise lines hire hosts through a company that screens applicants and matches them to the different lines. The major company supplying hosts is Laurette Blake The Working Vacation, 4277 Lake Santa Clara Drive, Santa Clara, CA 95054, (408) 727-9665. It works with eight cruise lines on host programs. Gentlemen who are interested should call the company for selection guidelines and procedures.

Talk Your Way Aboard

Cruise lines, especially those with longer sailings and a mature clientele, often bring aboard enrichment speakers.

Some companies do their own recruiting; others use speakers' bureaus or headhunters specializing in cruise-ship placements, or a combination.

If you're a celebrity such as news commentator Walter Cronkite or household-hints maven Heloise, it's relatively easy to travel free in return for speaking and mingling with passengers. It's also promising if you're an authority in your field of work.

A number of lines tap guest speakers from different professions, as well as celebrities. Royal Cruise Line's Odyssey Discovery Program links speakers to the cruise destinations if possible or to the theme of the cruise. The line may have speakers talking about world affairs or gardens of Europe, for instance. Photography experts often are on Alaska cruises.

Cunard has a World University Program, fielding distinguished speakers on a variety of topics for its ships, and Holland America Line has the Flagship Forum Lecture Series on European itineraries of the Maasdam.

Take note!

☞ **Make a video.** Potential speakers for a cruise may be asked to prepare a video to submit to the line or to the lecturer supplier. If you don't have a video camera, rent one from a camera store and recruit a friend to film you in action.

For its speakers and instructors, a cruise line usually provides a cabin for two and meals. The speaker's airfare may be included by some lines but not others. No airfare is provided for companions. A speaker may be able to join shore excursions at no cost if space is available.

Lecturers who use speakers' bureaus or headhunters may have to pay the company a fee based on length and cost of the trip, normally $25-$50 a day. Two of the best-known companies supplying lecturers are Lauretta Blake The Working Vacation of Santa Clara, CA, and Lectures International of Tucson, AZ.

Lecturer suppliers say speakers who are experts on destinations or certain regions of the world are in demand; cultural, historical, political and natural aspects are of interest. Areas of expertise that cruise lines are seeking include: sciences, from anthropology to zoology; health fields such as exercise psychology, nutrition, stress management, herbalism and massage; music; comedy;

beauty and fashion; psychological/family counseling; memory and time management; and cultural fields, such as history, art, wine, photography and regional studies.

Instructors in fitness and exercise, dancing, bridge, languages, computers, sports, and arts and crafts also are needed.

The competition for lecturers' and instructors' slots on cruise ships is ferocious. And just because you're an experienced lecturer doesn't mean you'll necessarily do well in a cruise ship's easygoing environment.

"We want enthusiasm, people with diversified lives, and the right sociability who can mingle with passengers after they're done speaking," says Lauretta Blake. Someone who has expertise in more than one topic, or a husband-wife team specializing in different fields, might have an edge.

Those who have an expertise to share may call individual cruise lines to check on their needs. Many lines, however, work through suppliers for their speakers. Contact Lauretta Blake The Working Vacation, 4277 Lake Santa Clara Drive, Santa Clara, CA 95054, (408) 727-9665, to check which areas of expertise are needed currently and to get an application form. Lectures International, P.O. Box 35446, Tucson AZ 85740, (520) 297-1145, responds to cover letters with resumes.

If you make it through the screening and board ship, be aware that the cruise line looks very carefully at how you perform, especially at passenger ratings, before inviting you back.

CHAPTER 11

Tax-Deductible Volunteer Vacations

You could deduct your next vacation from your taxes. Sound too good to be true? It's not.

Of course, there's a hitch. You can't just lie around the beach and expect Uncle Sam to accept a write-off for that vacation. But you could spend your vacation time working as a researcher or as a Good Samaritan, at a beach or elsewhere, and deduct the costs — legitimately.

Technically, no vacation, in the normal sense of the word, is tax-deductible. But doing qualified research or work projects benefiting the public while on your vacation can be deducted as a charitable contribution, if you're careful to meet all the Internal Revenue Service criteria.

These trips can be weekend excursions to territory only a short drive from home, a week or longer at a national park or wildlife refuge, or far-flung quests to exotic lands. Prices range from extremely low-cost to the luxury level. Volunteering in a park may require that you pay only your incidental living expenses, but a foreign research expedition can cost $1,000 and higher. Yet, the tax-deductibility factor makes even the costly trips an option to consider.

Helping America the Beautiful

The U.S. government offers some of the best bargains in volunteer vacations, providing opportunities to get close to nature at no fee. The National Park Service, the U.S. Fish and Wildlife Service and the U.S. Forest Service welcome volunteers. There's no pay for your work. You usually foot the bill for your living expenses, but your costs can be tax-deductible because your work benefits the public. In some cases, volunteers are provided free accommodations or are reimbursed for some living expenses.

Bob Reed has volunteered regularly in the summer for Colorado's Rocky Mountain National Park. He leads campfire programs on bighorn sheep, then prowls the alpine tundra with a pair of field glasses looking for the animals to point out to visitors.

"My job is to spot the sheep, which hide in the rocks, so that visitors can catch a glimpse of them," he explains.

The job requires sure-footed climbing, which helps keep him fit, he adds.

If he were to write a job description, it would say, "requires a real good sense of humor and a private income," he laughs. "The reward is personal and emotional. You have to look at it as doing something that's worthwhile and doing it for free."

Reed says his mileage between the park and his home in Grand Lake, CO, is tax-deductible.

Those who want to volunteer in the parks should plan ahead. Housing for volunteers is at a premium during the summer. It's easier to get a volunteer position then if you have an RV or camper of some kind. A park often can provide utility hookups though it may not have housing. Parks usually are better able to provide housing for volunteers who can work prior to Memorial Day or after Labor Day. If park housing or hookups are available, they're usually provided free; otherwise, volunteers have to make their own living arrangements.

The U.S. Fish and Wildlife Service oversees numerous refuges, where volunteer jobs vary according to the type of wildlife at the site. Volunteers may observe animal activity, identify birds, look for weather or human damage in the refuge, do bird banding and post boundary signs.

You don't need special skills to be a park, forest or refuge volunteer, spokesmen say. But when applying, you should list any special talents or interests because it can mean a difference in the tasks you're given. Some agencies will provide training, if needed.

Be precise about your expectations or what you would enjoy most. If you like being with people, say so because you might not enjoy the somewhat solitary task of bird identification. On the other hand, taking a group of giggling schoolkids on a nature hike won't be your cup of tea if you're longing for the peace and quiet of a secluded forest trail.

Volunteer arrangements are made with each individual park, forest or refuge. While some may reimburse volunteers for food and travel, others may not. Regulations vary from site to site. Contact the volunteer coordinator at the individual sites that interest you most. Some government agencies provide general information about volunteering; see sources of information at end of the chapter.

Research Projects

In the private sector, Earthwatch is the premier provider of volunteer travel for research work, fielding 150 expeditions a year in the United States and 50 other countries.

Tom and Delta Greene of Downers Grove, IL, went to Kenya, Nepal and Tonga on different trips as Earthwatch volunteers. Their work and living conditions varied widely.

"In Kenya, we studied the ecology of Lake Naivasha, working with British and Kenyan researchers. For two weeks we stayed in a comfortable lodge formerly used by Joy Adamson (of "Born Free" fame) as a research center. So that was not a roughing-it trip," Tom says.

Nepal, on the other hand, was a challenge, he says. The trip involved studying

> *Take note!*
>
> ☛ **Expect no luxury.** Whatever the work, the qualifying tax-deductible projects tend toward spartan and rugged travel, even if they take place in an otherwise exotic land. If you're concerned about lodging, clarify the exact meaning of such terms as "rustic."

small carnivores in Chitwan National Park, in the jungle.

"We trapped small animals, sedated them so we could take their measurements and sometimes put a radio on them. We trapped civets, mongooses, fishing cats and leopard cats, which are about the size of a house cat," he says.

Delta says they thought accommodations in the lodge were rather primitive — until they went to a field camp where they slept on the ground in lean-tos constructed for them by the Nepalese.

"We moved to our sites on elephants, which were there to protect us from rhinos and tigers as well as to transport us. It was not unusual for tigers to come quite close to camp," she recalls.

On a trip to Tonga, the Greenes helped save endangered giant clams.

"On all these trips, we've thought highly of our researchers and felt they were doing valuable and important work," says Tom. "You get a real sense of fulfillment and satisfaction that you've helped in something that can be important to the survival of a species, or to the ecology."

> **Take note!**
> ☞ **Be prepared to work.**
> Some volunteer vacations involve hard, physical labor. For many participants, the physical work is a welcome change of pace from sedentary office jobs and a chance to get outdoors.

Water-based projects attract scuba and photography enthusiast Dr. Eugene T. Rowe of Highland Springs, VA. The retired veterinarian tries to go where his talents are needed.

"I learn a lot. I have a great deal of fun, and I can write off the expense," he says.

One Earthwatch project took Rowe to the north coast of the Dominican Republic in the Caribbean. "The researcher found a shipwreck that probably dates to the 1600s. He's attempting to identify its nationality, cargo, and when and why it went down. I took extensive photographs of the wreck," Rowe says.

On another Earthwatch trip, Rowe stayed on dry land, to study volancoes on the Kamchatka Peninsula in the far eastern part of Siberia, on the Bering Sea jutting toward Japan. The group camped out in rugged conditions and ate plain food, he says. He collected soil samples and rock specimens — and got a close-up look at a culture and area that few tourists ever see.

Earthwatch research expeditions start as low as $599 for one week. Trips to the more exotic destinations can cost much the same as luxurious vacations because volunteers actually fund the project on which they work. Airfare to the sites usually is extra.

Earthwatch trips, however, are tax-deductible. Also, you can look for a corporate sponsor to pay your contribution. The sponsor gets the tax deduction, and you take the research trip. Sometimes companies will sponsor their employees, and some corporations have scholarship or fellowship programs that fund research trips for teachers or students.

Getting the Tax Deduction

Rules about deducting costs of travel have been tightened considerably in the past few years. At one time, if you spent just one day of your two-week vacation in work-related tasks, you could deduct the cost of your entire trip from your taxes. A French professor could claim a three-month vacation traveling in France as a deduction because it furthered education.

No more. Beginning in 1987 in the wake of Uncle Sam's massive tax reform, the Internal Revenue Service began to take a hard look at the practice of subsidizing the vacations of millions of Americans.

Wilson Fadely, a spokesman for the IRS in Washington, DC, says, "There were so many abuses going on — ads promoting all kinds of vacations as tax-deductible, even cruises to the Mediterranean. Congress said this has to halt — all these vacations can't be deductible."

So the IRS code — never known for simple statements — now says that no deduction is allowed for travel expenses away from home "unless there is no significant element of personal pleasure, recreation, or vacation in such travel."

Translation: Leisure travel must be genuinely work-oriented to qualify as tax-deductible.

Two kinds of leisure travel are still deductible under the tax reform: trips that directly relate to a traveler's profession, and work-oriented trips with organizations that qualify for charitable contribution deductions.

Also, since 1987, to claim any such tax-deductible travel, you must be filing a long tax form that allows you to itemize deductions.

For career-related travel deductions, consult a tax accountant or a local IRS office; the guidelines are extensive and vary with the kind of work.

For other leisure travel deductions, two basic criteria must be met: You must spend your time working, and you must be doing the work for an organization qualified by the IRS to receive charitable contributions.

Organizations that do research projects with the help of volunteers are sensitive about the term vacation. Earthwatch cautions participants that while they may be taking vacation time, the trips are work.

After an orientation, participants normally spend eight or even more hours a day on an environmentally oriented project. Participants do significant work, and the fees they pay for the trip fund the research and the scientists.

> **Take note!**
>
> ☛ **Gear up.** When looking at volunteer vacations, ask what equipment is needed and whether it is supplied or you must bring your own. Clothing or other gear bought specifically for the trip may be tax-deductible.

Educational or study trips with no hands-on research do not qualify for the tax deduction. If an expert acts as a travel guide and you merely follow, the costs are not deductible. For example: A trip spent with Earthwatch excavating a 13th-century castle in Dublin is deductible. A seven-day trip to France to study garden designs isn't. However, if a study trip has a required donation fee to the organization, check to see if that specific amount is tax-deductible even though the cost of the trip is not.

Don't expect to take a regular vacation, tack on a few days with a research project and then deduct all of your expenses. If you travel directly to and from your deductible trip, then all of the costs incurred during the travel are deductible, including plane tickets and meals. If you choose to make a side trip, like visiting Aunt Martha, before or after the legitimately deductible work project, you cannot deduct any of your transportation costs.

Caveat: Don't overdo it on first-class tickets and accommodations because deductions above a certain level raise red flags with the IRS.

While the IRS code says there can be no "significant element of personal pleasure" in tax-deductible travel, few people sign up for some activity they know they're going to hate, even if they do get a big tax deduction for it. It's doubtful, however, that the IRS would disallow an otherwise qualified deduction if you admit that you enjoyed your trip.

> **Take note!**
> ☛ **Calling all ages.** People from their 20s to 80s take volunteer vacations. Many participants are retirees, and many sign up for repeated trips.

The IRS does want proof that you actually worked on a specified project that qualifies for a deduction. Keep documents to back up your claim. Besides cancelled checks and airline tickets, keep a daily journal of the tasks you perform and the number of hours you spend on them. In the case of an audit, this log is important proof of the deductibility of your trip.

The IRS spells out the type of organizations that qualify to receive charitable contributions under Section 501 (c) (3) as "corporations and any community chest, fund, or foundation organized and operated exclusively for religious, charitable, scientific, testing for public safety, literacy or educational purposes."

The fee you pay for a research or work project is considered a donation to the organization. But, don't expect to claim a deduction for a church-sponsored tour of cathedrals in Europe. If your religious group, however, goes to a Guatemalan village to build a church, it likely qualifies as a donation and is deductible. Some fees are totally tax-deductible while others may be only partially deductible, depending on what they cover.

Earthwatch provides a letter specifying that it qualifies under Section 501 (c) (3) to receive charitable donations and says as far it knows, none of its projects ever has been disallowed by the IRS. Some participants, however, have been asked for clarification of their deductions in the form of letters or testimonials from the scientists under whom they worked, in addition to their own receipts and daily journal.

Don't assume that all organizations doing research trips meet the IRS criteria. For instance, donations to a non-profit organization aren't necessarily tax-deductible — unless the organization also qualifies under IRS rules as a charity. Ask the organization doing a research trip if it qualifies under Section 501 (c) (3). If it's not a well-known group, verify the information with a tax accountant or an IRS office.

Besides private organizations, governmental agencies can receive charitable contributions, under provisions of Section 170 in the tax code. For instance, if you volunteer to man a fire tower for the U.S. Forest Service, count coyotes at a wildlife refuge or help visitors to one of the many national parks on your vacation, all or at least part of your expenses may be deductible. But check with your tax accountant about the specific volunteer work you will be doing, the documentation needed and to what extent expenses are tax deductible.

For more information from the IRS, call (800) 829-3676 and request Publication 17, "Your Federal Income Tax," and Publication 526, "Charitable Contributions."

Also, before signing up for any work-oriented travel that you think is tax-deductible, it's wise to check with your tax accountant or a local IRS office for clarifications and updates on regulations.

Getting Information

For information on volunteer vacations, contact the sources listed below. In addition to these sources, vacation volunteering opportunities may be available through your local museums, art centers, historical societies, hospitals and churches.

● Earthwatch, 680 Mount Auburn St., Box 403, Watertown, MA 02172, (617) 926-8200. Expeditions start at $599.

● University Research Expeditions Program (UREP), University of California, Berkeley, CA 94720, (510) 642-6586. Trips average $1,200.

● Appalachian Mountain Club Trails Program, P.O. Box 298, Gorham, NH 03581, (603) 466-2721. Does trail maintenance mainly in the Northeast but some in the West. Programs are seven to 10 days, and fees of $70-$200 cover meals and housing. Club fees are $40 a year for adults, $65 for entire family.

● Tahoe Rim Trail, P.O.Box 4647, Stateline, NV 89449, (702) 588-0686. Trail builder's hot line: (702) 588-8799 for recorded information on work parties, which are weekends only mid-May to mid-October, depending on weather. No fee charged.

● National Park Service. Call individual parks for volunteer opportunities and regulations.

● U.S. Fish and Wildlife Service, Attention Volunteer Coordinator, 4401 N. Fairfax Drive, Room 670, Arlington, VA 22203, (703) 358-2029. Provides a volunteer brochure and list of national wildlife refuges.

● U.S. Forest Service, Volunteering in the Forest, P.O. Box 96090, Washington, DC 20090, (703) 235-8855. Provides packet of information.

Seeing the USA For Free

While there's probably "no free lunch" on a vacation trip, you'll have better luck when it comes to sightseeing and family entertainment. Nearly every travel destination in the United States has wonderful things to do that are free. We offer the best of the freebies in this section.

CHAPTER 12

The Best Sightseeing From New York To Hawaii

Many of the following freebies deliver enough entertainment to serve as the focus of an entire trip. Indeed, a few cities — such as Washington, Philadelphia and San Antonio — make it hard to spend money because they offer so many free attractions. Other suggestions focus on a single, simple pleasure unique to a destination, something you shouldn't miss when you are in the area. Either way, you'll still have change in your jeans at the end of the trip.

To cut vacation costs even more, remember that almost all zoos and museums offer free admission on certain days and that the vast majority of America's beaches and some state and national parks don't charge admission.

Now, the envelope please. Here, in no particular ranking, are our nominations for our country's 25 best free travel experiences, categorized by location.

Boston, Massachusetts

The three-mile-long Freedom Trail starts at the Boston Common Visitor Information Center. On this self-guided tour, visitors follow a painted red line that connects 16 major historic sites significant to the Colonial and Revolutionary War eras. Stops that offer free admission include the Park Street Church (where the song "America" was first sung on July 4, 1831), Granary Burying Ground (with the graves of Paul Revere, Benjamin Franklin, John Hancock and Samuel Adams), King's Chapel (1754), Old Corner Bookstore (in business since the mid-1800s, browsers welcome), Faneuil Hall (still a thriving marketplace), Old North Church (1723) and the USS Constitution (Old Ironsides). Paul Revere's home also is on the trail; it has an admission fee.

Prefer a guide? National Park Service rangers give free, 90-minute tours over much of this territory from late March through late November, starting from the Boston National Historic Park Visitor Center at State and Devonshire streets.

Information: National Park Service, (617) 242-5642.

New York, New York

Rockefeller Plaza is loaded with gardens, plazas and pocket parks; pick up a free walking tour brochure in the main lobby at 30 Rockefeller Center and enjoy this city within a city at Fifth Avenue and 50th Street.

Many other landmark buildings offer art exhibits and free entertainment. Concerts and dance performances take place among the palm trees at the indoor Winter Garden at the World Financial Center in Lower Manhattan, and the *beaux-arts* New York Public Library has special exhibitions as well as free guided tours at 11 a.m. and 2 p.m., Monday through Saturday.

> **Take note!**
> ☞ **Wear the right clothes.** Dress properly if you are going to visit a church or solemn shrine such as the USS Arizona Memorial at Pearl Harbor. Visitors to the Arizona, for example, are requested to wear appropriate dress — shirts and footwear are required at all times.

The free visitor gallery of the New York Stock Exchange is one of the best shows in town. To witness the often frantic activity visible in the "pit" on the floor below, line up at the 20 Broad Street entrance for a ticket. Get there early, tickets become available by 9 a.m. and they're often gone by midmorning.

Afterwards, visit Federal Hall and Fraunces Tavern (both have ties to George Washington), search out the graves of Alexander Hamilton and Robert Fulton in Trinity Church's tiny cemetery, and/or tour the Federal Reserve Bank. End your day of no-cost sightseeing with a stroll through nearby South Street Seaport and the revitalized Fulton Fish Market. On weekends, browse for bargains at the Sixth Avenue Antiques Market, between 24th and 27th streets

Information: New York Convention and Visitors Bureau, (800) NYC-VISIT.

Philadelphia, Pennsylvania

Known as America's most historic square mile, Independence National Historical Park offers more than a dozen free attractions in the heart of the city. Prime sites include Carpenters' Hall, where the First Continental Congress met in 1774, the Liberty Bell Pavilion, Independence Hall, Todd House (the home of Dolley Madison) and the Bishop White House, a restored upper-class home built in 1786-87. Near the park is the Edgar Allan Poe National Historic Site, where fans of the writer are treated to a slide show and tour of his home.

Love art? Don't miss the outstanding Atwater Kent Museum nearby at 15 S. Seventh St., home to more than 40,000 objects that span the city's 300-year history. Admission is free on Saturday ($2 Tuesday through Friday).

Information: Independence National Historical Park, (215) 597-8974; Philadelphia Convention and Visitors Bureau, (215) 636-3300.

Washington, DC

No museum in the world compares to the Smithsonian Institution, which includes the "old red castle," Arts and Industries Building, National Air and Space Museum, the Freer and Sackler art galleries, National Museum of

American History, National Museum of Natural History, National Museum of American Art, National Portrait Gallery, Renwick Gallery, Hirshhorn Museum and Sculpture Garden, National Zoological Park, Anacostia Museum and the National Museum of African Art. Take advantage of free tours at each building; call Smithsonian Information, (202) 357-2700, or for recorded information, (202) 357-2020.

Want to tour the White House? Get tickets eight to 10 weeks in advance from your congressman or, in spring and summer, line up really early for tickets (some get there as early as 6:30 a.m.) at the White House Visitor Center on 15th Street near E Street. Tickets aren't required in winter; those who line up at the Visitor Center by 11:30 a.m. generally are assured of admission. Tours operate from 10 a.m. to noon Tuesday-Saturday; call the White House Visitors Office tour line, (202) 456-7041. Tours may be cancelled at the last minute due to official events.

Other major free sights include the U.S. Capitol, (202) 225-6827 for tours; Arlington National Cemetery and Arlington House, (703) 692-0931; Bureau of Engraving and Printing, (202) 874-3188; Federal Bureau of Investigation, (202) 324-3447; and *The Washington Post*, (202) 334-7969.

Information: Washington, DC, Convention and Visitors Association, (202) 789-7000.

Norfolk, Virginia

The world's largest naval base allows tours of active-duty ships every weekend afternoon year-round; visits include command centers, the bridge, weapons systems and living quarters. Call (804) 444-7955. Afterwards, visit the Hampton Roads Naval Museum in historic Pennsylvania House on the base, (804) 444-8971. Fun-filled locales in the city include the Waterside, a festival marketplace on the waterfront, and Town Point Park, site of free concerts and festivals almost every weekend.

A free brochure from the Norfolk Convention and Visitors Bureau outlines three walking tours, covering such sites as the Douglas MacArthur Memorial and the cobblestone streets of the Freemason Historic District, Norfolk's oldest standing neighborhood.

Information: Norfolk Convention and Visitors Bureau, (800) 368-3097.

Charleston, South Carolina

Self-guided walking tours through this town's charming and extensive historic district are best begun at the Visitor Reception and Transportation Center at the corner of Meeting and Ann streets. With a map from the Charleston Convention and Visitors Bureau in hand, you'll discover some 70 pre-Revolutionary buildings, 136 structures built in the late 18th century and more than 600 others constructed pre-1840. Fort Moultrie, part of Fort Sumter National Monument, lies 10 miles east of town. This 1776 coastal fortification has been restored and has a free visitor center with film and slide shows that focus on the Revolutionary War.

Information: Charleston Convention and Visitors Bureau, (800) 868-8118.

Kennedy Space Center, Florida

Watching the space shuttle launch is just one of the free things available at Kennedy Space Center, but it's the best. The earth trembles and rockets roar as the shuttle lifts off and ultimately disappears into space. Spaceport USA, the visitor center, has numerous free displays and exhibits, including a space shuttle orbiter that visitors can climb aboard. The bus tours and IMAX movie at the spaceport have small admission fees.

Information: For launch status, free car passes and locations where launches are visible from public highways, call Spaceport USA, (407) 452-2121.

Miami Beach, Florida

Every Saturday and Sunday in the late afternoon, a number of cruise ships exit the Port of Miami via a channel bordered by South Pointe Park. Passing in single file review en route to the Caribbean, these floating resorts — some nearly as long as three football fields and 10 stories tall — offer drop-jaw glamour as they pass almost close enough to touch. Watson Island is another great vantage point. Do what Miami residents do and bring a tailgate picnic. A few ships leave on Mondays and Fridays.

Information: Greater Miami Convention and Visitors Bureau, (800) 283-2707.

> **Take note!**
> ☞ **Be kind to your feet.** For sightseeing, wear comfortable, low-heeled shoes that you have already broken in. Your favorite tennis shoes or other rubber-sole footwear are acceptable gear, even when sightseeing in cities.

Key West, Florida

Applauding the sunset from Mallory Square, a downtown dock that faces due west, is a nightly tradition year-round. Craft and food vendors are out in force, along with a strange and varied cast of volunteer performers to whom all the wharf is a stage. Contortionists, fortune tellers, magicians, bagpipers, jugglers, even animal trainers do their thing, and then pass the hat.

Information: Key West Visitor Center, (800) LAST-KEY.

Indian Shores, Florida

The Suncoast Seabird Sanctuary near St. Petersburg treats more injured birds each day than any other wild bird hospital in North America. Patients include pelicans, egrets, owls and hawks — often suffering injuries such as maimed wings and crippled legs — who are nursed back to health and then released. The sanctuary also is home to more than 600 permanently injured birds.

Information: Suncoast Seabird Sanctuary, (813) 391-6211.

Vicksburg, Mississippi

Models at the U.S. Corps of Engineers Waterways Experiment Station in this historic Mississippi River town re-create to scale the major river and dam systems in the United States, complete with water wave action machines. One highlight of the 90-minute guided tour is a working model of Niagara River and Falls. Tours are at 10 a.m. and 2 p.m. weekdays.

Information: Waterways Experiment Station, (601) 634-2502; Vicksburg Convention and Visitors Bureau, (800) 221-3536.

San Antonio, Texas

Begin with an early morning visit to Mission San Antonio de Valero (better known as the Alamo) and then follow the Mission Trail to four other living relics of San Antonio's 18th-century Spanish past: missions Concepcion, San Jose, San Juan and Espada. Next stop is lively Market Square, brimming with Mexican crafts, culture, food and music. Then enjoy the color and crowds along the River Walk en route to the craft shops and art galleries of La Villita, the "little town" where San Antonio began more than two centuries ago.

Information: San Antonio Convention & Visitors Bureau, (800) 447-3372.

Claremore, Oklahoma

The life, times and legends of Oklahoma's best-known native son live on at the Will Rogers Memorial, a 20-acre museum and garden complex that also includes his grave. Eight exhibit galleries chronicle his life as a cowboy, entertainer, journalist, actor, humorist and philosopher; there are daily showings of many of his movies. One small case contains bits salvaged from the 1935 plane crash in Alaska that claimed his life. His birthplace, 12 miles north of Claremore on State Highway 88, also is open daily.

Information: Will Rogers Memorial, (800) 324-9455.

Colorado Springs, Colorado

Set at the scenic foot of the Rampart range of the Rockies, the U.S. Air Force Academy offers free guided tours June through Labor Day and self-guided tours year-round. If you are there by noon on weekdays during the August-May school year, you'll see approximately 4,000 cadets form their units and march to lunch. Colorado's most visited man-made attraction, the architecturally distinctive Cadet Chapel is open for viewing; for church service schedules, call (719) 472-4515. There's an outstanding visitor center with displays, photos and a 15-minute film that recount the history of the academy and describe the daily life of a cadet. For information, call the Visitors Center, (719) 472-2025.

Feeling frisky in spite of the city's 7,280-foot altitude? You can hike to the top of nearby Pikes Peak for the view that inspired the song "America the Beautiful."

Information: Colorado Springs Convention and Visitors Bureau, (800) 368-4748.

Grand Junction, Colorado

Thirty miles west of Grand Junction via I-70, Rabbit Valley "Trail Through Time" is a 1.5-mile, self-guided tour focused on fossils of ancient flora and fauna from the Jurassic Age, 140 million years ago. You'll see skeletal portions of an 80-foot-long Diplodocus and a 50-foot Camarasaurus as well as anthropologists at work.

Information: Dinosaur Valley, (303) 241-9210.

Arizona

The Navajo Nation, largest of all Indian reservations, sweeps across most of northeast Arizona. Within its borders is the Hopi Indian Reservation. Both tribes welcome visitors, opening many of their ceremonies and dances to the public. A free "Indian Country" brochure gives information on the tribes and notes the crafts at which each tribe excels.

Information: Arizona Office of Tourism, (800) 842-8257.

Las Vegas, Nevada

Would you believe a volcano? Easily seen from the sidewalk, the centerpiece of the tropical lagoon fronting the Mirage Hotel is a 55-foot-high volcano that erupts with steam, fire and simulated lava every evening from dusk into the wee hours. Beginning with a subterranean rumble that soon turns into a roar, it builds into a fiery simulation of a South Seas volcano. This show lasts several minutes and erupts every 15 minutes.

Information: Las Vegas Convention and Visitors Authority, (702) 892-0711.

Los Angeles, California

Got stars in your eyes? You can be in the audience for a taping of your favorite TV show by calling Audiences Unlimited, (818) 506-0067, or Audiences Associates, (213) 467-4697, for reservations and free tickets. Next, visit Mann's Chinese Theatre courtyard to trace hand and footprints of more than 150 stars. Then move on to the Hollywood Walk of Fame, where 1,300 terrazzo stars are embedded in the sidewalks along 10 blocks of Hollywood Boulevard between Vine and La Brea. Wind up with a visit to Forest Lawn Memorial Park in Glendale, the last resting place of Lucille Ball, Bette Davis and other stars.

Information: Los Angeles Convention and Visitors Bureau, (213) 624-7300.

San Francisco, California

Walking even part way across the Golden Gate Bridge, a 3.5-mile round-trip jaunt on a wide pedestrian walkway, is an "only-here" experience. All of the Pacific lies to the west, giant ships glide silently below, and the bridge literally pulses beneath your feet as if it were a living thing. Afterward, visit Fort Point National Historic Site underneath the south ramparts of the bridge. Now a museum within the Golden Gate National Recreation Area, the building dates from 1857.

Information: San Francisco Convention and Visitors Bureau, (415) 391-2000.

Honolulu, Hawaii

Poignant and unforgettable, tours of the USS Arizona Memorial at Pearl Harbor begin at the visitor center operated by the National Park Service in cooperation with the U.S. Navy. After you view a 20-minute documentary film that includes rare footage of the surprise attack by the Japanese on the American fleet in Pearl Harbor on Dec. 7, 1941, a Navy shuttle boat takes you to a memorial bridge that straddles the sunken USS Arizona. Some 1,102 men still are entombed below, and oil continues to seep from the rusting hull. Go early; this is a take-a-number operation, and crowds later in the day make for long waits. Tickets may be gone by noon.

Information: USS Arizona Memorial, (808) 422-0561.

Seattle, Washington

Watching Boeing 747s take shape from a catwalk high above the assembly floor is fascinating. Ninety-minute tours of portions of Boeing's huge manufacturing facility in nearby Everett are offered weekdays, but fair warning: Folks begin lining up at 7 a.m. for tickets. Call Boeing's Everett Tour Center, (206) 342-4801. Afterwards, head for Pike Place Market on Seattle's waterfront. Founded in 1907 and located in a nine-acre national historic district, it offers everything from the best fresh fish, produce and flowers in town to the latest in T-shirts, crafts and cafes. Just wandering through is fun — don't miss the flying fish show at Pike Place Fish.

Information: Seattle Visitor Information, (206) 461-5840.

Coulee Dam, Washington

What may be the world's largest screen — the mile-wide, 300-foot-high face of Grand Coulee Dam — comes alive with a spectacular 36-minute laser show nightly from Memorial Day through September. Paced by contemporary music such as "Chariots of Fire" and Neil Diamond's "America," the show focuses on the history of the area and the dam. Best scene: A giant laser-created eagle swoops down to snatch a salmon from the very real Columbia River. Best viewing is at or near the Visitor Arrival Center immediately below the dam on State Highway 155, 85 miles west of Spokane.

Information: Visitor Arrival Center, (509) 633-9265.

Keystone, South Dakota

For pure majesty, catch the early morning light on the four great granite faces of the Mount Rushmore National Memorial — George, Thomas, Teddy and Abraham never looked more impressive — and then return in the evening for the light and sound show (mid-May through mid-September). The result of six years of intermittent sculpting between 1927 and 1941, these massive faces measure 60 feet from chin to forehead. This 1,246-acre memorial also includes a visitor center and sculptor Gutzon Borglum's studio, where carving techniques are demonstrated in summer months.

Information: Mount Rushmore National Memorial, (605) 574-2523.

Amana Colonies, Iowa

Although most of the museums carry a modest admission charge, there are many free things to do in these seven historic villages, founded in 1855 by

Germans seeking religious freedom. First, get your bearings via advice and a free video presentation at the Amana Colonies Welcome Center in Amana. Then catch the free tour at the Amana Woolen Mill, portions of which date from the mid-19th century, (319) 622-3432. Other freebies include tours and samples at the 10 wineries and a brewery and samples of cheese and sausage for the asking in the Amana meat shops. Don't miss the Amana Arts Guild Center in High Amana, a gallery museum shop featuring locally produced crafts and fine art.

Information: Amana Colonies, (800) 245-5465.

Soo Locks, Michigan

One of the world's largest and busiest locking systems raises and lowers lake freighters and ocean-going vessels 21 feet, linking Lake Superior with the lower Great Lakes and, ultimately, the Atlantic Ocean. Visitors watch the action from an observation platform.

Information: UP (Upper Peninsula) Travel and Recreation Association, (800) 562-7134.

Ways to Save on Sightseeing

Beyond the many free sights in America, you will find ways to cut the cost of attractions that have admission fees.

A number of popular cities have discount cards or coupons that save on sightseeing, lodging and food. Some discounts are tied to particular times of the year. For example:

Orlando Magicard: Available free, this discount card comes with a list of merchants and their discounts — some offering 50 percent off or two-for-one savings. To receive the Orlando Magicard, call (800) 551-0181. For more information, contact the Orlando/Orange County Convention and Visitors Bureau, 6700 Forum Drive, Suite 100, Orlando, FL 32821, (407) 363-5871.

Kissimmee-St. Cloud Vacation Guide: This 79-page book provides information on more than 130 hotels and motels in the Walt Disney World area. Coupons provide discounts of up to 50 percent. For the book, call (800) 362-5477. For other information, contact the Kissimmee-St. Cloud Convention and Visitors Bureau, P.O. Box 422007, Kissimmee, FL 34742.

Golden Gate Park Explorer Pass: Available for $12.50, this discount card provides one free admission to each of five museums and cultural attractions in San Francisco's Golden Gate Park. Obtain a pass from any of the museum locations or from the San Francisco information center at 900 Market St., San Francisco, CA 94102, (415) 391-2000.

Williamsburg, VA: This popular destination has three seasonal brochures — an "early bird" brochure for January-March, a fall brochure for September-November and a holiday brochure for December through early January. These contain coupons good for savings up to 25 percent at local merchants, hotels and restaurants. For information, contact the Williamsburg Area Convention and Visitors Bureau, 201 Penniman Road, Williamsburg, VA 23185, (800) 368-6511.

Palm Beach, FL: Seasonal savings are offered April-December in a free coupon book titled "$500 Worth of the Palm Beaches Free." The book has merchant, lodging and restaurant discounts. For more information or to receive a coupon book, contact the Palm Beach County Convention and Visitors Bureau, 1555 Palm Beach Lakes Blvd., Suite 204, West Palm Beach, FL 33401, (800) 554-7256.

When planning a trip, check your destinations for possible cards or coupon books. Major cities and popular sites are most likely to offer them.

Most state tourism offices offer free travel guides, and many of them contain money-saving coupons. For example:

Discover Nevada Bonus Book: This guidebook has valuable coupons good at various shops, hotels and restaurants statewide. The Bonus Book is available at most Nevada chambers of commerce and visitor welcome centers or by contacting the Nevada Commission on Tourism, 5151 S. Carson St., Capitol Complex, Carson City, NV 89710, (800) 638-2328.

Ohio Pass: This guide comes with more than $3,000 worth of coupons good at shops, lodging and restaurants across Ohio. For more information or to order the Ohio Pass, contact the Ohio Division of Travel & Tourism, P.O. Box 1001, Columbus, OH 43216, (800) 282-5393.

Check with tourist offices in the states you plan to visit to see if they offer such money-saving vacation guides. The following chapter contains a list of all state tourism offices.

CHAPTER 13

Getting Information

State tourism offices offer a wide variety of free literature for travelers. When contacting the state, ask about travel discount books, coupons or cards also. For literature or travel kit requests, use the "800" number when provided; for other inquiries use the information numbers or write to the state tourism offices at the addresses provided.

State	For literature	For information	Address
Alabama	800-252-2262	334-242-4169	P.O. Box 4927, Montgomery, AL 36103
Alaska	907-465-2010	907-465-2010	P.O. Box 110801, Juneau, AK 99811
Arizona	800-842-8257	800-842-8257	2702 N. Third St., Suite 4015, Phoenix, AZ 85004
Arkansas	800-628-8725	501-682-7777	1 Capitol Mall, Little Rock, AR 72201
California	800-862-2543	916-322-2882	801 K St., Suite 1600, Sacramento, CA 95814
Colorado	800-265-6723	800-265-6723	225 W. Colfax, Denver, CO 80202
Connecticut	800-282-6863	860-258-4355	865 Brook St., Rocky Hill, CT 06067
Delaware	800-441-8846	302-739-4271	P.O. Box 1401, 99 Kings Highway, Dover, DE 19903
Florida	904-487-1462	904-487-1462	126 W. Van Buren St., Tallahassee, FL 32399
Georgia	800-847-4842	404-656-3590	P.O. Box 1776, Atlanta, GA 30301
Hawaii	800-464-2924	800-464-2924	2270 Kalakaua Ave., Suite 801, Honolulu, HI 96815
Idaho	800-635-7820	208-334-2470	700 W. State St., P.O. Box 83720, Boise, ID 83720
Illinois	800-223-0121	800-223-0121	James R. Thompson Center, 100 W. Randolph St., Suite 3-400, Chicago, IL 60601
Indiana	800-289-6646	317-232-8860	1 N. Capitol Ave., Suite 700, Indianapolis, IN 46204
Iowa	800-345-4692	515-242-4705	200 E. Grand, Des Moines, IA 50309
Kansas	800-252-6727	913-296-2009	700 S.W. Harrison St., Suite 1300, Topeka, KS 66603
Kentucky	800-225-8747	502-564-4930	500 Nero St., Capital Plaza Tower, Suite 2200, Frankfort, KY 40601
Louisiana	800-334-8626	800-633-6970	P.O. Box 94291, Baton Rouge, LA 70804
Maine	800-533-9595	207-623-0363	P.O. Box 2300, Hallowell, ME 04347
Maryland	800-543-1036	410-767-3400	217 E. Redwood St., Ninth Floor, Baltimore, MD 21202
Massachusetts	800-447-6277	617-727-3201	100 Cambridge St., 13th Floor, Boston, MA 02202

State	For literature	For information	Address
Michigan	800-543-2937	800-543-2937	333 S. Capitol, Suite F, Lansing, MI 48909
Minnesota	800-657-3700	612-296-5029	100 Metro Square, 121 Seventh Place E., St. Paul, MN 55101
Mississippi	800-927-6378	601-359-3297	P.O. Box 1705, Ocean Springs, MS 39566
Missouri	800-877-1234	314-751-4133	P.O. Box 1055, Jefferson City, MO 65102
Montana	800-847-4868	800-548-3390	1424 Ninth Ave., Helena, MT 59620
Nebraska	800-228-4307	402-471-3796	P.O. Box 98913, Lincoln, NE 68509
Nevada	800-638-2328	800-237-0774	5151 S. Carson St., Capitol Complex, Carson City, NV 89710
New Hampshire	603-271-2666	603-271-2666	P.O. Box 1856, Concord, NH 03302
New Jersey	800-537-7397	609-292-2470	20 W. State St., CN826, Trenton, NJ 08625
New Mexico	800-545-2040	800-545-2040	491 Old Santa Fe Trail, Santa Fe, NM 87503
New York	800-225-5697	518-474-4116	1 Commerce Plaza, Albany, NY 12245
North Carolina	800-847-4862	919-733-4171	430 N. Salisbury St., Raleigh, NC 27611
North Dakota	800-435-5663	800-435-5663	604 East Blvd., Bismarck, ND 58505
Ohio	800-282-5393	614-466-8844	P.O. Box 1001, Columbus, OH 43216
Oklahoma	800-652-6552	405-521-2409	2401 N. Lincoln Blvd., Will Rogers Bldg., Oklahoma City, OK 73105
Oregon	800-547-7842	503-986-0000	775 Summer St. N.E., Salem, OR 97310
Pennsylvania	800-847-4872	717-787-5453	453 Forum Building, Room 453, Harrisburg, PA 17120
Rhode Island	800-556-2484	401-277-2601	7 Jackson Walkway, Providence, RI 02903
South Carolina	803-734-0122	803-734-0122	1205 Pendleton St., Columbia, SC 29201
South Dakota	800-732-5682	605-773-3301	711 E. Wells Ave., Pierre, SD 57501
Tennessee	800-836-6200	800-836-6200	P.O. Box 23170, Nashville, TN 37202
Texas	800-452-9292	512-463-8586	P.O. Box 5064, Austin, TX 78763
Utah	800-200-1160	801-538-1030	Council Hall, Capitol Hill, Salt Lake City, UT 84114
Vermont	800-837-6668	802-828-3236	134 State St., Montpelier, VT 05602
Virginia	800-847-4882	804-786-4484	1021 E. Cary St., 14th Floor, Richmond, VA 23219
Washington	800-544-1800	360-586-2088	101 General Admin. Bldg., P.O. Box 42500, Olympia, WA 98504
West Virginia	800-225-5982	304-558-2286	2101 Washington St. E., Charleston, WV 25305
Wisconsin	800-432-8747	800-372-2737	P.O. Box 7606, Madison, WI 53707
Wyoming	800-225-5996	307-777-7777	I-25 at College Drive, Cheyenne, WY 82002

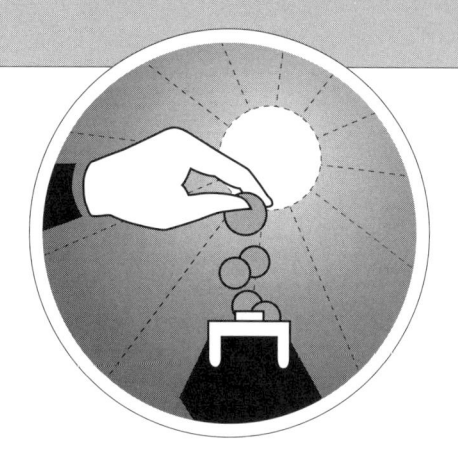

Guide to Off-Season Discounts

The timing of your vacation can make a big difference in the impact on your pocketbook. Prices plummet in the off-season, and the crowds have gone. In the following chapters, we tell you when to cash in on all the high-season amenities at the off-season rates.

CHAPTER 14

Sea Escapes

The sand and surf may be a mob scene during high season at the nation's most popular seaside resorts, but off-season the beaches are all yours. Hotels and restaurants slash prices as crowds head home after Labor Day, shops clear out merchandise to make room for next year's hot items and lines at popular recreational attractions shorten considerably.

While on some coasts the ocean might be too cold for swimming, you still can collapse on the beach or walk for miles with an unobstructed view of the sea.

U.S. Virgin Islands

Off-season: April-October. Many resorts cut prices 30 percent or more starting in mid-April, making resorts that were pricey suddenly affordable luxury.

Weather tips: The islands have two seasons, wet and dry. Temperatures hover in the 80s year-round, and easterly trade winds ease the humidity and bugs. Hurricane season starts June 1, with August-October bringing higher chances of storms usually.

The scene: Postcard images abound on the three sister islands of St. Thomas, St. Croix and St. John. Crystal white beaches bordered by red hibiscus stretch for miles under tree-covered hillsides accented with red rooftops. White sails skim an aquamarine sea so clear you can see right down to the coral reefs.

Settled by Danes, St. Thomas and St. Croix are dotted with historic structures and ruins. St. John is the smallest of the three and composed mostly of national parklands.

Each island is distinctive. Historic Charlotte Amalie on St. Thomas is famous for its duty-free shopping, with crowds elbow to elbow Wednesdays and Saturdays, when a number of cruise ships dock. Beware, though, even in the off-season, when everything's on sale, you can spend a bundle faster than you can say, "Charge it!"

Take note!
☞ **Island alert.** Beware: In the U.S. Virgin Islands, traffic moves on the left side of the road. When walking, be sure to look to your right before stepping off the curb.

It's fun to explore the town by foot. Cobblestone alleys and narrow streets lead to historic Market Square with its vendors. The "99 Steps" (actually 101), a staircase "street," leads to Blackbeard's Castle, once the pirate's hideout and now a guest house. Outside town, Coral World's three-level underwater tank lets you see marine life close-up, and palm-fringed beaches invite you to explore the sea yourself.

You can hop a floatplane for St. Croix, where sugar cane fields stretch to the horizon. Christiansted, the island's historic hub, is packed with shops along palm-shaded sidewalks. Explore the rain forest interior or spread your beach towel at Cane Bay, a breezy north-shore beach where you can lounge on sugar-white sand or snorkel in warm waters year-round past elkhorn corals to a 200-foot drop-off called Cane Bay Wall.

Diminutive St. John, the jewel of the U.S. Virgin Islands and a quick ferry ride from St. Thomas, is encircled by a scenic roller-coaster road. In Cruz Bay, the island's compact, colorful harbor town, The Fish Trap restaurant offers a bargain feed in its treehouse setting. Try the conch fritters and fish chowder, then board an open-air safari bus to sample some beautiful beaches. Hawknest has an old sugar mill and great views, while Trunk Bay has an underwater snorkel trail for beginners.

Information: U.S. Virgin Islands Division of Tourism, 1270 Avenue of the Americas, Suite 2108, New York, NY 10020, (212) 332-2222.

Miami Beach, Florida

Off-season: Easter to mid-December, generally, with summer bringing the lowest prices. Watch for conventions that can make lodging hard to find and pricier. Savings can range up to 50 percent.

Weather tips: Spring and fall usually are pleasant, although September and October bring frequent rain showers and the threat of hurricanes. Daytime highs are in the 80s-90s.

The scene: Miami Beach, the "American Riviera" comprised of 17 islands in Biscayne Bay, was a sandy wilderness populated mostly by mosquitoes and snakes until a land boom in the 1920s. Today, the 7.5-mile stretch of pastel hotels overlooks shining beaches and the Atlantic Ocean.

Take note!

☞ **Taking a toll.** When driving in the Miami area, keep coins and small bills handy to pay tolls on highways and bridges.

A boardwalk stretches from 21st to 46th streets for scenic ocean-front strolls, and piers extending into the sea are popular with anglers. While the town and beaches are never what you'd call deserted, during low season you'll have far less trouble locating a patch of ocean-view sand.

It's free to spread your towel anywhere along 10.5 miles of sparkling sands. Like Rio de Janeiro, each beach attracts its own crowd — from seniors and families to topless maidens from the University of Miami in search of a total-body tan. The surf is Caribbeanlike and balmy in summer but can be chilly and rough in winter.

You'll enjoy discounts at hotels and shops and can look for bargains at more than 30 factory outlets. The Miami Free Zone is an international wholesale trade center, and Cauley Square in Goulds, a quaint complex of clapboard, coral rock and stucco buildings that once housed railroad workers, offers one-of-a-kind antiques, crafts and clothing at discount prices.

You can take your pick among 30-plus area golf courses and 11 tennis centers or escape the sun at Miami Beach Garden Center and Conservatory, a cool oasis within a large park.

Information: Greater Miami Convention and Visitors Bureau, 701 Brickell Ave., Miami, FL 33131, (800) 283-2707.

Florida Panhandle

Off-season: After Labor Day until the second week of March. Rates drop 50 percent and sometimes more, with $60 the average nightly hotel rate and about $500 the weekly rate for two-bedroom condos.

Weather tips: It's sunny year-round with daytime highs in the 80s in fall and 60s-70s in winter. Occasional cold snaps can bring chilly weather, but it rarely lasts more than a few days. Bring a jacket and windbreaker, and you'll need a wet suit in the brisk surf late fall through spring.

The scene: The 24-mile Emerald Coast, a pristine, affordable Florida destination, was named for its beautiful seas. It has shocking white beaches, 60 percent of which are preserved in seaside parks and beach overwalks for sun-drenched solitude. The "Redneck Riviera" is a bargain spot any time of year but especially off-season.

A sense of childlike innocence pervades this area. Here are some of the world's best shelling beaches, thanks to a ribbon reef of limestone that captures thousands of shells up to 20 inches long. You can enter sand castle contests, watch dancing dolphins or befriend a sandpiper.

Grayton Beach State Park, just east of Destin, is considered one of the nation's prettiest beaches; off-season, it's your private sanctuary. Nearby is Seaside, a fairy-tale town of pastel Victorian houses and white picket fences. Stop at the open-air market for fresh fruit or buy a cone at the old-fashioned ice cream parlor. Collect your thoughts — and seashells — on solitary marsh, beach and dune trails at St. Andrews State Park near Panama City.

Two-lane highways wind past beaches scattered with dunes, pines and sea oats, tiny pocket beaches with pavilions and gazebos, sunken forests, moss-draped rivers for tubing and 10 amusement parks with bumper boats and water slides.

Destin, the "world's luckiest" fishing village, still is in the swim off-season with 20 species of edible fish — as local restaurants testify. Hop a schooner and cast your line — the crew will clean your catch free.

For a unique Christmas with sand instead of snow, where Santa rolls into town on a surfboard instead of a sleigh, visit Destin and neighboring towns a month before and during Christmas. Enjoy a twinkling procession of festively bedecked boats parading through Destin Harbor as local celebrants cheer and wave.

Information: Emerald Coast Convention and Visitors Bureau, P.O. Box 609, Fort Walton Beach, FL 32549, (800) 322-3319.

Myrtle Beach, South Carolina

Off-season: Labor Day to Memorial Day. Visitors encounter lower rates in fall and spring, but the lowest prices are in winter when rates may drop 50 percent or more. Seniors can take advantage of 10 percent discounts at other times when booking weeklong stays.

Weather tips: Fall and spring are warm and pleasant, and winters are mild. In December, air temperatures average 53 degrees; other months are warmer.

The scene: Part Coney Island and part Miami Beach, Myrtle Beach is the hub of South Carolina's 60-mile Grand Strand, with outdoor recreation and night life yearlong. There are hefty discounts in winter, when daytime temperatures normally are in the 60s.

After Labor Day, the summer crowds thin to a trickle, making the wide beaches ideal for beach bumming and wet-suit swimming and surfing. Many resorts and restaurants stay open year-round.

If you long for a quiet place to practice your swing, Myrtle Beach is the unofficial off-season golf capital of the country, with more than 70 golf courses carved from wooded sandhills.

Offshore waters along the South Carolina coast are warmed by the Gulf Stream, making for great fishing early spring through December.

Downtown is lined with high-rise hotels and T-shirt and fudge shops — all offering slashed prices off-season. Nearby Murrells Inlet is a picturesque fishing village with fishing charters and great seafood restaurants as well as Brookgreen Gardens, set on four former Colonial rice plantations. The gardens include more than 2,000 different plants and 500 sculptures.

On nearby historic Pawleys Island, home to Pawleys Island hammocks handmade here since 1880, weathered summer cottages peek from oak and oleander groves. At quaint Georgetown you can trace the history of the area at the Rice Museum, housed in a gracious structure topped by an 1842 clock tower.

Beginning in November, Myrtle Beach and neighboring communities celebrate the holidays with the Christmas Connection, a festival of parades, light displays, arts and crafts shows and Santas on surfboards.

Information: Myrtle Beach Area Chamber of Commerce, P.O. Box 2115, Myrtle Beach, SC 29578, (803) 626-7444 or (800) 356-3016.

Block Island, Rhode Island

Off-season: Columbus Day to Memorial Day. After Labor Day, weekday rates drop, then all rates fall after Columbus Day. Expect to pay about 30 percent less than in high season. Many resorts and restaurants close during off-season.

Weather tips: Off-season brings sunny, brisk sweater weather, with blazing foliage in fall. Expect temperatures in the 60s in September, 50s in October and May and cooler in other months, though winters usually are mild. Winds can be strong.

Take note!

☞ **Don't 'harvest' the oats.** Along the Grand Strand of South Carolina, tall sea oats grow in the sand dunes, providing needed vegetation. Don't pick the oats for home decorations — it's illegal to cut, break or destroy them. Violators are subject to a fine.

The scene: Just 13 miles off the coast of Rhode Island, this island feels like a chip off the old block, with its well-tended farms and fenced pastures. But unlike the mainland, there's little hustle-bustle to mar the Block's historic ambiance. The island looks and feels much the way it did a century ago.

Hop a ferry (reservations usually aren't needed in fall) for the island, where guest houses line a Victorian waterfront and quaint cottages dot hillsides. The historic Southeast Lighthouse, built in 1874, blinks a warm welcome 35 miles to sea from its precarious perch 180 feet above sea level on Mohegan Bluffs.

Come fall, the fishing is great at Great Salt Pond and the main harbor remains speckled with cabin cruisers and avid sport fishermen. Cast your line or, for the best catch, stop by Ballards Inn, an old-fashioned, family-run restaurant where the meals go from sea to plate all in the same day. The restaurant closes in mid-October until Memorial Day.

After Labor Day, three-mile Crescent Beach is quiet. While it's too cold to swim, by afternoon it's warm enough to spread a beach towel. Or head to Mansion Beach and have the brimming tide pools to yourself.

Wander "The Maze" at Lapham's Bluestone bird sanctuary, a sea of wings in fall, or visit Sachem Pond, which is fringed with autumnal colors. Or, stroll the island's moorlike meadows and hike to Southeast Lighthouse for spectacular views of the sea.

Information: Rhode Island Tourism Division, 7 Jackson Walkway, Providence, RI 02903, (800) 556-2484. Ferry information, (401) 783-4613.

Cape Cod, Martha's Vineyard and Nantucket, Massachusetts

Off-season: Labor Day through June. Rates dip in September, then fall up to 50 percent after mid-October, although Thanksgiving may bring a boost in prices. In establishments that stay open in winter, you often find cozy rooms with fireplaces.

Weather tips: Expect temperatures of 50-55 in spring and fall and 25-40 in winter. Heavy winds and rain can make it feel colder.

The scene: Cape Cod's main attractions are timeless. Rugged coasts offer well-preserved towns where church steeples and weather vanes pierce the sky and village greens are surrounded by antique shops and restaurants serving clam chowder, Wellfleet oysters and butter-sweet bay scallops.

Take note!
☞ **Go carless.** There's no need for a car on the island of Nantucket. Leave it at the ferry terminal on Cape Cod. It's easy to walk or bike most places on the island, but there are taxis to take you to farther points.

After Labor Day, the bustling crowds go home and the cape becomes a series of quiet small towns where fire-warmed inns welcome, rather than turn away, tourists. Even seasonally mobbed hot spots like the Brewster Fish House, a former carnation farm, and the Lobster Pot in Provincetown, with its glassed-in dining room overlooking the sea, slash prices. And in coastal Yarmouth Port, you can have your pick of B&Bs once occupied by sea captains.

Route 6A, bumper-to-bumper in summer, is devoid of traffic off-season. Sandwich, a perfectly restored New England village and the cape's oldest at Route 6A's western terminus, looks little changed over the years. The route passes cranberry bogs, split-rail fences, museums, historic lighthouses, shops and galleries.

At the Upper Cape, you can walk through a quiet forest to Pilgrims' graves at Cove Cemetery in Eastham or hike to Pilgrim Spring near Pilgrim Heights where the first settlers found fresh water. The trails at Cape Cod National Seashore wind through forests to 30 miles of dune-backed white beaches. Even Provincetown, the cape's flamboyant mecca for alternative lifestyles, tames down, and you won't find any lines at Pilgrim Monument, a 252-foot granite tower commemorating the Pilgrims' 1620 landing.

Off the cape's south shore is Martha's Vineyard, whose six towns range from the polished former whaling port of Edgartown, with tidy streets and chic boutiques, to Oak Bluffs, where 300 gingerbread cottages crowd around Methodist Camp Ground, an open-air tabernacle. Pick a pristine beach or follow scenic roads for panoramic views.

Farther south is the island of Nantucket, former whaling center. In fall, the pace slows, and it's easy to explore the open moorlands or wander along uncrowded cobblestone streets. In the quaint seaside village of Siasconset, lined with Pooh Bear cottages, it's so quiet you can hear the waves breaking against the shore.

Information: Cape Cod Chamber of Commerce, P.O. Box 16, Hyannis, MA 02601, (508) 362-3225.

Northern Oregon Coast

Off-season: October-May except holidays. Expect rates to drop 20 percent to 40 percent, sometimes more. Some places close during winter.

Weather tips: Oregon's rainy season kicks off in November; gray skies and brisk winds make this a hale-and-hardy vacation spot in winter. Fall temperatures are in the 40s-50s and dip into the high 30s in winter. In spring, wildflowers sprout from cliffs.

The scene: The northern Oregon Coast, as brooding off-season as it is sunny in summer, is most dramatic as it winds south from Astoria to Newport for 133 miles. Off-season, you'll likely have the road to yourself as you pass by towering monoliths of rock tortured by the sea, lonely headlands, pocket beaches facing steel-blue waters, haunted lighthouses and wind-swept beach towns lined with homey ma-and-pa establishments — many of which button up for the winter. However, watch for historic bed-and-breakfast lodgings that keep their porch lights on.

The mighty Columbia River meets the sea at Astoria, and strong currents sank nearly 2,000 ships over the decades. You can see some belongings of ill-fated passengers among other interesting exhibits at the Columbia River Maritime Museum.

Down the coast, Seaside's two-mile promenade, dating from the 1920s and lined with stately mansions, is abandoned by summer beach bums, although the pace quickens a tad during May, when the nearby artsy town of Cannon Beach holds its annual sand castle contest. In the backdrop is Haystack Rock, a finger of stone jutting 235 feet above the sea. It lures summertime rock climbers and then often maroons them when the tide rolls in.

If Depoe Bay, the world's smallest navigable harbor, looks familiar, you probably saw "One Flew Over the Cuckoo's Nest." In Spouting Horn, the sea thunders and sprays through a cleft in the rock — and there are no crowds hovering to spoil the view.

In Newport, you'll get quick service at Mo's Original Diner, an Oregon coast institution serving gravy-thick chowder and steaming crab. The diner once was a hangout for Paul Newman and Henry Fonda.

Information: Oregon Tourism Commission, 775 Summer St. N.E., Salem, OR 97310, (800) 547-7842 or Central Oregon Coast Association, P.O. Box 2094, Newport, OR 97365, (800) 767-2064.

Monterey/Big Sur, California

Off-season: Late October through April. Because the Monterey area is popular year-round, many lodgings drop rates only slightly off-season, but check for specials. Expect 20 percent to 30 percent discounts at times. Lowest rates are late November through January, the latter a good month for whale watching.

Weather tips: Fall is warm and dry with temperatures in the 80s. Winter is cool and often overcast or rainy with temperatures in the mid-60s.

The scene: From the Monterey Peninsula, about two hours south of San Francisco, Big Sur winds an undulating cliffside path between weathered trees and raging surf. It's often a traffic jam in summer, but off-season you can drive for hours without encountering anyone at a scenic turnoff.

Waves pound the beaches and replenish tide pools, and cathedrallike redwoods soar to the sky. In autumn, the deciduous trees and underbrush turn beautiful muted shades.

Monterey, the rugged fishing town of Steinbeck fame, is cooler and quieter in fall. The path from Fisherman's Wharf to Cannery Row, the sardine district now restored to studied quaintness, reverts to a jogging path for locals. Even the Monterey Bay Aquarium, the town's big attraction now, is free of lines, offering an unobstructed window on the sea. Nearby is charming Pacific Grove, a storybook town of Victorian mansions-turned-B&Bs that are booked solid in summer.

> *Take note!*
> ☞ **Pay-per-view.** The famous scenic Seventeen-Mile Drive on the coast between Monterey and Carmel, CA, is a private road. Pay a toll of $6.50, please, and you will see the often-photographed Lone Cypress tree.

Off-season, specifically winter, brings thousands of migrating monarch butterflies to flutter and nest in the cypress and oak trees.

Carmel, a snooty town that formerly was an important religious center for Spanish California and an early 20th-century artists' colony, empties of summertime status shoppers. Locals rather than tourists can be found off-season in Clint Eastwood's homey eatery, The Hog's Breath Inn, where you can get a Dirty Harry Burger or a 12-ounce steak. You might even find the owner downing a burger.

From Point Lobos State Reserve, a 1,250-acre headland, you can observe sea lions, otters, seals and, in winter, migrating whales. Off-season, Big Sur feels like the rural town it is, and you actually can get a sea-view seat at Nepenthe, a dramatic cliffside restaurant purchased by Orson Welles for Rita Hayworth. It's easier to get a tour at the Hearst San Simeon State Historical Monument, an opulent Spanish-Moorish estate built by publishing mogul William Randolph Hearst near San Luis Obispo.

Information: California Office of Tourism, 801 K St., Suite 1600, Sacramento, CA 95814, (800) 862-2543.

La Jolla, California

Off-season: October-May. Prices dip 25 percent or more.

Weather tips: Early morning fog is not unusual in this beach town, but it gives way to beautiful clear blue skies most of the year. Winter daytime temperatures average 65 and drop to a cool 49 at night.

The scene: A fashionable cove by the sea, La Jolla (Spanish for "The Jewel") is Southern California's answer to St. Tropez, with year-round flower-bedecked streets lined with chic shops and eateries.

La Jolla Cove, with its crystal waters, affords excellent if chilly swimming and diving in winter. Divers and snorkelers enjoy La Jolla's Underwater Park, a state ecological reserve just off Cove Beach.

If you'd rather stay dry, La Jolla is a mecca for golf and tennis, with numerous courses, tennis clubs and resorts and several off-season tournaments.

For a unique tour, visit La Jolla Caves, formed by incessant pounding of waves against La Jolla's sandstone cliffs and unearthed in 1902-03 by pick and shovel. Off-season there's no line at "Sunny Jim" cave, accessible via 133 steps from the Cave store and aptly named for the rock formation around the entrance that silhouettes the profile of a man's head against blue sky and turquoise sea.

Born to shop? La Jolla has everything from Saks Fifth Avenue to Spoiled Rotten, a unique children's clothing store. Or take a guided walking tour with docents (call the town council for details), rent a bike and pedal La Jolla's scenic bicycle paths, beachcomb on miles of pristine beaches or stroll Coast Walk and watch the pelicans sail from the bluffs to the sea. Refuel with the locals on cappuccino and sinful pastry.

Even off-season, La Jolla is no snoozing beach town. It boasts the La Jolla Museum of Contemporary Art and the world-famous Scripps Institution of Oceanography, and you can choose from a number of music, dance and theater offerings.

Information: La Jolla Town Council, 1055 Wall St., La Jolla, CA 92037, (619) 454-1444.

Maui, Hawaii

Off-season: September to mid-November and first three weeks of December are quietest. Summer is a shoulder season, drawing many families. To get best bargains, be flexible about dates and check air-hotel packages. With supersaver rates, pricey hotels become reasonable. Also look for discounts that give the fourth night or seventh night free, or provide meals or a rental car free. Such discounts often can be found year-round although hotels may limit the number of discounted rooms.

Weather tips: Temperatures are in the 80s year-round; summer and fall are more humid. Winter is the rainiest time of year, especially on the eastern coast, although a string of rainy days is rare.

The scene: Maui, the second-largest island in the chain, offers contrasts ranging from trendy surfing towns such as Paia and Wailuku to native villages in flower-scented hills where local farmers till their land with horse-drawn plows and continue to speak Hawaiian.

While the island is virtually seasonless, the first three weeks of December are quiet as mainlanders stay home to prepare for the holidays.

In West Maui, you will find pineapple fields, fishing villages and classy hotels, first-rate snorkeling and swimming and hiking trails. Lahaina, a whaling town on the National Register of Historic Places, has a notorious past, with stories of lusty whalers butting heads with missionaries determined to save souls.

Relax with a tropical fruit snow cone by Lahaina's towering Banyan Tree, the largest of its kind in the United States, and enjoy a private performance as resident mynah birds sing a screeching symphony at sundown. Visit the Brig Carthaginian II, a replica of a ship that brought missionaries to Hawaii in the early 1800s. It houses a museum describing the journey.

Follow winding Haleakala Highway from sand to snow in winter, finally arriving at Haleakala (House of Sun), the island's immense dormant volcano and the centerpiece of the 27,284-acre Haleakala National Park. For a private, panoramic sunrise, drive to the glass-enclosed lookout at Puu Ulaula, Maui's high point.

Finally, explore the heart of Old Hawaii on infamous Hana Highway. Its hairpin curves take you past lush foliage, crashing waterfalls and hillside farms. Howard Cooper, owner of 60-acre Helani Gardens, has erected signs throughout to explain his philosophy; during off-season, the crusty recluse may even come down from his treehouse to give you a private tour.

At Hana — don't blink or you'll miss it — grab a snack at Tutu's, a seaside shack frequented by fishermen and locals, and then take the rutted, rocky road to Oheo Gulchaka. Here you can take a solitary skinny dip in the Seven Sacred Pools; despite the name, there's nothing holy about the water.

Information: Maui Visitors Bureau, P.O. Box 580, Wailuku, Maui, HI 96793, (808) 244-3530.

Take note!

☞ **Heavenly Hana.** The tiny old Hawaii town on Maui may be called heavenly but the road to Hana is not. It's a spectacular coastal drive but a twisting, torturous narrow road. While the round trip is only about 110 miles, count on it taking the entire day.

CHAPTER 15

City Getaways

To some, the idea of taking a city vacation off-season sounds like an oxymoron. But you won't miss a thing. In fact, with fewer tourists around, you'll have more to yourself of what makes these 10 destinations sizzle.

Visit the best of America's cities off-season (even Manhattan dims her lights for a few months) and you'll get a slice of Americana with a distinctively regional twist. Chances are that you'll encounter shorter lines at restaurants and attractions and some enticing sales at ritzy department stores.

Orlando and Disney, Florida

Off-season: Early September until just before Thanksgiving and generally the first three weeks of December. The last three weeks of January and into early February usually are slow periods that may bring lower rates; May sometimes is quiet, too. Expect 30 percent or more off the top rates. With the large number of hotels in the Orlando area, comparison shop for the best deal. Some hotels may have a convention and not lower rates, while other places may be facing low occupancy when you want to go and reduce their rates.

Weather tips: Temperatures in fall are mild, although September can still be hot. Bring a jacket in January. May should be warm and pleasant.

The scene: Mickey, Goofy and Tinker Bell await you at Walt Disney World, which includes four distinct theme parks: Epcot Center, Disney-MGM Studios, Typhoon Lagoon and the Magic Kingdom.

Lines can be as long as Santa's list during the Christmas season and anytime school's out; holidays should be avoided. Give yourself five days to see the entire park and start early in the day — the afternoons generally are crowded.

If you've been to Disneyland in California, you'll find the Magic Kingdom similar here. Still, if you have young children in tow, this is the place to go first. For new experiences, head to Epcot Center, where Future World's seven pavilions offer 12 grades worth of knowledge — if only school had been like this. Ride into the prehistoric past at the solar-powered Universe of Energy. It's like stepping into Jurassic Park. Follow the mind of a 12-year-old through the Wonders of Life. Ride through the human body and tour The Making of Me to watch the egg race for the sperm to the tune of Wagner's "The Ride of the

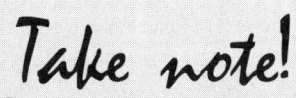

Take note!

☞ **Beat the Disney crowds.** Holidays and holiday weekends draw the biggest crowds to Walt Disney World. Mondays, Tuesdays and Wednesdays are the busiest days at the Magic Kingdom, Thursdays and Fridays at the Disney-MGM Studios Theme Park. The quietest time: Sunday mornings.

Valkyries." At the World Showcase, sample life — and food — from 11 countries.

Wandering around Disney-MGM Studios will take you back to Tinseltown in the 1930s-40s, with Hollywood Boulevard lined by palm trees, pastel buildings and flashing neon.

When you've seen enough (if you can ever see enough) of Walt Disney World, head to Universal Studios Florida, Busch Gardens, Cypress Gardens, Sea World and the surrounding towns. The Church Street Exchange in downtown Orlando combines history and great shopping in a decorative Victorian-themed festival marketplace. At Old Town in nearby Kissimmee, buy a nickel Coke at the General Store and try not to spend all your money at more than 70 specialty shops that re-create turn-of-the-century Florida.

Information: Orlando/Orange County Convention and Visitors Bureau, P.O. Box 690355, Orlando, FL 32869, (800) 551-0181.

Washington, DC

Off-season: Mid-December through January and July through August. Avoid April, when visitors come to see the cherry and apple blossoms, and holidays, when the capital bursts with special events. Expect savings of 20 percent to 30 percent on lodging. Check hotels for packages that reduce nightly rates, and look into hotels in the suburban areas of Virginia and Maryland.

Weather tips: Steamy in summer and cold in winter, DC is a place to visit for history, not weather.

The scene: Going through life without touring DC seems downright unpatriotic. But there's more than towering marble monuments, memorials, foundations and statues.

The capital is packed with museums of art, history and science that feature everything from George Washington's false teeth to atom smashers. Quaint Georgetown has chic eateries where you might catch a supping senator.

But all roads lead to the Capitol, so start there. Take the monorail linking the Senate and House — and don't miss the bean soup in the Senate dining room.

Tour five state rooms at the White House and visit the National Museum of Natural History, a treasure trove of life sciences ranging from anthropology to marine zoology. And at the National Museum of American History, you can see Washington's choppers, Eli Whitney's cotton gin, Alexander Graham Bell's telephone and mannequins wearing first ladies' gowns (from Martha to Hillary). The National Air and Space Museum houses America's aerodynamic treasures including Charles Lindbergh's Spirit of St. Louis, the Wright brothers' Kitty Hawk flyer and a model of Skylab.

At nearby Arlington National Cemetery, the eternal flame flickers over JFK's grave and a solitary soldier guards the Tomb of the Unknown Soldier.

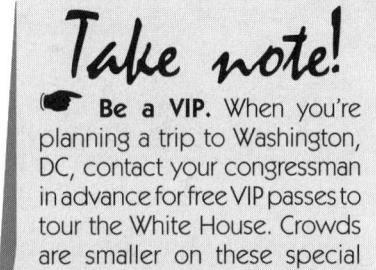

Take note!

☞ **Be a VIP.** When you're planning a trip to Washington, DC, contact your congressman in advance for free VIP passes to tour the White House. Crowds are smaller on these special tours.

If time allows, beyond the city you will find the rolling green Shenandoahs, laced with trails, and the hills of West Virginia, which are dotted with small farms.

Information: Washington, DC, Convention and Visitors Association, 1212 New York Ave. N.W., Washington, DC 20005, (202) 789-7038.

New York City

Off-season: Last three weeks of January through March. Spring and summer are shoulder seasons, with summer particularly drawing tourists. You can find discounts up to 50 percent at times. Many New York hotels offer weekend discounts throughout the year on a limited-availability basis.

Weather tips: Winters can be cold and snowy. Weather is mild April through early June. Summers can bring hot, humid days occasionally.

The scene: The world's leading tourist destination, New York is more than the Empire State Building and Rockefeller Center. Manhattan has something for everyone — from gourmet cuisine to hot dogs in Central Park, rap to opera, flea markets to Fifth Avenue and museums for every imaginable interest (and taste).

Take note!
☞ **Broadway bargains.** In New York City, try your luck at getting half-price tickets to Broadway and off-Broadway shows. At the Times Square TKTS booth, half-price tickets for matinees go on sale at 10 a.m. and for evening performances at 3 p.m.

For a grand overview, head to the World Trade Center and ride the elevator a quarter of a mile up for panoramic views. Or ride an elevator to the top of the classic Empire State Building and peer down on canyons of steel.

Hop the Staten Island Ferry to the Statue of Liberty and Ellis Island, the entry point for more than 12 million immigrants between 1894 and 1954 and now a museum. Wander Wall Street, deserted on weekends, and stroll past a bright patchwork of Oriental shops, pseudo pagodas, bright banners and temple bells to The Bowery, a former Indian trail-turned-skid row.

Don't look for hippies in Greenwich Village. The city's former bohemian enclave has been reborn as a trendy brownstone neighborhood with ritzy boutiques and eateries.

Speaking of ritzy, don't miss Fifth Avenue, where you can dream and window shop. For culture, head to the New York City Opera or the New York City Ballet at Lincoln Center, offering a four-block smorgasbord of the performing arts, or the Joffrey Ballet and Dance Theatre of Harlem at The City Center, a Moorish-style building at West 55th Street and Broadway.

Walk, cycle or skate through Central Park, the city's 840-acre greenbelt with fountains, ponds, statues, monuments, a zoo and wooded pathway. It's a beautiful refuge for the well-heeled and homeless alike — but a place to avoid at night.

Information: New York Convention and Visitors Bureau, 2 Columbus Circle, New York, NY 10019, (800) NYC-VISIT.

Chicago, Illinois

Off-season: November through March. Look for savings of 30 percent or more. Check for weekend hotel packages.

Weather tips: Daytime temperatures normally are in the 30s-40s in winter, but then do drop lower — much lower when you figure in the wind-chill factor of the Windy City. Spring temperatures push into the 50s.

The scene: A frontier outpost in the early 1800s, Chicago grew to prominence as the main link between the established East and the ever-moving frontier. It burned to the ground in 1871, but rebounded with grace and style to become the financial and cultural heart of Middle America.

Chicagoans seem edgy about the city's gangster past, although tour buses can take you to mobster hideaways. Most locals will point instead to a towering skyline of a city replete with the world's best modern architecture, from Frank Lloyd Wright homes to the 110-story Sears Tower, which dominates miles of prairie. You can ride the elevator to the 103rd-floor Skydeck observatory for a scenic overview.

Then head to the Loop, business headquarters for many American corporations and home to a wide range of museums, from the Art Institute of Chicago to live theater at the circa-1920s Chicago Theater.

Near the South Side, visit the Prairie Avenue Historic District, with its 19th-century mansions where the elite lived. Or try on ethnic masks and touch fish skeletons from the dinosaur age at the Field Museum of Natural History.

See Chicago burn again and explore its 19th-century days at the Chicago Historical Society Museum on the North Side. While you're in the neighborhood, visit Lill Street, where more than 40 potters work their wares.

For a fascinating side trip just outside the city, head for Brookfield Zoo, a 200-acre park of woods and good fishing lakes with an indoor rain forest, special preserves for wolves, a bison prairie and the Frank Lloyd Wright Home and Studio. The self-taught architect designed everything here from the rafters to the chairs.

Information: Chicago Office of Tourism, 78 E. Washington St., Fourth Floor, Chicago, IL 60602, (312) 744-2400.

New Orleans, Louisiana

Off-season: Memorial Day through Labor Day. Expect to find rates cut 50 percent and sometimes more, although availability may be limited.

Weather tips: Be prepared for rain, heat and humidity. Bring plenty of light, cool clothes.

The scene: The home of Dixieland jazz and Cajun cooking, New Orleans is at once sordid and sublime — a mixture of shanty towns and French-inspired red brick facades with wrought-iron balconies.

Along the restored riverfront you'll find the Aquarium of the Americas, Plaza d'Espana with its fountains, and the Riverwalk Mall, which is lined with shops and eateries. In the picturesque Warehouse District, turn-of-the-century brick structures have been converted to trendy apartments and shops.

Most of the history and action in New Orleans centers around the French

Quarter, the heart of the original French colonial settlement. Don't miss historic Jackson Square with its charming cast-iron and brick buildings. For authentic *cafe au lait* (half coffee with chicory and half hot milk) head over to Cafe du Monde.

Take a mule-drawn coach ride down Decatur Street. Included in the price is a running commentary from your driver, which may be heavier on fiction than fact. Or take a tour on the Canal Street ferry. A streetcar named Desire once rolled down Royal Street. Today you can board a streetcar along St. Charles Street or the Riverfront.

The Old U.S. Mint houses fascinating relics, including Louis Armstrong's first horn and instruments from the original Dixieland Jazz Band.

Voodoo is history in New Orleans, but you can learn about the religion, which infiltrated from Africa in the early 1700s, on a voodoo walking tour of the French Quarter. Or you can visit historic plantations, Indian burial grounds and gloomy bayous on a voodoo swamp tour. Don't be surprised if the old black magic puts you in a spell.

Information: New Orleans Metropolitan Convention and Visitors Bureau, 1520 Sugar Bowl Drive, New Orleans, LA 70112, (504) 566-5011.

Denver, Colorado

Off-season: Thanksgiving through March. Expect savings up to 50 percent.

Weather tips: Blizzards occasionally blow in from the Rockies, dumping about 60 inches of snow over the winter. But generally you can expect Denver's Rocky Mountain highs to be in the 40s in January and in the 50s in November and March. Some winters seem almost spring-like, with a hot sun melting snow within hours.

The scene: This former cowtown is friendly, relaxed and clean, despite the infamous brown smog clouds that sometimes linger overhead.

For a scenic overview of Denver and environs on clear days, head to the State Capitol. From the rotunda, you can see west to the Rockies, east to the Great Plains and, below, modern-day Denver. Stroll past Victorian mansions to the U.S. Mint. Denver made its fortune in gold and still has more than any other city. Watch money being printed but, sorry, no free samples.

Don't miss the Denver Art Museum, which resembles a medieval castle with slitlike windows. The museum houses top collections, including an American Indian exhibit.

Remember "Unsinkable" Molly Brown, the heroine of the Titanic lifeboat immortalized in a musical? Her Pennsylvania Street mansion, purchased by nouveau rich gold miner Johnny Brown, is open for touring.

At 16th Street Mall, a pedestrian area several blocks long, you'll find

> *Take note!*
> ☞ **Dine for less.** New Orleans is famous for its fine restaurants, which can be pricey and hard to get into for dinner. Try them for lunch, when they're less crowded and the offerings usually are less expensive.

galleries, curio and silversmith shops; Larimer Square is a step into a Wild West street.

Information: Denver Metro Convention and Visitors Bureau, 1555 California St., Suite 300, Denver, CO 80202, (800) 645-3446.

Palm Springs, California

Off-season: June through September. Most hotels lower their rates substantially during summer months, and you are almost sure to find great deals at all the luxurious hotels and resorts, with savings of 50 percent fairly common.

Weather tips: Summer is extremely hot and dry, although nights cool down; June and September are the best bets.

The scene: Take a hot, dry desert and add water. The result is Palm Springs, a desert oasis just 120 miles from Los Angeles.

The area long has been home to the Agua Caliente Indian Tribe (it owns every other square block now, making it among the richest tribes in the nation). The chic desert oasis has drawn Hollywood stars and celebrities since the 1930s, along with hordes of tourists — lured by the area's bright sun, blue skies, natural hot springs (all owned now by elegant resorts) and drop-dead scenery.

The desert rolls through Palm Springs, then rises in jagged cliffs and crags through five ecoclimates to Mount San Jacinto State Park, with subalpine terrain topped by a snowcapped peaks in winter. The Palm Springs Aerial Tramway just outside town takes you on a thrilling cable car ride from the scorching desert floor to cool mountain heights. It's a great way to beat the heat on summer afternoons.

Early morning or late afternoon is the best time to explore the outer bounds of Palm Springs on foot. Just southeast of town are the Indian Canyons, ancient canyon oases where rushing streams and waterfalls tumble down rocky gorges you can hike and wade in summer. Palm and Andreas canyons offer the easiest trails. Or rent a four-wheel-drive and take a wild ride through specially designated jeep areas.

Information: Palm Springs Desert Resorts Convention and Visitors Bureau, 69930 Highway 111, Suite 201, Rancho Mirage, CA 92270, (619) 770-9000.

San Francisco, California

Off-season: Late fall through early spring, except holidays. Expect savings of about 30 percent. Be flexible about dates because it's a popular convention city. Weekends offer reduced rates.

Weather tips: Mild climate year-round but rainy and foggy autumn through spring. You often need a light coat in evenings.

The scene: San Francisco considers itself the cultured cousin of uncouth Los Angeles to the south. In fact, say you love L.A. and they're likely to "tsk!" you and walk briskly away.

Beyond the rivalry is a hilly town blessed with charm. Forget the hippies — they can't afford the high rents in Haight-Ashbury, which has grown from the free-love haven of the '60s to a gentrified yuppie bastion.

Not that San Francisco has lost its soul. The cable cars still ride steep hills halfway to the stars, offering stunning views of the city, bay and Golden Gate Bridge. There's also Chinatown, a funky composite of colorful chaos, neon signs and Chinese kites flapping in the wind.

For a magnificent overview of the city, hike or hop a cable car to Nob Hill and watch the sun set over the ocean. Nob Hill, the city's old-money section, was once home to the robber barons who ran the Central Pacific Railroad.

Down below is Union Square, San Francisco's shopping district, where boutiques, restaurants and cafes stretch for blocks. In the daytime, clutch your purse and take a fascinating clip down Geary Street. The city's theater district is like Broadway West.

Or, to see historic structures from the 1930s, roam charming Jackson Square Historic District, a former rough-and-tumble waterfront neighborhood that became a haven for artists in the 1930s. Mark Twain, Rudyard Kipling and Randolph Hearst all rented office space in Montgomery Block, the building that once stood on the site now occupied by the Transamerica Pyramid — a local landmark or eyesore, depending on whom you ask. Sun Yat-Sen (you'll see his statue in Chinatown) is said to have orchestrated the overthrow of the Manchu Dynasty from his second-floor office here.

> **Take note!**
> ☞ **Call it cool.** San Francisco is cool, in many ways but particularly in its weather. Daytime temperatures rarely get above 70 degrees, usually hovering in the low 60s and often breezy. It also tends to be a dressy city. Leave the shorts home and opt for a casual chic wardrobe.

Consider the short boat ride across San Francisco Bay to Alcatraz, a rocky islet that once housed the country's most feared high-security prison. Both Al Capone and Machine Gun Kelly were incarcerated here. The jail closed in 1963 because of exorbitant operating costs. Today, however, you can take an hour-long, self-guided audio tour of the abandoned prison — and even spend a moment or two in solitary confinement.

Information: San Francisco Convention and Visitors Bureau, 201 Third St., Suite 900, San Francisco, CA 94103, (415) 974-6900.

Seattle, Washington

Off-season: Late autumn through early spring. Hotels offer supersaver rates, discounted up to 50 percent, Nov. 15 through March and sweeten the deal with a discount coupon book January through March. Call the hotel hot line, (800) 535-7071, for details.

Weather tips: Chilly and damp with mostly overcast skies, rain and occasional snow in winter. Early spring can be sunny and mild one day, gloomy and chilly the next.

The scene: Rain, rain go away? Not in Seattle — and especially during off-season, when it can drizzle day after day. The locals call it "liquid sunshine" and go about their business.

But no amount of rain can quite take the bloom off Seattle's spectacular setting between the Cascades and Puget Sound. When the sun peeks through the clouds, try to catch a glimpse of Mount Rainier and see the snowcapped Olympic peaks mirrored in Puget Sound. Rain or shine, ferries ply the sound, whisking you to mountainous isles that seem a world removed from the bustling city.

Should you catch a chill, Seattle's omnipresent Starbucks coffee shops and corner stands will warm you. Order a non-fat double mocha (hold the whipped cream), and you may pass for a local.

The busy stalls and cafes at Pike Place Market are a good place to start your visit. Farmers and fishermen brought their bounty here in the early 1900s. During the Depression the place went to seed, but Seattlites rallied for restoration. Today, the market is a city landmark with street entertainers, stalls piled high with lobsters, fruit, jewelry, ethnic foods and, of course, coffee stands.

A few blocks inland is Pioneer Square, Seattle's historic district. Although the homeless have put deep roots into some of the park benches, it's still charming, with gigantic trees and red-brick buildings housing boutiques and cafes.

The square is home to Seattle's strangest but most popular attraction, the Underground Tour, which starts at Doc Maynard's Tavern. The dusty tour, replete with sly jokes concerning former illustrious residents, takes you into underground passages through the remains of buildings destroyed in a fire in 1889. Since high tides were a problem anyway, the street level was raised one story and the ground floors went underground.

Stroll through the University District, a lively hodgepodge of cafes, bookstores and ethnic restaurants near the University of Washington. On sunny days, the hilltop campus, which looks more like a national park than a seat of learning, offers views of the sound and Mount Rainier. It is quite possibly one of the most beautiful ivory towers in the world.

Information: Seattle/King County Convention and Visitors Bureau, 520 Pike St., Suite 1300, Seattle, WA 98101, (206) 461-5800.

Honolulu, Hawaii

Off-season: September to mid-November and early December. Mid-February to April sometimes is slow. Summer is a shoulder season drawing many families. To get best bargains, be flexible about dates and check air-hotel packages and special promotions, such as those that offer the fourth night or seventh night free. Many hotels offer specials year-round but they're available on a limited basis. Supersaver rates can make the pricey resorts reasonable.

Weather tips: Temperatures are fairly constant, with highs of 70s-80s and the mercury rarely dropping below 60 even in winter.

The scene: With a beautiful setting between the sea and dramatic cliffs, Honolulu is about as scenic as cities get. The real lure, however, is the cultural crossroads of shopping and dining.

For an overview of the city, take the elevator in the Aloha Tower on Pier 9 to the top, where you can see a few of Honolulu's popular attractions, including Pearl Harbor and the Punchbowl.

Most of Pearl Harbor is closed to visitors, but the sunken USS Arizona has become a shrine. The hull is marked by a simple white memorial that was financed in part by Elvis Presley's 1961 Honolulu concert. The memorial honors the more than 1,100 crew members who were entombed here when the Japanese bombed the harbor in 1941. Access is via ferry; free tours run from 8 a.m. to 3 p.m., with tickets given on a first-come, first-served basis.

One of the best views of the area is from the National Memorial Cemetery of the Pacific, high above the city in the caldera of an extinct volcano called Punchbowl — once an ancient burial ground. Many servicemen who died in Pacific battles are buried here, as is Hawaiian shuttle astronaut Ellison Onizuka.

To the east is photogenic Diamond Head. A hiking trail leads up to a panoramic view and passes through tunnels that were built during World War II. Down below is Waikiki, a frenzied collage of beach-front hotels, restaurants, Midwesterners in Bermuda shorts, Californians in thongs — and every imaginable sort of shop and store. The place is about as far from native Hawaii as Oshkosh. Even Waikiki Beach, a narrow, crowded strand, is from somewhere else. The sand, they say, was shipped in.

Information: Hawaii Visitors Bureau, 2270 Kalakaua Ave., Suite 801, Honolulu, HI 96815, (808) 923-1811.

In several of the cities included here, and other popular tourist destinations, you can find discounted hotel rooms through reservation services. See Cutting the Cost of Lodging section for tips on finding hotel bargains and a list of reservation services that offer accommodations at a discount.

Take note!

☞ **Pick your beach.** Honolulu's Waikiki Beach actually is a string of beaches, each attracting a slightly different crowd. Toward Diamond Head, you will see more Honolulu residents — including some celebrities. Tourists are on the beaches across from the large hotels, with some stretches drawing the young bikini crowds, others families and others the more sedate sun-worshippers.

CHAPTER 16

Mountain Highs

When the days get short and the temperatures fall below freezing, America's ski resorts gear up for their prime season: mid-December through March — or April at some Western U.S. resorts with high peaks.

With such a limited season, it's always been hard for skiers to find true bargains, but the advent of snow-making equipment has extended the ski season. Today, ski resorts offer several windows for economizing on winter vacations.

Once the snow melts, prices in ski resorts go downhill and summer vacationers can find good deals. Generally, ski resort rates are lower from spring through fall, but summer has become a popular second season and no longer offers the greatest savings.

Some mountain regions are known better as summer destinations and therefore offer their lowest prices in winter.

The following guide will help both winter and summer vacationers get a mountain high at bargain rates.

Ski Vacations

Off-season: Opening day, sometime in October or early November, to mid-December, although Thanksgiving week may be busy. The last two to three weeks of skiing in the spring also are considered off-season. Expect savings of 20 percent to 30 percent off high-season rates. Some resorts tag the last three weeks of January and first week of February as a "value" season with slight discounts off high-season prices.

Weather tips: Inconsistent weather is the catch, a problem not exclusive to the off-season, though. Usually, Mother Nature cooperates with some early snowfall — but many resorts today have state-of-the-science snow-making capability that allows them to operate despite the whims of nature.

The scene: For those tired of waiting in long lift lines and paying dearly for the privilege, early-season skiing can be a chance to rediscover what you liked about the sport in the first place. Late fall and early winter often bring the best of all worlds — fresh snowfalls and, at many resorts, almost deserted mountains.

There's usually no need to make reservations far in advance; lodging remains a last-minute buyer's market until the year-end holidays. No snow, no go.

Killington, Vermont's largest ski area, has extensive snow-making, allowing it to operate 63 percent of its runs without a flake of natural snow. And the quality? Like packed powder in midwinter, the resort spokesman says — minus the lift lines and crowds. Until the Christmas holidays, you'll be making tracks by yourself on many runs.

Killington discounts its lift tickets by 45 percent or even more at times during the early and late seasons, and you'll find hotels reducing rates by up to 30 percent.

Out West, ski resorts at higher elevations often get snow beginning in September and enhance it with their snow-making as needed. While most resorts open in early November, some slopes have lifts running in early October.

The Western resorts offer a variety of savings in the off-season, ranging from reduced rates on tickets to free ski days in addition to lower hotel rates.

In Colorado, Vail and its sidekick resort Beaver Creek cut the price of an adult ski ticket by 35 percent from their opening in early November until just before Thanksgiving, and you'll find hotels discounted up to 40 percent.

> **Take note!**
> ☞ **Fun for non-skiers.** Non-skiers married to skiers needn't despair at vacation time. Most popular ski resort towns have a myriad of non-skiing activities, such as sleigh rides, dog-sledding, ice skating, shopping, historical walking tours, live entertainment and more.

In Summit County, you get a free lift ticket for Keystone, Arapahoe Basin and Breckenridge when you purchase one night's lodging at Keystone before mid-December; rates start at $65 a night. In the late season, after mid-April, a night's lodging and ski ticket drop to as low as $49 at Keystone. Lift tickets for the early season are discounted as much as 40 percent.

At Aspen and Snowmass, early birds can expect about 50 percent of the mountain runs open and discounts of 25 percent on lift tickets. Winter Park cuts its lift tickets by about 35 percent in the early and late seasons.

Telluride spices its early and late seasons with free skiing when you stay at lodges participating in the program; outside those packages, lift tickets are reduced by about 33 percent in the off-season.

Crested Butte tops the offerings with free skiing for everyone in early and late seasons, except during Thanksgiving, when you must buy lodging to ski free. In the early season, you'll find free skiing and three nights' lodging for as low as $91 per person, and as low as $70 in the late season.

In Utah, Park City lets you ski free until mid-December when you book a minimum of four nights at one of 18 participating lodgings. In case snowfall is light, Park City has snow-making on 42 percent of its runs. For the late season, the resort discounts lift tickets by about 25 percent.

Note: While the early and late ski seasons always bring good deals, the amount of discounts will vary from year to year, and free-ski programs are subject to change.

White Mountains, New Hampshire

Off-season: Early April (or after snow season) through mid-June. Savings can range up to 50 percent.

Weather tips: They don't call spring the "mud season" for nothing, so bring waterproof boots, an umbrella and a warm jacket in April and early May. From mid-May to mid-June is the best time. Temperatures range in the 40s-60s. If you plan to hike at higher elevations, dress warmly. Sudden storms can quickly transform a placid spring morning into a freezing winter afternoon.

The scene: The 770,000-acre White Mountain National Forest is a wilderness mecca for hikers, climbers and nature lovers. Gorges slash through rock-strewn flanks, and rivers rush down steep valleys. The area is delightfully compact. You can drive in a few hours from the discount shopping malls in North Conway to the rugged Presidential Range, where tundralike summits house endangered plants and moose. In spring, hillsides and meadows are carpeted with wildflowers.

Stately mansions and white clapboard bed-and-breakfast inns dot the area. Many are furnished with quilt-covered poster beds and serve home-style country breakfasts. The Covered Bridge House in Glen has its own 1851 covered bridge.

Shop 'til you drop in North Conway's vast discount outlets, then hop aboard the town's antique steam train and roll past forests, cornfields and rivers.

For the highest views around, drive to the top of Mount Washington for awesome views; at 6,288 feet, it's the highest point in the northeastern United States. Or leave the driving to the historic Mount Washington Cog Railway, a steam-powered train that's been chugging to the summit since 1869. It runs May through October.

Near Franconia Notch is Frost Place, Robert Frost's 1915 home where you can peer at memorabilia and signed editions of the poet's works. And, nearby is Old Man of the Mountains, the likeness of a face in a natural granite formation that was immortalized by Daniel Webster and Nathaniel Hawthorne and a three-cent stamp.

The Kancanmagus Highway winds 34 miles through some of the Northeast's most spectacular scenery, including trails that lead down to wedding cake waterfalls that plunge through potholes and flumes. Watch for moose in marshy, boggy areas along the highway.

Don't miss Jackson, a town that looks like it was lifted from a sampler. In spring, hike the trails past gurgling streams bloated with snow melt and tiny wildflowers poking from the ground.

Information: Jackson Chamber of Commerce, P.O. Box 304, Jackson, NH 03846, (800) 866-3334. Supervisor, White Mountain National Forest, 719 Main St., Laconia, NH 03246, (603) 528-8721.

Green Mountains, Vermont

Off-season: After Easter to mid-June, mid-October to the day before Thanksgiving. Expect discounts of 30 percent to 40 percent.

Weather tips: Early spring is chilly and often rainy. Late fall is sweater weather, and you can expect some snow.

The scene: Vermont is the sort of nostalgic, small-town America where we all wish we had grown up. There are white steepled churches and red barns, covered bridges and clapboard houses, snowy woods, maple syrup and mountains and green forests galore. In fact, *verd mont* is French for "green mountain."

Perhaps no town is more Vermont than Stowe, which huddles in the shadow of 4,393-foot Mount Mansfield, the state's highest peak. On a clear day, you can see 50 to 70 miles. The town is quintessential Vermont, with a white-spired meeting house, gingerbread cottages and village greens.

> **Take note!**
> ☛ **Sweet time.** Late winter and early spring is maple sugaring time in New Hampshire and Vermont. Visit a sugarhouse to see the sap being boiled down and taste sugar-on-snow, syrup drizzled over scoops of snow.

The hills still are alive with the sound of music. Although the original Trapp Family Lodge, filmed for "The Sound of Music," burned down years ago, the new lodge features musical performances and Austrian tea rooms that serve buttery cookies, cakes and pastries.

For a grand overview of the area, take Route 108, also called Mountain Road (closed in winter) to Smuggler's Notch. For $12 a car you can drive the Mount Mansfield Auto Toll Road (open May through October) to the summit. An intrepid, 4.5-mile gravel road (no road warriors or student drivers, please), it winds to the top through heavily wooded slopes. Or, ride the Mount Mansfield Gondola ($9) to the summit.

Early spring also is a great time to rent bikes and pedal along the five-mile scenic Stowe Recreation Path past a mountain stream, cornfields, woodlands, pastures and old-time swimming holes. Or head for the hills. Mount Mansfield is laced with hiking and biking paths, but remember, as the T-shirts warn, "Vermont Ain't Flat!"

Information: Stowe Area Association, P.O. Box 1320, Stowe, VT 05672, (800) 24-STOWE.

The Adirondacks, New York

Off-season: Early spring and all winter. Rates sometimes are slashed more than 60 percent. Many hotels and attractions are closed after the fall foliage season, but recreational opportunities abound.

Weather tips: Mild and sometimes rainy in early spring with temperatures in the 40s-50s. Winters are cold, often with snow and below-freezing temperatures.

The scene: In the early 18th century, before the hot springs lured the rich and famous, Saratoga and environs were the exclusive domain of loggers, fur trappers and a few New York millionaires and mobsters who built extravagant backwoods retreats.

By the late 18th century, Saratoga had become one of society's favorite gambling and horse-racing resorts. Nestled in the rugged Adirondacks amid evergreen forests and sparkling lakes, the town is a stone's throw from Adirondack Park.

In spring, the best off-season time to visit, the Saratoga streets are relatively quiet. For vicarious thrills, head to the National Museum of Thoroughbred Racing with its video-simulated race featuring famous horses and jockeys. Or peek back in time at Casino and Congress Park, which houses a historic 1870 casino with Italian gardens.

Saratoga also is the dining center of the area. Don't miss the Irish stew and folk tunes at The Parting Glass pub, or Cafe Lena, a folksy hangout where musician Don McLean first played the song, "American Pie."

Several scenic drives are particularly beautiful in spring. Drive 20 miles north to Glens Falls and follow the Central Adirondack Trail (Route 28) northwest along the Fulton Chain of Lakes. Take time to hike or rent a canoe and explore the back country. Don't miss the Adirondack Museum, where you'll find 22 buildings filled with historic treasures, including a miniature collection of old lake boats.

Another wonderful drive is the Dude Ranch Trail, a 40-mile loop that starts 40 miles north of Saratoga in Lake George. The drive is studded with guest ranches, so hang up your spurs and stay awhile.

In winter, you can cross-country ski at Mount Van Hoevengert, where a network of trails connects Lake Placid, Saranac Lake and Keene. Contact Adirondack Ski Touring Council, (518) 523-1365, for details. Or go downhill skiing at Whiteface Mountain Ski Center near Lake Placid.

Information: Saratoga County Chamber of Commerce, 494 Broadway, Saratoga Springs, NY 12866, (518) 584-3255.

Shenandoah Mountains, Virginia

Off-season: Generally November to May. You will find savings of about 30 percent. In Charlottesville, home of the University of Virginia, you can expect higher room rates during special college events.

Weather tips: Spring and late fall are pleasant, while winter can be cold with snow. April is garden month but often is rainy. Some visitor attractions close in the off-season.

The scene: Two ridge-top routes more famous than the mountains themselves open up the Shenandoahs: Skyline Drive, a 105-mile route that winds southwest through Virginia, and Blue Ridge Parkway, which begins at the southern terminus of Skyline Drive and extends 469 miles south to the Smokies.

Take note!
☛ **Jefferson's arch.** The Natural Bridge, a landmark near Lexington, VA, so impressed Thomas Jefferson that he bought the arch and surrounding 157 acres. Often called one of the seven wonders of the world, it still is privately owned.

Late summer through fall, both are bumper-to-bumper with visitors, especially on weekends. But April through mid-May, you can poke along without horns honking or car fumes camouflaging the fragrance of the rhododendrons.

You can exit the main roads and idle along two-lane roads through quaint towns lined with historic inns, bed-and-breakfast lodgings and ma-and-pa eateries. In April, brake for local garden tours or cast your line in a gurgling trout stream.

History buffs should explore a few of the old towns sprinkled through the region. In Winchester, an apple-producing center, the office where George Washington worked as a surveyor is a museum. Woodrow Wilson's home is in

Staunton, and Thomas Jefferson's gracious Monticello and James Monroe's Ash Lawn are near Charlottesville.

Near the West Virginia border is Hot Springs and The Homestead, a legendary resort built in 1891. South of Lexington near Interstate 81, you can walk or drive across Natural Bridge, a natural limestone span.

Information: Shenandoah National Park, Route 4, Box 348, Luray, VA 22835, (540) 999-3231.

Ozark and Ouachita Mountains, Arkansas

Off-season: Generally November through February, although Christmas can be busy. Savings can be up to 40 percent.

Weather tips: November and March are normally pleasant sweater weather with some rain; winter brings some snow and freezing temperatures.

The scene: The Ozarks are synonymous with homespun pleasure — just ask President Clinton, who spent his childhood here. Crooked highways wind through velvet mountains and past historic hamlets where the neighbors gather on porches at night to sing folk tunes and strum instruments, often made locally.

Road warriors can spend days exploring the Ouachita and Ozark mountains, doing a big loop from the Hot Springs area northwest to Eureka Springs and east to Mountain View.

Hot Springs grew up a century ago around a series of thermal pools that attracted celebrities and still draws droves of modern-day spa-goers. Head for the Fordyce Bathhouse Visitor Center to get a historic prospective, then stroll along Bathhouse Row, lined with historic spas, two of which are still operating.

Follow Highway 7, considered one of the nation's most scenic routes, north from Hot Springs to Harrison, then go west to Eureka Springs, the bed-and-breakfast capital of the world. Crooked lanes wind past historic hotels, Victorian gingerbread houses, churches and regional craft shops selling Ozark pottery and quilts.

A half-day drive but worth the detour is Pea Ridge National Military Park, the stirring site of the 1862 Civil War battle that saved Missouri for the Union. Park roads wind past wind-swept prairies and patchy woodlands lined with split-rail fences, where cannons rust in the brush.

Much of the unique lifestyle of the Ozarks is preserved at the Ozark Folk Center near Mountain View, about 130 miles east of Eureka Springs. Craftsmen ply age-old crafts like blacksmithing and pottery-making at the folk center. Head for the front porch of the Wild Flower Hotel, a hangout for local fiddlers and banjo players, and settle in a spell to listen to the music of the mountains.

Information: Arkansas Department of Parks and Tourism, One Capitol

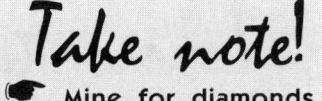

> *Take note!*
> ☛ **Mine for diamonds.** About an hour southwest of Hot Springs, AR, is Crater of Diamonds State Park, the only diamond mine in the world open to the public. Explore old buildings from the mining days and keep your eyes peeled for a diamond in the rough.

Mall, Little Rock, AR 72201, (800) NATURAL. Superintendent, Hot Springs National Park, P.O. Box 1860, Hot Springs, AR 71902, (501) 624-3383.

Rocky Mountains, Aspen, Colorado

Off-season: April through Memorial Day and late fall until mid-December. Rates are highest in ski season; summer and early fall offer discounts but not the greatest savings. Off-season savings often are 40 percent to 60 percent off the ski season rates.

Weather tips: Early spring can be "mud season," but late spring and fall bring warm, sunny days and cool nights. Bring a sweater.

The scene: In 1890, a mini silver rush brought thousands of prospectors to Aspen. During their three-year stay, they erected a slapdash town with 70 saloons, 12 churches and an opera house. By 1893 the silver mines were depleted and most prospectors moved on to golder pastures or turned to ranching and potato farming.

Today, the authentic Victorian town remains synonymous with silver, glitter, glamour and stars. Cher, Jack Nicholson, Goldie Hawn and John Denver all call this pristine mountain town home.

Spring through fall, Aspen throws open its lodges and shutters to mere mortals, with even the most rarefied lodges slashing prices.

The town's historic past and scenery are as free as the colorful wildflowers that grow waist-high on the ski mountains. The flowers continue through fall, a quasi off-season when prices tend to be a little higher than summer but crowds dwindle — you can have to yourself an entire mountainside of quivering aspen splashing gold against the evergreens.

Aspen is easily explored on foot — or you can rent a pair of in-line skates and be mistaken for a local as you roll by graceful Victorian and gingerbread mansions, galleries, sleek window displays and elite boutiques and restaurants.

To get a closer look at Aspen's most precious commodity (the mountains), ride a gondola to the top of Aspen Mountain and hike or mountain bike down — Aspen has countless sports rental shops. Or, hike through the colorful Maroon Bells, mineral-streaked twin peaks that soar 14,000-plus feet. Go fishing in Upper Frying Pan River or take a guided rafting trip down the Roaring Fork River.

Drive scenic, roller-coaster roads to Woody Creek, home of Hunter Thompson. Order a burger at the funky Woody Creek Tavern and don't be surprised if the irreverent author himself wanders in after his routine round of target practice. Don't worry — he leaves his gun by the door.

Summer and early fall visitors can enjoy numerous festivals.

Information: Aspen Chamber Resort Association, 425 Rio Grande Place, Aspen, CO 81611, (800) 26-ASPEN.

Sangre de Cristo Range, Northern New Mexico

Off-season: Taos has lower rates generally April to mid-December, except holidays; summer prices are lower than ski season but not the lowest of the year. Santa Fe rates tend to be lower November-April, except holidays; summer is peak season. Because the Santa Fe-Taos area is so popular year-round, rates don't fluctuate widely. You can find savings of 25 percent to 30 percent at select times.

Weather tips: Crisp, clear air and sunny weather year-round, with temperatures of 35-70 in the spring. In November, temperatures are in the 40s-60s but can dip below freezing, particularly in Taos.

The scene: These sister mountain towns nestle above 7,000 feet in dramatic landscapes that are rich with history and culture. Their cobblestone side streets are filled with art galleries, museums and shops showcasing American Indian, Mexican and Southwestern arts and crafts. And both towns easily can be explored on foot.

> *Take note!*
>
> ☛ **Photographic tip.** For a fee, visitors can enter the Taos Pueblo outside Taos, NM, a mud-and-straw structure dating back more than 400 years. Don't take pictures of the Indian residents without asking permission, however, and be prepared to tip them.

Taos, the smaller of the two, lies in the shadow of the Sangre de Cristo Range. Summer crowds belie the fact that Taos actually is a small town of just 4,000 residents — mostly artists, musicians and craftspeople. Eucalyptus trees shade neighborhood streets dotted with Spanish mission-style homes and quaint B&Bs. The business district radiates around Taos Plaza, established by the Spanish around 1617.

Outside town are two leading tourist attractions: Taos Pueblo, the country's largest existing multistory pueblo, which has been inhabited continuously for centuries, and the Kit Carson Home and Museum, former abode of the famous mountain man, scout and trapper.

Explore the area via the scenic Enchanted Circle Drive, which winds past sagebrush flats and mesas to Wheeler Peak, at 13,161 the state's highest point.

Santa Fe is much larger, with 60,000 residents, though still easily explored. Most of its museums, galleries, shops and restaurants are centered around Santa Fe Plaza, the city's tourist hub. Developed in 1609 as a bull ring, the plaza was the official end of the Santa Fe Trail and once hosted fiestas and fandangos.

Serious consumers in search of fine crafts, silver jewelry and antiques should explore Canyon Road. If you love good art, don't miss The Museum of Fine Arts, with paintings by Mexican and American Indian masters. Food lovers will find it much easier to get into Santa Fe's fine restaurants in the off-season.

Cristo Rey Church is worth a visit. The mud-and-straw brick building was hand-built by parishioners in 1940 to commemorate the 400th anniversary of Coronado's exploration of the West and is believed to be the largest adobe structure in the United States.

Nearby is Loretto Chapel. Built in 1873, the chapel is world-famous for its Miraculous Staircase, spiral steps built without any visible support.

Information: Taos County Chamber of Commerce, P.O. Drawer I, Taos, NM 87571, (800) 732-8267. Santa Fe Convention and Visitors Bureau, 201 W. Marcy, Santa Fe, NM 87504, (800) 777-2489. Taos Ski Valley Inc., P.O. Box 90, Taos Ski Valley, NM 87525, (505) 776-2291.

Sawtooth Mountains, Idaho

Off-season: Spring through fall. Lowest rates are April through May and mid-October through mid-December. Expect savings of 30 percent or more.

Weather tips: Spring, or mud season, has rainy days — but when the sun comes out, you'll think you're in heaven. Summer is sunny, dry and sometimes hot, while fall is nippy.

The scene: Sun Valley opened in 1936 as the St. Moritz of the Rockies and was aptly named for the bright winter sun that sends skiers home with a Florida tan. Early photographs lining the lobby hallway inside Sun Valley Lodge show skiers descending Bald Mountain (Baldy) stripped to the waist.

The weather and advanced ski terrain lured a celebrity lineup of the time, including Gary Cooper, Claudette Colbert, Errol Flynn and Ernest Hemingway.

Today, Sun Valley is the antithesis of Aspen, preferring Old World charm and manners to modern-day glitz and glamour. While the stars are still around — it's not uncommon to see Mariel Hemingway or Brooke Shields or Clint Eastwood huddled over cappuccino at a sidewalk cafe — you're not likely to see any of them in fur coats. Parkas, blue jeans and cowboy boots are more like it.

> **Take note!**
> ☞ **Festival time.** In Sun Valley, ID, spring introduces a season of festivals that lasts through fall. The hills come alive with music in July and August.

Down a cold one at Grumpy's in Ketchum (watch for the sign that says, "Sorry, We're Open"), then light out of town along the 68-mile stretch of Sawtooth Scenic Byway, which runs from Ketchum through the Sawtooth Wilderness area and over Galena Summit. Self-tour cassette tapes are free for the borrowing at the Sawtooth National Recreation Area headquarters and the ranger station in Stanley. Try to time your drive from Ketchum so you arrive at the summit around sunset. The view of jagged peaks silhouetted against the sun is awesome.

From tiny Homer, a one-block town with a population of 70 not counting the cows, follow the winding road to Stanley, a picturesque ranching town that's quiet unless a plane is landing at the makeshift airstrip — a fenced pasture.

With plentiful wildlife and some of the best fly-fishing in the United States (try Silver Creek and Wood River for trout and steelhead), Sun Valley is a sportsman's paradise, provided you have a license and abide by the local catch-and-release policy. Otherwise you may go to jail.

Catch a chairlift up mountains and hike down, ride horseback on trails winding through the back country and canoe or white-water raft area rivers.

Sun Valley hosts ice shows at its historic rink behind the lodge every Saturday night June through September. Get a front row seat and watch such stars as Nancy Kerrigan, Scott Hamilton and Katarina Witt spin and twirl. The rink is open to the public the rest of the week, so rent skates, take a few lessons and practice your own version of the triple axle.

Information: Sun Valley Co., Sun Valley Road, Sun Valley, ID 83353, (800)

635-8261. Sawtooth National Forest, 2647 Kimberly Road E., Twin Falls, ID 83301, (208) 737-3200.

Wasatch Range, Utah

Off-season: May and October. Rates usually are lower in summer than in ski season but not the lowest of the year. Off season rates plummet 60 percent or more sometimes.

Weather tips: Both May and October are sunny, mild and dry, with daytime temperatures of 60s-80s and nighttime temperatures dipping to the 40s-50s.

The scene: Nowadays there's little evidence of Park City's rip-roaring past as a silver-mining town, complete with a Chinatown, red-light district and bars built up near-vertical streets. It was a rare prospector who could stop for a drink at each tavern in town and still make it home on two feet.

All that remains of Park City's hell-raising past are 64 turn-of-the-century buildings, all listed on the National Register of Historic Places and nudged helter-skelter between museums, boutiques, restaurants, factory outlet malls, inns and B&Bs.

While the town is elbow-to-elbow with skiers in winter, the crowds thin out in summer and fall — and the scenery gets even better. Wildflowers carpet ski slopes that are laced with hiking and mountain biking trails. You can golf at Park Meadows Golf Club (a championship course designed by Jack Nicklaus) or take in one of the town's many festivals.

Road warriors will enjoy the scenic drive along Route 140 into Brighton Basin and down Big Cottonwood Canyon, or the more rugged jaunt over Guardsmen Pass; the gravel road is accessible to most vehicles. Both routes offer a wildflower smorgasbord late spring through fall.

Paradise regained? Not quite. Despite her chastised present, Park City still packs a few sins under her belt. To name one: Mrs. Field's cookies, which makes its headquarters here. Just try to avoid those bags of discounted seconds and you'll see what we mean.

Information: Park City Chamber of Commerce, P.O. Box 1630, Park City, UT 84060, (800) 453-1360.

Sierra Nevada, California/Nevada

Off-season: April through May and October through November. Expect savings of about 30 percent at times.

Weather tips: The weather is mild and sunny, with daytime highs in the 50s-60s and lows dipping to freezing.

The scene: Lake Tahoe looks like it dropped from heaven, starting with its namesake, a world-famous looking-glass lake surrounded by evergreens, cliffs and canyons and towered over by snowcapped peaks. A scenic loop lets you view the lake and mountains from many angles.

For the best overviews, take the trams in Squaw Valley or Heavenly Valley, or drive or hike up Mount Rose Highway near Incline Village.

The scenic loop tunnels through stone at Cave Rock, which protrudes into the lake. It is said that American Indians once buried their dead under the outcropping, although any kid can tell you the outcropping is really the underwater home of Tahoe Tessie, the lake's friendly monster.

As for what to do, most of the area's recreational opportunities can be reached via this 72-mile loop, including the tramways and nature trails that take off in all directions.

Lake Tahoe's most spectacular beaches include D.L. Bliss State Park and Meeks Bay on the California side and Zephyr Cove (complete with a beautiful lodge) and Sand Harbor at Nevada Lake Tahoe State Park on the Nevada side. While Lake Tahoe is never tropical, it's warm enough for a quick dip in summer.

You can get another perspective on the beauty of the area from the Tahoe Queen, an old-fashioned glass-bottom paddle wheeler that skims around the lake.

Whether touring by land or lake, don't miss Emerald Bay, an aquamarine jewel. Fannette Island pokes like a peak from the bay and is crowned improbably by a storybook tea house that was built in 1920 and modeled after Vikingsholm, a Scandinavian castle. A one-mile trail leads to the 38-room castle. Guided tours are available in summer.

For side trips, Truckee has a historic downtown lined with quaint boutiques, an old-fashioned five-and-dime and hometown bakeries. Nearby Donner State Park pays a poignant tribute to the ill-fated Donner Party, stranded here in the winter of 1846.

If you can find the time, take corkscrew Route 207 (also known as the Kingsbury Grade) to Genoa, a quasi-ghost town that is Nevada's oldest settlement. Genoa boasts the oldest saloon in the state. It also has plenty of charming B&Bs, so you won't have to stumble down in the dark.

Information: South Lake Tahoe Chamber of Commerce, 3066 Lake Tahoe Blvd., South Lake Tahoe, CA 96150, (916) 541-5255, or Lake Tahoe Visitors Authority central hotel reservations, (800) AT-TAHOE.

CHAPTER 17

Park Retreats

We know 50 places you can go for vacation and, believe it or not, you own them all. From Acadia to Zion, America's national parks are calling you to experience wind-swept beaches, towering peaks and the awesome scenery you thought existed only on postcards.

And here's some good news: Despite their vastly popular beauty, even national parks take a few months off to hibernate. Whether they snooze all winter (or summer) or take a quickie nap between seasons, go the right time and you'll enjoy the country's prize jewels at their usual radiance — minus the crowds.

You'll also have a good chance of obtaining accommodations in the popular national park lodges, which sometimes seem impossible to book in high season. However, there may be no off-season savings advantage; some charge the same rates year-round. Others close in the off-season.

In many of the parks, some campground facilities remain open in the off-season. However, treacherous roads and weather extremes make off-season camping in some parks best left to the most intrepid travelers.

Acadia, Maine

Off-season: Mid-October to mid-May. Savings can be about 40 percent at nearby Bar Harbor.

Weather tips: Temperatures are 30-70 in the spring and fall and below zero to mid-30s in winter. Weather conditions can change rapidly. Average snowfall in the park is 60 inches, but major accessible areas are at or near sea level and rarely receive snow.

The scene: At this rugged park along the central coast of Maine, crashing waves shatter the silence of pine forests. Along the jagged shoreline of rocky coves and inlets, squirrels dart from the trees and scamper along the beach. At Thunder Hole, a granite chasm, waves explode in spray, but only steps away is a shaded sanctuary where nothing seems to move except the mist.

While the park is busy in summer and fall, it reverts to a hushed wilderness with few visitors from Columbus Day through May.

Before the winter snow and in spring, you can walk along Sand Beach or hike on Great Head Trail near Sand Beach. For a scenic driving tour, follow Sargent Drive along the shores of Somes Sound, with glacier-carved granite walls dropping to the sea.

In winter, you can hike, snowshoe or cross-country ski on footpaths and carriage roads past ponds with beaver lodges and mountain views. The east side of Eagle Lake Loop is open to snowmobilers.

Bring your telescope for winter stargazing and watch for the Northern Lights, when the sky shimmers with strange pulsating images of red, green and white. Also in winter, look for small land birds, white-tailed deer and snowshoe hare as well as moose, bear, red fox, otter and coyote.

Acadia is known as the warbler capital of the United States, and in spring several species, as well as the rare peregrine falcon, can be seen and heard. Also in spring, wild strawberries, bluets, white starflowers and purple violets dot the park's network of trails. The four-mile Hadlock Pond Carriage Road loop showcases some of spring's best wildflower displays.

Information: Acadia National Park, P.O. Box 177, Bar Harbor, ME 04609, (207) 288-3338.

Great Smoky Mountains, North Carolina/Tennessee

Off-season: November through April. Expect savings of about 30 percent.

Weather tips: Temperatures vary according to elevations, which range from 840 to 6,643 feet. Mild days and cool nights are the normal pattern in late spring and early fall. Winter temperatures can dip below zero at upper elevations. March is wet.

The scene: Time seems suspended in these mountains, among the oldest on Earth. From a distance, rounded ridges spanning the North Carolina and Tennessee borders recede into the horizon like shadowy silhouettes, blurred by a bluish haze that turns the park's peaks into floating islands. Trails wind to moonscape balds where you can see ridge after ridge march to the horizon.

Crowds throng from late April through fall, when wildflowers carpet the slopes, followed by a blazing autumnal display. But go November through April, and you'll have the park mostly to yourself.

While winter temperatures vary from moderate to bitter cold, the Newfound Gap Road, the park's 35-mile scenic thoroughfare, remains open unless there's ice and snow. With no summertime haze obscuring the view, you can see for miles.

Smoky Mountains National Park once was home to mountain folk who lived quietly in secluded coves and hollows. The gap road leads you past stone walls that mark the boundary of former pastures, a solitary apple tree revealing a long-forgotten orchard, and Cades Cove, a collection of log cabins, weathered barns and white churches that from a distance appears to be a living community. But as you draw closer, you see that there are no lights in the cabins or voices in the churchyard — nor have there been since Cades Cove was taken over by the park and frozen in time as part of its legacy.

Information: Superintendent, Great Smoky Mountains National Park, Gatlinburg, TN 37738, (615) 436-1200.

Take note!

☞ **Get a pass.** A Golden Eagle Pass costs $25 and admits the holder and an accompanying party free to all parks for the calendar year. Those age 62 and older can get a Golden Age Passport good for life for $10, with proof of age. The Golden Access Passport provides free admission to the disabled. All are available at parks.

Big Bend, Texas

Off-season: Generally June to September and December through February, with the exception of the Christmas holidays. Rates remain the same year-round at the park lodge but drop about 20 percent in nearby motels.

Weather tips: Summers are hot, with daytime highs of 90-100, but the humidity stays relatively low and nights are cool. Winter temperatures are cooler, with daytime highs near 60 and nights in the 20s-30s. Snow is rare, and light if it falls.

The scene: Named for the U-shaped bend of the Rio Grande that runs through the park, Big Bend National Park is the Lone Star State's last great wilderness area. Here the frontier spirit of American Indians, cavalrymen, cowboys and Mexican bandidos lives on.

Rugged and remote — the closest airport is more than 230 miles away and the nearest hospital is 108 miles — this diverse national park houses harsh desert plains, green valleys and deep canyons, forested mountains and towering pinnacles.

The park is busiest mid-March through late April, as visitors come to see the desert wildflowers, blooming cactuses and migratory birds.

For the best views in the park, drive the 30-mile Ross Maxwell Scenic Drive, which winds by the Chisos Mountains (highest peak 7,835 feet) down to Santa Elena Canyon on the Rio Grande. The shorter but equally spectacular seven-mile road up Chisos Basin winds steeply through canyon country and red rock cliffs to Chisos Mountain Lodge, which overlooks the basin and is open year-round.

Big Bend is a gigantic living history museum. Hike trails to discover old mines and ranches as well as spectacular views — always take water — or join one of the river-rafting trips. Bring a swimsuit for a midwinter dip in the hot springs at the now-abandoned Hot Springs Post Office. American Indians claim these mineral waters have restorative powers.

Information: Superintendent, Panther Junction Visitor Center, Big Bend National Park, Big Bend, TX 79834, (915) 477-2251.

Yellowstone, Wyoming

Off-season: May and September. The park has two seasons, summer and winter. Winter, though not peak, is popular and requires advance planning because park access and lodging are limited. Only one road, from the North Entrance east to Cooke City, MT, is open to cars year-round. Park lodging rates remain constant; rooms are reasonably priced but often hard to get. Reserve early. Rates at nearby motels drop about 20 percent in the off-season.

Weather tips: Expect cool days and cold nights in the off-season. Snow is possible at higher elevations year-round; September can be cloudy and wet.

The scene: While people outnumber the bison in July and August, Yellowstone's wild beauty shows off best in the off-season.

In May and early fall, there's little traffic along the park's Grand Loop, which takes you past Yellowstone's most prominent attractions. Explore boardwalk trails that lead past gurgling mudpots, hot springs and shooting geysers. Hike into meadows to see early wildflowers or the changing colors of fall and catch sight of some of the wildlife.

In spring, you can view baby bison, moose, elk and other new arrivals feeding under the watchful eyes of their mothers. But keep your distance from all animals — remember, they are wild.

Park lodging is shuttered by early October, and snows normally have closed most park roads by Nov. 1. But from December into March, parts of the park reopen, bringing to view a totally different Yellowstone, its landscape and animals cloaked in snow.

In the winter, shuttles operate from Bozeman's airport to Mammoth Hot Springs and the West Yellowstone entrance where they connect with snow-coach (tracked vehicle) transportation into the park. The park also can be entered from the south, via Jackson, WY. TW Recreational Services, (307) 344-7311, has winter packages including snowmobile tours, cross-country ski tours and winter wildlife tours in the park.

You can explore trails independently on cross-country skis or snowshoes, with rental equipment available from Mammoth Hot Springs Hotel and Old Faithful Snow Lodge. At Old Faithful, the park's most famous geyser, the Lone Star Geyser Trail winds nine miles past crystallized streams and hot springs to several other trails ranging from easy to difficult. Detailed brochures are available at the visitor center.

Just outside the park near the east entrance is Pahaska Teepee Resort, (307) 527-7701, a national historic site where Buffalo Bill Cody built his hunting lodge in 1901. In the winter, warm up in heated log cabins and cross-country ski its network of groomed trails; ski and snowmobile rentals are available. It's closed Oct. 15-Dec. 15, then open until March 15. It closes then until May 15, when it opens for summer.

Information: Superintendent, Yellowstone National Park, P.O. Box 168, Yellowstone National Park, WY 82190, (307) 344-7381.

Glacier, Montana

Off-season: Mid-September through May. In winter, you can enter the park for limited distances on either end of the Going to the Sun Road. Park lodging rates remain the same, but nearby motels offer savings of about 30 percent off rates, which normally are $50-$60 a night.

Weather tips: Weather can be described in one word: unpredictable. Be ready for anything, including rain, hail and snow. Temperatures late fall through spring range from the 30s to the low teens and below. Heavy snow coats the park in winter.

The scene: Situated in northwestern Montana near the Canadian border, Glacier is a fair-weather friend whose main attraction — the Going to the Sun Road — brings hordes of motorists from mid-June to early September.

Take note!
☛ **Park fees.** Most national parks now charge an entrance fee, ranging from $3 to $10 per vehicle and good for seven consecutive days.

But arrive in mid-September just before the park lodges close and you'll have the park, scenic highway, trails and awesome autumnal display to yourself. You'll also have your pick of rustic lodging.

Going to the Sun Road, a winding mountain route flanked by precipitous mountainsides, coils from lush stream beds and shimmering aspen to the snow-covered summit of the Continental Divide. En route are sharp spires, toothed ridges, abrupt cliffs and razor gorges with crashing waterfalls.

From the numerous turnouts, you can tiptoe to the edge and peer down into hushed valleys where streams tumble free over stony staircases. The road passes numerous trailheads of varying difficulty that are hikeable until the first snow.

If you're more of a Sunday driver than a road warrior, consider boarding one of Glacier Park's vintage 1936 red buses with roll-back tops — and leave the switchbacks to them. The buses usually run from early June until late September.

By December, Glacier is hibernating under several feet of snow and drawing cross-country skiers and snowshoers. The park's free guide, "Ski Trails of Glacier National Park," describes 14 trails in the park.

Most park lodges and local hotels are closed in winter; an exception is Glacier Highland Resort, about half a mile outside the park. The old but spotless motel keeps 13 units open throughout the winter.

Information: Superintendent, Glacier National Park, West Glacier, MT 59936, (406) 888-5441

Grand Canyon, Arizona

Off-season: November through February, except holidays. Park lodging rates remain the same; nearby accommodations drop rates up to 40 percent.

Weather tips: On the South Rim, weather conditions can change rapidly. Be prepared for snow and some road closures because of ice. The North Rim is closed in winter.

The scene: The "Temple of the World," the Grand Canyon instills reverence in all who see it. Clouds, sun and shadows seem to repaint buttes and gorges from dawn until dusk. The canyon walls go from blood red at sunset to deep purple as night falls.

In summer, car traffic is restricted in parts of the South Rim, but once the crowds are gone, you're free to roam. The South Rim, 81 miles north of Flagstaff, has the most services, sights and amenities and is accessible year-round. The North Rim, 210 miles from Flagstaff through lonely but scenic country, is open May through October depending on snow.

You can tour the South Rim by car, guided bus tours, foot, bicycle, mule and plane. In nearby Tusayan you can get a dazzling introduction at the IMAX Theater featuring the film, "Grand Canyon, Hidden Secrets."

The 25-mile East Rim Drive offers a good sampling of the park via scenic turnouts with views of the canyon and its Anasazi and pre-Columbian Indian ruins.

Walk along the 10-mile Rim Trail (paved in parts) for non-stop views and historic landmarks. El Tovar Hotel, built in 1905 of native stone and pine logs, is considered one of the finest national park hotels. The Yavapai Museum traces the canyon's geologic history and offers dramatic views through polarized picture windows. When exploring, remember the altitude here is about 7,000 feet.

To see the canyon from top to bottom, take a guided mule trip to Phantom Ranch and overnight where famous artists and authors once rested, (520) 638-2401.

For a historic journey, climb aboard the steam-powered train in Williams, south of the park, and ride to the canyon in restored vintage rail cars. The train operates daily, (800) THE-TRAIN.

Information: Superintendent, Grand Canyon National Park, P.O. Box 129, Grand Canyon, AZ 86023, (602) 638-7888.

Yosemite, California

Off-season: Late October to mid-March, except holidays. Park hotels drop rates about $20 except for holidays and weekends. Rates at places outside the park drop as much as 40 percent.

Weather tips: Autumns are quiet and crisp, yet daytime temperatures in the valley often are a balmy 60-70. Winters bring a coat of snow.

The scene: In 1919, stagecoach passengers rode through a tunnel bored in a giant sequoia to an incomparable vista of a deep green gorge enclosed by 3,000-foot stone walls and waterfalls crashing from angelic heights — the same view visitors see today.

While the seven-mile-long, mile-wide Yosemite Valley houses two of the world's 10 highest waterfalls and the largest single granite rock on earth (El Capitan), it's just a slice of the 750,000-acre park. You'll also see giant sequoias and rugged wilderness with meadows, forests, lakes and rock domes.

While Yosemite Valley is packed all summer with traffic jams, tour buses and noxious fumes, the crowds thin from Thanksgiving through mid-March, when heavy snowfalls blanket the high country and periodically dust the valley floor.

Mariposa Grove Road is open year-round except for intermittent winter closures. Tuolumne Grove, Glacier Point Road and Tioga Road are closed mid-November through late May.

Snow lovers should head to Badger Pass for alpine skiing and independent or ranger-led cross-country and snowshoe walks as well as ski schools, (209) 372-1000. Follow marked cross-country trails at Crane Flat and Mariposa Grove, go sledding at Crane Flat or Goat Meadow or settle into Ostrander Ski Hut.

For a milder winter experience, hike around Yosemite Valley; daytime temperatures hover in the mild 40s and snow rarely accumulates. Ask park rangers about conditions on trails to waterfalls and vistas — the winter route to Vernal Fall via Mist Trail is awesome. Or hibernate before a fire at the Ahwahnee, a historic hotel where picture windows and log beams frame majestic views of cliffs, waterfalls and snowcapped peaks.

Yosemite Pioneer Christmas, usually the closest weekend to Christmas, offers caroling, candlelight tours and other activities in the Wawona area of the park, (209) 372-0563. Or enjoy gourmet cuisine at Chefs' Holidays in January and

February, (209) 454-0555, when celebrated chefs put on free cooking demonstrations; a chefs' banquet is $75 per person.

For affordable yet elegant lodging, settle into the Groveland Hotel, (209) 962-4000, a turn-of-the-century charmer with gourmet dining nestled in a historic gold rush town 23 miles from the park. Rates remain constant all year at $85-$105, including continental breakfast.

Information: Superintendent, Yosemite National Park, P.O. Box 577, Yosemite, CA 95389, (209) 372-0264.

Take note!

☞ **Food for thought.** Most dining establishments in the parks are casual and offer reasonably priced fare. The parks are a natural for picnicking, too; general stores in or near the parks have snack foods.

Death Valley, California

Off-season: Summer. Crowds also may be thin Labor Day through the end of October, when temperatures cool just enough to make outdoor exploring feasible. Lodgings in and adjacent to Death Valley rarely lower rates, but in nearby towns, accommodations may cut prices in summer.

Weather tips: Temperatures in September and October are 90-110 at midday but drop to a comfortable 62-81 by late afternoon. Early mornings and late afternoons are ideal for outdoor exploring, hiking and cycling. Summers are extremely hot, with temperatures reaching 120. Always carry water.

The scene: Blame it on Hollywood, but most people think Death Valley is a vast sweep of sand, broken only by an occasional cow skull or snake, a forbidding place that responds to every human need with "no!"

But America's quintessential desert offers far more than moonscapes. Salt flats shimmer in the shadow of snowcapped peaks, and sand dunes change moods by the hour — from blinding white at high noon to pitch-black under thunder clouds. Barren mountains house the rusted, century-old remains of tumble-down mining camps that howled on Saturday nights, only to wither away to slag heaps.

Although we wouldn't recommend long treks during the scorching summer off-season, it's a perfectly acceptable time to visit because most of Death Valley's grandeur can be viewed from inside the air-conditioned comfort of a car. Most of the park's historic attractions also are air-conditioned.

Although you'll need to book a room in advance from fall through spring, the park's wide open spaces never allow the visitor to feel crowded.

You'll need a car to do the park justice, since attractions are miles apart. Death Valley Museum offers information and an overview of the area's culture and history, and a scenic drive leads to Badwater, the lowest point in the Western Hemisphere.

At the park's northern edge is Scotty's Castle, a Mediterranean-style hacienda with a 56-foot clock tower. The historic home is named after Walter Scott (Death Valley Scotty), a self-described prospector as notorious for his laziness as his long-winded mining tales. Employees in period costumes lead living-history tours through the mansion and grounds.

In the northeastern corner is Rhyolite, a ghost town known as "the queen city of Death Valley" during the early 1900s gold rush boom. For a scenic view of the entire valley and mountains, follow the spiral road to 11,049-foot Telescope Peak, the park's high point.

To explore by foot, head to the dunes area east of Stovepipe Wells and roam an ocean of sand, particularly dramatic at sunset, when the dunes turn crimson to purple. The Salt Creek Nature Trail is a bird-watcher's haven. Take a guided horseback ride or carriage ride at Furnace Creek Ranch, or tee off, play tennis and swim in a spring-fed pool (80 degrees year-round) at Furnace Creek Inn. It was built in 1927 for well-heeled tourists and exudes an aura of wealth and old money.

Information: Superintendent, Death Valley National Monument, Death Valley, CA 92328, (619) 786-2331.

Denali, Alaska

Off-season: Mid-September to mid-May. The first two weeks of September and mid-May through early June are considered shoulder seasons, when you can see the most for slightly less. Rates drop about 30 percent to 50 percent in the shoulder seasons. All park facilities and roads are closed during the official off-season from mid-September through mid-May.

Weather tips: In autumn, it's sunny and cool with temperatures in the 40s-50s during the day and 30s or colder at night. In spring, it's rainy and cool with trees just starting to leaf in mid-May and early June. In winter, the park is snowbound and frigid; access is by dogsled, cross-country skiing and snowshoeing only.

The scene: The park basically has one season — summer, when 16- to 20-hour days afford maximum sightseeing. For moderate temperatures and fewer crowds, visit during the park's shoulder seasons, the first two weeks in September and from mid-May to early June. Summer crowds June-August can lead to two- and three-day waits for shuttle passes — the only way to get around the park.

A wilderness of tundra, blue glacier pools and snowfields, Denali is best-known for 20,320-foot Mount McKinley, the highest mountain in North America. The 88-mile road into the park's heart is unpaved after 14 miles and accessible only by shuttle buses, which stop where you can disembark to picnic, hike or visit historic attractions. Throughout the park, wildlife — including grizzlies, Denali caribou, moose and 159 species of birds — abounds.

The park is laced with footpaths. Most maintained trails are located near the park entrance at Riley Creek and include treks through dense spruce forest. Rangers offer free daily walks at Eielson Visitor Center at Mile 66 on the Park Road, and you may follow them on off-road discovery hikes. Check at the visitor center for information.

You also can do flightseeing tours or get a close-up view of Denali's icy white water on guided rafting trips.

The Denali National Park Hotel is utilitarian, with rustic touches and a location close to the shuttles, or you can settle into luxurious rustic comfort at the grand Harper Lodge Princess Hotel, whose log-cabin interior is richly furnished. Big wood decks overlook the Nenana River.

Information: Superintendent, Denali National Park and Preserve, P.O. Box 9, Denali Park, AK 99755, (907) 683-2294.

Hawaii Volcanoes, Hawaii

Off-season: There is no real off-season, but there generally are fewer visitors from fall into spring. Lodging prices remain constant year-round in and adjacent to the park, but accommodations in resort areas offer special packages year-round. A number of bed-and-breakfast lodgings are adjacent to the park.

Weather tips: Temperatures are 60s-70s. June, July and September are dry; November and December are the rainiest months. Though snow is rare, below-freezing temperatures are recorded on peaks; with parts of the park at elevations of 4,000 feet, mornings and evenings can be cool.

The scene: Set in the south part of the island of Hawaii, this 377-square-mile park ranges from arid moonscape expanses of hardened lava to Tarzan jungles. Lava oozing down precipitous slopes and hitting the sea with a sizzling cloud of steam is one of Earth's greatest live performances.

From Hilo, head south on Route 11. Just before the park, you'll pass through a Wizard of Oz hamlet called Volcano Village, where cottages are set among giant ferns and tropical flowers.

For an overview of the park, stop at Kilauea Visitor Center, which includes the Volcano House hotel and art center featuring local work, much of it inspired by the park's fiery beauty. The hotel offers rooms with a view of 4,000-foot Kilauea caldera, the collapsed summit of one of the park's two active volcanos, and a dining room that serves award-winning cuisine with a five-star view. Golf enthusiasts can tee off at the nearby Volcano Golf Course.

The 11-mile Crater Rim Drive circumnavigates the caldera, about three miles across at its widest. You can take short paths to the edge and peer down into a steaming moonscape. The Jaggar Museum, the park's second visitor center located about three miles from the entrance, offers up-to-the-minute reports on volcanic activity and video displays of crews and rangers at active lava sites.

Follow old and recent lava flow to the sea via 50-mile (round-trip) Chain of Craters Road. There are no services en route, so fill the tank and take plenty of water. The narrow ribbon of asphalt runs between black lava fields and the sea, then parallels the coast for several miles before ending at the foot of the 1989 lava flow that swallowed the road and nearby Wahaula Visitor Center.

From here, you can walk an ever-changing pathway to a black sand beach to watch active lava flow into the sea in a molten waterfall. Listen to the hiss and watch the steam billow into huge mushroom clouds. Come at sunset when the lava flow becomes a vivid neon show of reds, oranges and purples.

Information: Superintendent, Hawaii Volcanoes National Park, HI 96718, (808) 967-7311.

CHAPTER 18

Foreign Affairs

Those faraway places with strange-sounding names may sound hopelessly out of reach, but during off-season they can be as accessible and affordable as many destinations in the United States.

Resorts throughout the Caribbean traditionally have "summer sales," offering savings on their rooms, and winter brings greatly reduced airfares to Europe and some hotel discounts.

Often, varying your departure date by only a few days can save you hundreds of dollars. So it's wise to stay flexible when you start making your travel plans and to always ask about seasonal price differences.

Some cities, such as London, have so much international business traffic that many hotels have similar rates year-round but may offer unannounced specials or packages.

Check out the off-season bargains below and you'll be saying *adios*, *au revoir* or *arrivederci* before you know it. Prices may vary due to fluctuation in the exchange rates.

Western Europe

Off-season: Generally November until late March. April, May and October are shoulder seasons, bringing some lower prices but not as low as winter. In some capitals, you may find lower hotel rates in August, when many Europeans take vacation and leave the cities to tourists. Airfares to Europe are the highest in summer and lowest in winter. Expect savings of about 30 percent on both airfare and accommodations by traveling in the off-season.

Weather tips: Northern areas are chilly in fall and spring, cold and snowy in winter. Central Europe has nippy days in fall and spring and varied winter weather, ranging from crisp and clear to cold and wet days. With a year-round Mediterranean climate, southern Europe is warmer and sunnier, but winter can bring cool days.

Take note!
☛ **Picnic in Paris.** Cut your food costs in Paris while enjoying the scenery. Buy bread, cheese and wine in a corner store and picnic in one of the gardens, by the Eiffel Tower or along the Seine.

For extensive information about cutting the cost of travel to Europe and a sampler of savings in particular destinations, see the following Bargain Hunter's Europe section.

Rio de Janeiro, Brazil

Off-season: April through November, except July. Winter in the states, which is summer in Brazil, is high season, with peak rates during *Carnaval* celebration immediately preceding Ash Wednesday, usually in February. In off-season, you can find savings up to 50 percent sometimes. Airfares are lower after *Carnaval* until early June and again from early August to early December.

Weather tips: Brazil's fall and winter temperatures are in the 60s (the natives wear sweaters and shun the beach).

The scene: Rio! You can almost hear the waves lapping and the taxis honking. While the typical tourist hops into a swimsuit and promptly heads for Copacabana, Ipanema and Leblon — chic neighborhoods that boast Rio's most beautiful strands (as well as semiclad bodies) — there's more to soak up in this glittery city than the sun. Besides, the water is much too polluted for swimming, and the threat of pickpockets is omnipresent.

Take note!

☞ **When in Rome.** Eating in an Italian *trattoria* or *pizzeria* will cost less than dining in a *ristorante*. Also, watch for signs designating an *enoteca*, a wine shop, which usually has light fare.

For a spectacular overview of Rio, board a glass-enclosed cable car to Sugarloaf, a hunk of towering granite in Guanabara Bay offering panoramic views. Hang on tight; the winds can be fierce up here.

For another bird's-eye view of Rio, take the Corcovado Railroad to the mountaintop with the famed 120-foot Christ statue, which stands with arms outstretched to the sea and city, as if blessing it. The train climbs through tropical foliage with views of mountain and sea below. You also can drive up on narrow, winding roads through Tijuca Forest, an enchanting tropical reserve with crashing waterfalls.

Don't miss Rio's spectacular Botanical Garden, with 8,000 types of plants and an awesome entrance lined with royal palms. And leave time for shopping. Just a block from the sea, Rio metamorphoses into a cluttered jumble of noisy, crowded streets jam-packed with boutiques, galleries, outdoor markets, restaurants and local characters ranging from street urchins to screaming transvestites. Take a good street map and cling tightly to your purse.

If you want a little peace and quiet, a rare commodity in Rio proper, head south to Sao Conrado, an outlying beach that rests in an idyllic natural amphitheater. The beach is surrounded on three sides by thickly forested mountains and granite hills. Once situated on your private patch of paradise, you may find it hard to pry yourself away. Blame it on Rio.

Information: Brazilian American Cultural Center, 16 W. 46th St., Second Floor, New York, NY 10036, (212) 730-1010.

Montego Bay, Jamaica

Off-season: May to mid-December (especially May, June and July). Expect savings of 35 percent and as high as 50 percent sometimes.

Weather tips: Temperatures usually are 78-85 year-round but can go higher in summer, when the humidity also rises.

The scene: Off-season Jamaica is no problem, as the locals would say. With a year-round balmy climate and more than 200 miles of beaches — many of them empty — this tropical isle is the perfect spot to escape the rat race. Tarzan jungles and rain forests carpet its lush slopes, waterfalls crash from unseen heights and you can spend the day staring at the beautiful sea.

That's not to suggest that Jamaica is a snooze. Music throbs from neon discos, where scantily clad dancers sway to reggae, and from Montego Bay to the Blue Mountains, bustling outdoor markets are filled with high-decibel wheeler-dealing and bargaining.

And, of course, there's the beach. Doctor's Cave Beach near Montego Bay has five miles of sugary-white sands, while Walter Fletcher Beach has calm waters for swimming.

For a peek at historic Jamaica, visit a few "great houses" — elegantly restored plantations. Then drive into the Blue Mountains and visit Pine Grove, a working coffee farm with an inn that serves the freshest Blue Mountain coffee on Earth — you can even pick your own beans.

Montego Bay's open-air crafts stalls are a great place to pick up Jamaican rum, hand-loomed fabrics, wood carvings, paintings, silk batiks and reggae tapes. Restaurants are pricey, but for a memorable meal, head to Negril, home of the best jerky (fiery wood-smoked beef). Stop at a shanty and get it straight from the flames — served with a paper cup of rum.

Information: Jamaica Tourist Board, 801 Second Ave., 20th Floor, New York, NY 10017, (212) 856-9727.

Quebec City, Canada

Off-season: Fall and spring have the lowest rates. The Christmas holidays, Winter Carnival in February and nearby skiing push rates up from mid-December into March, although not as high as the peak summer season. Look for packages that cut rates about 35 percent. Also, factor in the U.S. dollar's favorable exchange rate with the Canadian dollar; at press time, you got Canadian $1 for less than U.S. $.80. Thus, a hotel room priced at Canadian $135 and discounted 35 percent would end up costing about U.S. $70.

Weather tips: Autumns are cool and beautiful, and winters are cold — but often sunny and crisp for winter sports.

The scene: Quebec City is the crown jewel of Quebec, rich in history, culture and beauty and full of Old World charm. The only remaining walled city in North America, it occupies a regal perch high above the St. Lawrence River and is capped by the Citadel, which stands on Cape Diamond, the city's high point.

Quebec's best sights are behind the wall in Old City, a dense, double-decker cloister of buildings divided into Upper and Lower Town. The best and maybe only way to explore is by foot, so bring a comfy pair of walking shoes, and get a

Take note!
☛ **Safety first.** When sightseeing anywhere, but particularly in major cities, it's wise to wear a money belt or pouch to hide your valuables. Carry only the amount of money you think you will need that day.

walking-tour booklet from the tourist office — every other building has a tale to tell.

Don't miss (actually, you can't) Chateau Frontenac, an imposing castlelike hotel with a steep green copper roof that dates to 1893, and the Citadel, the historic fort that is still an active military base. Behind the Frontenac, a boardwalk edges along the cliff for spectacular views.

Beyond the Citadel and outside the walls is the National Battlefields Park, a pleasant place to stroll with hills, gardens and monuments. It's hard to believe that several bloody battles between the British and the French took place here.

In Lower Town, historic Place Royale, the town's 400-year-old cobblestone square, is encircled by buildings with Normandy-style roofs, dormer windows and chimneys — formerly the homes of wealthy merchants. Lower Town also houses a number of historic churches and estates plus sidewalk cafes, restaurants, hotels, souvenir shops and a farm market.

Quebec in autumn is a leaf-watcher's delight, and during her frosty winters, you can ice skate for 2.4 miles along the river, cross-country ski inside the battlefields and parks or downhill ski at nearby resorts.

If your feet get weary or your nose a little cold, take a horse-drawn carriage tour and snuggle underneath a warm blanket, then drop by Cafe Loft for sinful pastries.

Information: Tourism Quebec, P.O. Box 979, Montreal, Quebec, Canada H3C 2W3, (800) 363-7777.

Canadian Rockies

Off-season: October to mid-December and April into May have the lowest rates. From mid-December to mid-April prices are higher at the ski areas, although not as high as in the peak summer season. Expect savings of about 30 percent, with best rates usually through hotel packages. The U.S. dollar's favorable exchange rate with the Canadian dollar enhances the savings.

Weather tips: Autumns are a blaze of color, and winters are sunny and "brrr." Sudden snow may close passes. The Icefields Parkway between Lake Louise and Jasper is snow-covered nearly all winter but packed so hard you almost forget you're driving on snow. You'll have no problem, provided your car has snow tires or chains.

The scene: From Wild West Calgary to Banff Springs' elegant tea rooms and ski resorts and Jasper's snow-clad peaks, Alberta is a gem with many facets.

Off-season, the aspen shimmer gold against the evergreens, and the brisk air is ideal for hiking. Winter transforms the area into a hushed white wonderland; while the ski resorts may be packed, the rest of the area sleeps quietly under a blanket of snow, with opportunities for cross-country skiing, snowshoeing, ice skating and dog-sledding excursions.

While at heart a Wild West town with the world's largest outdoor rodeo each summer, downtown Calgary is Alberta's sophisticated lady, with galleries, museums and restaurants galore.

For stellar scenery, head northwest. First stop is Banff, a storybook town with the historic castlelike Banff Springs Hotel and nearby hot springs at Cave and

Basin Centennial Centre. For great views, ride the glass-enclosed Sulphur Mountain Gondola to the 6,500-foot summit and hike down. In winter, there's good skiing in the area.

Just 35 miles north is Lake Louise, where the milky green water reflects the image of Chateau Lake Louise, one of Canada's grand dame hotels, complete with tea rooms and fancy restaurants overlooking the water. In the dead of winter, the lake is frozen and you can cross-country ski in the woods. Down the road a few miles is Moraine Lake, an aquamarine stunner surrounded by 10 peaks. You won't have to buy a postcard; just take home one of the older Canadian $20 bills on which the lake and surrounding peaks are pictured.

From Lake Louise, the famous Icefields Parkway heads north to Jasper past snowcapped peaks, alpine lakes and glaciers. In autumn, look for moose, elk and mountain goats migrating down from the high country for the winter. Beyond Sunwapta Pass, the road's high point, is Columbia Icefield, the largest accumulation of ice in the Rockies. It feeds nine major glaciers as well as rivers that flow to three different oceans. Climb aboard a snow coach for a narrated tour into the icefield itself.

Jasper has a pretty little downtown packed with boutiques and restaurants and a charming train depot that starred in "Dr. Zhivago." Visit in winter and you'll likely shiver from the cold like the film characters did.

Information: Alberta Economic Development and Tourism, 10155 102nd St., Commerce Plaza, Third Floor, Edmonton, Alberta, Canada T5J 4L6, (800) 661-8888. Ask for a Winter Vacationer's Guide, which offers information on ski and back-country packages.

> *Take note!*
> ☞ **Regional fare.** Dine on foods and drinks that are popular in the region. These usually are better prepared and will cost less than Americanized foods.

Acapulco, Mexico

Off-season: Generally mid-April to mid-December, with summer bringing the lowest rates. Expect savings of 40 percent and sometimes more. Often the more luxurious hotels give the bigger discounts.

Weather tips: Off-season is the rainy — and hot — season, but the showers usually are short-lived and clouds often clear quickly to reveal blue sky.

The scene: Life's a beach in Acapulco, with balmy seas, constant sunshine and year-round temperatures in the 80s. Grab a towel and head for Playa Revolcadero, a wide, sprawling beach with restaurants, hammocks and horseback riding.

Beaches in Acapulco often are crowded, and the water may be polluted and/or rough, so swim at your own risk or just enjoy the view. For more solitary sunbathing, head to Pie de la Cuesta, about 15 minutes outside town, a broad beach where *palapas* (beach shacks) provide *mucho sombra* (shade) and you can dine in authentic, if rustic, restaurants.

Away from the balmy surf are championship golf courses, tennis courts, food and craft markets, legendary night life and restaurants featuring fresh seafood.

Action centers around the Costera Miguel Aleman, a broad, eight-mile boulevard hugging the sea. Start a tour with the *zocalo*, home of colonial Acapulco and the Fort of San Diego. Shop for silver at Taxco El Viego, housed in a large colonial building. Take the 10-minute walk up to La Quebrada (near Mirador Hotel), where five times daily, you can watch Acapulco's cliff divers pray before a shrine before plunging 130 feet into the sea, sometimes in pairs and carrying torches at sunset.

Cap the night with chuckles and good Mexican cuisine at Carlos 'n' Charlie's, a Mexican restaurant with prankster waiters, a jester menu and painted tools and gadgets hanging from the ceiling. The stuffed shrimp, ribs and oysters, however, are no laughing matter.

Information: Mexican Government Tourism Office, 405 Park Ave., Suite 1401, New York, NY 10022, (212) 421-6656 or (800) 44-MEXICO.

Australia and New Zealand

Off-season: May through October (fall and winter), although September and October may be busier. Expect savings of 30 percent to 40 percent at some destinations.

Weather tips: Most major cities in both countries enjoy temperate climates year-round, with winter daytime temperatures ranging between the high 30s to low 60s. But the geography ranges from snowfields and glaciers to subtropical rain forests and deserts, so go prepared for all weather if you're touring widely. The summer months actually are a better time for trips to the Great Barrier Reef, off the northeast coast of Australia.

The scene: Australia is far more than Crocodile Dundee. Take Sydney, a worldly city with skyscrapers and mansions overlooking the sea. Get an overview from the Sydney Tower, then visit the celebrated Opera House on the harbor and take in the numerous museums and art galleries.

North of Sydney is subtropical Cairns, where sightseeing boats depart for the Great Barrier Reef. Balmy off-season temperatures are perfect for exploring reefs, cays and tiny tropical islands.

Southwest of Sydney is Adelaide. Off-season buzzes with art and cultural festivals; outside the city is Australia's wine country and Flinders Ranges, desert mountains of exceptional beauty. On the West Coast, separated by miles of arid and largely inaccessible Outback, is modern, sunny Perth, Australia's answer to Los Angeles with pristine beaches, boating, surfing and nightlife.

Also Down Under is New Zealand, considered by many to be the most beautiful country on Earth. No larger than Colorado, its two islands offer every

> **Take note!**
>
> ☛ **Plane talk.** On long overseas flights, take a bottle of water and drink frequently. Avoid carbonated and alcoholic drinks. Stand up and walk around the plane every hour or two so that your body won't get so stiff.

scenery and climate, plus Victorian cities with elegant architecture as well as quaint villages set in sweeping landscapes.

To sample New Zealand's myriad moods, start on the North Island and head to Ninety Mile Beach, a dazzling expanse of tropical sands ending in a cluster of islands. Then go down to Rotorua, a Yellowstone-type park with geysers and mudpots.

The next stop is South Island, known for its Southern Alps, scenic fiords and pristine lakes. Christchurch, the main city, exudes a proper British air. Wander Hagley Park past botanical gardens and shop for fine woolens and crafts at the Galleria.

The historic Fox Glacier Hotel is an ideal place from which to take sightseeing flights to Fox Glacier and 12,315-foot Mount Cook — and if the weather's good, even land on a glacier to play in the snow. Near Queenstown, a little jewel on a lake surrounded by mountains, go skiing or watch bungee jumpers fling themselves nearly 100 feet off a historic bridge near the picturesque village of Arrowtown.

Farther south is postcard-perfect Milford Sound, a spectacular fiord where hundreds of waterfalls crash down jagged cliffs. Book well in advance for guided four-day treks along the famed 33-mile Milford Track. The packages include lodging and meals at a hostel-type lodge; for information and reservations, contact Mount Cook Line, (800) 446-5494.

Information: Australian Tourist Commission, 1000 Business Center Drive, Mount Prospect, IL 60056, (708) 296-4900. New Zealand Tourism Board, 501 Santa Monica Blvd., Suite 300, Santa Monica, CA 90401, (800) 388-5494.

CHAPTER 19

Chart of Travel Seasons

Off-season is the most cost-efficient time to travel, when discounts are easy to find. One week — even one day sometimes — can mean the difference between high prices and bargains, thus saving hundreds of vacation dollars.

We've charted travel seasons for popular destinations, both domestic and foreign. The seasons are: high, when rates peak; shoulder, the in-between months, when prices dip; and low, the best cost-saver time to go. Calculations were made with information from airlines, hotels and tourist offices. Not all destinations show holidays as high periods, but vacationers can expect increased prices in many places for Easter, Thanksgiving and Christmas-New Year's.

When prices are highest, lowest at foreign destinations

	January	February	March	April	May	June	July	August	September	October	November	December
Australia/New Zealand												
Bahamas												
Bermuda												
Caribbean												
Hong Kong												
Japan												
Mexico												
South America												
Canadian Rockies												
Western Europe/England												

[1]Within high season, Jan. 10-Feb. 10 usually are slightly lower priced. [2]High season starts late June for Northern beaches. [3]Shoulder season has lower weekday rates; weekend rates remain higher. Lower rates can be found year-round when conventions aren't in town. [4]Dates apply to most parks in the top two-thirds of the country. Summer

122   DISCOUNT TRAVEL HANDBOOK

When prices are highest, lowest at U.S. destinations

	January	February	March	April	May	June	July	August	September	October	November	December
Alaska	Low	Low	Low	Shoulder	High	High	High	High	Shoulder	Low	Low	Low
Appalachian Mountains	Low	Low	Low	Shoulder	Shoulder	High	High	High	High	High	Shoulder	Low
Arizona/California desert areas	High	High	High	High	Low	Low	Low	Low	Shoulder	Shoulder	High	High
Catskills, NY	Low	Low	Shoulder	Shoulder	Shoulder	High	High	High	High	High	Low	Low
Colorado/Utah resorts[1]	High	High	High	Shoulder	Low	Low	Shoulder	Shoulder	Low	Low	High	High
Eastern Seaboard beaches (Massachusetts to Florida)[2]	Low	Low	Low	Shoulder	Shoulder	High	High	High	High	Shoulder	Low	Low
Great Lakes resorts	Low	Low	Low	Low	Shoulder	High	High	High	Shoulder	Low	Low	Low
Hawaii	High	High	High	High	Shoulder	Shoulder	High	High	Low	Low	Shoulder	High
Las Vegas, NV[3]	High	Shoulder	Shoulder	Shoulder	High	High	High	High	High	High	High	High
National parks[4]	Low	Low	Low	Shoulder	Shoulder	High	High	High	Shoulder	Shoulder	Low	Low
New Orleans, LA	High	High	High	High	Low	Low	Low	Shoulder	Low	Shoulder	High	High
New York City	Low	Low	Low	Shoulder	Shoulder	Shoulder	High	High	High	High	High	High
Orlando, FL	High	Low	Shoulder	Shoulder	Shoulder	High	High	High	Shoulder	Shoulder	Shoulder	High
Ozark Mountains (Missouri/Arkansas)	Shoulder	Shoulder	Shoulder	Shoulder	Shoulder	High	High	High	Shoulder	Shoulder	Low	Shoulder
South Florida/Keys	High	High	High	Shoulder	Low	Low	Low	Shoulder	Shoulder	Low	Shoulder	High
Southern California (except desert areas)[5]	Shoulder	Shoulder	Shoulder	Shoulder	High	High	High	High	Shoulder	Shoulder	Low	High
Washington, DC	Low	High	High	High	High	Shoulder	Shoulder	Shoulder	High	High	Shoulder	High

is low season for parks in the desert areas of the Southwest and in some Southern parks. [5]For Palm Springs area, see Arizona/California desert areas. Summer often brings lower rates in San Diego because there are fewer conventions then.

High | Shoulder | Low

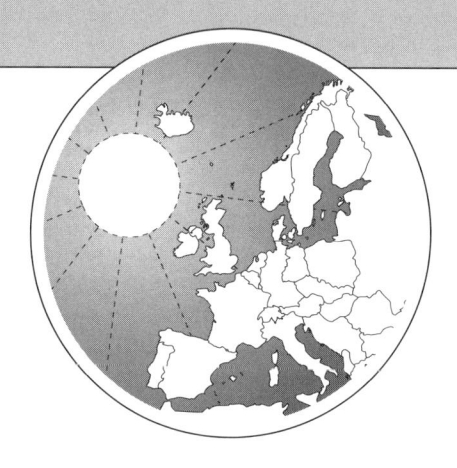

Bargain Hunter's Europe

Don't let reports of astronomical prices for a hotel room or a drink on the Champs-Elysées deter you from a longed-for European trip. There are numerous ways to enjoy Europe within a reasonable budget, but you need to do some homework first. The next 12 chapters are packed with tips that will cut your costs while giving you a memorable travel experience.

CHAPTER 20

Cost-Cutting In Europe

Americans heading to Europe on vacation can take some money-saving hints from the Europeans themselves, who long have been known for pinching their pounds, marks, francs and lire.

For instance, Europeans often choose smaller hotels rather than big-name international chains. They leave the driving to someone else in cities, where they walk and take advantage of mass-transit systems. And, they eat in smaller restaurants where the tab for a good regional meal won't give you indigestion.

The following 10 tips will help you cut costs in Europe — and give a closer feel for the countries you visit.

1. Travel when others don't.

Those who are flexible about their travel times can gain the greatest savings by going in the off-season when flights are less expensive. There's the added benefit of fewer tourists.

Airlines traditionally slash their trans-Atlantic fares to the lowest in midwinter. Round trips can be less than $500 a person — and sometimes the promotions include three-or four-night hotel stays.

Of course, there's a hitch — the weather can be cold and rainy or even snowy. But you also will find a full slate of cultural activities — such as theater and opera performances.

If you don't want to go in winter, time your trip in what's called the "shoulder" season, between summer's highest prices and winter's lowest. May and September are ideal; you save money, miss the crowds and usually luck out with mild weather.

> **Take note!**
> ☞ **What city is this?** Prepare to encounter different names for European cities from the Anglicized versions we know. Vienna is *Wien*, Munich is *Munchen*, Florence is *Firenze*, Lisbon is *Lisboa*. And when you're in France, London is called *Londres*.

2. Package your trip.

Those who buy in quantity save money. Thus, the individual traveler who books a package can tap into the group-rate savings that tour operators get with their volume business.

There are packages for everybody — whether you're an independent who never wants to set foot on a tour bus or whether you want to be fully escorted through every site.

For independent travelers, packages are good deals because they get you a hotel rate lower than any you could negotiate yourself.

There are several choices of independent packages, none requiring you to travel as a group. Through airlines, look for air-hotel packages, which give reduced rates on the basics — overseas flights, transfers between the airport and hotel, and accommodations. You can choose from luxury to budget lodging. Through tour operators, look for "hosted" packages, which usually cover hotels, breakfasts and maybe a city tour. While a "host" is there to assist, you're free to do what you want whenever you wish.

For those who want escorted tours, there are hundreds of options, from trips that provide lots of freedom to ones that program your every move.

> **Take note!**
>
> ☞ **What's the tab?** Commas replace decimal points in many European countries, so the number after the comma denotes the fractional currency, such as our pennies. A bill (or price tag) that reads 60,50 francs means 60 francs and 50 centimes. Also, commas and decimal points sometimes are reversed to our system — 2.500,50 means 2,500 francs, 50 centimes.

3. Go country.

Take a tip from your home travels, where vacationing in the country or smaller towns and cities is less expensive than going to the big cities. The same is true in Europe. For instance, in 1995, the latest U.S. government per-diem rate for lodging and food in London was $246, but the average per-diem in smaller towns in Great Britain was $199. In France, the per-diem was $283 in Paris but dropped to $147 in smaller towns.

Yes, you say, but you want to see London and Paris. Do so, but spend fewer days in the cities and more in other less-expensive scenic or historic areas of the country.

4. Take advantage of free literature.

Most European countries have tourist offices in the United States, and some are fountains of information helpful in planning a trip.

Many of the countries have literature specifically for budget-conscious travelers. For instance, the British Tourist Authority offers "London Accommodation for Budget Travelers" and "Britain: Bed & Breakfast" among its many publications. To obtain them, contact the BTA, 551 Fifth Ave., Suite 701, New York, NY 10176, (800) 462-2748. Also inquire about any newly published money-saving pamphlets.

Some tourist offices also offer special cards that entitle you to discounts on hotels, attractions and/or transportation. Check individual countries for availability.

For addresses and phone numbers, see the list of European tourist offices in Chapter 31, "Getting Information."

5. Travel like the locals do.

Take the subway or hop aboard a bus. Most cities in Europe have excellent mass transit, in the form of subways, buses, trams and rail lines. They're often the fastest, cheapest transportation. The subway systems, while sometimes overwhelming to Americans unaccustomed to mass transit, aren't hard to master.

You can cut your per-trip costs — and save the hassle of buying a ticket each time — with advance planning. BritRail offers a London Visitor Travelcard good on buses and subways for three, four or seven days for $25, $32 and $49 respectively. Buy cards through a travel agent before you leave home; call BritRail, (800) 677-8585, for more information.

In Paris, at the Metro station, buy a *carnet*, or booklet, of 10 tickets for 44 francs (slightly less than $9 at an exchange rate of 5 francs to U.S. $1); money-saving passes also are available.

Prices are subject to change.

6. Pull out the plastic cards.

Networks of automated teller machines have gone international, allowing travelers to put a debit card in a machine halfway around the world and get money from their home checking account — in local currency, nonetheless. By using debit cards, travelers save commissions charged when exchanging currency and usually get the best rate of exchange. (There may be a usage fee with the card, though.)

Take note!

☛ **What day is it?** In Europe, dates are written with day, not month, first and frequently separated by periods — 30.6.95 instead of 6/30/95. Watch for a new wrinkle — computerized bills that show the year/month/day — 95.6.30.

You also can use some credit cards to withdraw from your checking account or to charge a cash withdrawal to your account.

Don't rely on getting all your needed cash through ATMs, though. ATMs may be hard to find, particularly outside major cities. Check with the bank that issued your debit card to see how widely accepted it is. MasterCard and Visa also offer debit cards that access your bank account.

When using traveler's checks, save on fees by cashing larger amounts at a time. If you cash $200 at one time, you'll save three commission charges and other fees over what you'd pay if you cashed $50 at a time.

Use a charge card for major purchases or bills. You'll save transaction fees and frequently get a better exchange rate.

7. Eat where the price is right.

First, determine if your hotel price includes breakfast. It does in many instances. Breakfast may range from continental — coffee and croissants only — to a full English breakfast, so hearty that it can keep you going until dinner.

If your breakfast is not included, get around high hotel restaurant costs by asking at the desk, or scouting the neighborhood yourself, for a nearby cafe or bakery to get coffee and rolls. Or, take along a travel coffeemaker — the little filter-type ones that use real coffee grounds are great — and do your own breakfast, stocking up on fresh fruit and breads from nearby stores.

Save money on other meals in several ways. Luncheon menus are usually less expensive than dinner ones, so eat heavier at lunch. Most restaurants post their menus at the door or on a window; shop around for places with food you like in your price range. Tap into regional dishes and reasonable prices by ordering *prix fixe* (fixed-price) meals, which usually include choices in three courses. For more information, see Chapter 29, "Dining Out for Less."

8. Don't overtip.

Most restaurants in Europe include service (gratuities) in the bill. Look for such words as *service compris* or *servicio incluido*, on the menu or at the bottom of your bill. Ask if you don't see any note, or you could be double-tipping.

If service is included, you don't need to give any more tip, but many people leave small-denomination coins received in change. For instance, if the bill were 99.10 francs, leave the 90 centimes in change.

Take note!
☞ **Beware of the numbers 1 and 7.** In Europe, the 1 is written with an upward stroke on the left, making it look somewhat like 7 as written in the United States. In Europe, the 7 is distinguished by a slash across the descending leg.

9. Don't call home.

Phone calls from European hotels can rival the room rates. Hotels frequently tack surcharges onto already high phone rates. If you don't see an explanation of the rates in your room, call the operator and get specifics before making any calls.

Before leaving home, check with your long-distance phone supplier about special numbers to access an international operator and tap into lower rates by using your calling card. Even when using a calling card, you still may be subject to a small surcharge by the hotel. Clarify the fee; it's usually a flat rate per call.

10. Check about refunds on purchases.

Most European countries have a value-added tax (VAT), similar to our sales tax except the tax is built into the prices of the goods and services. The taxes range as high as 25 percent.

Foreign visitors may be eligible for a refund of a percentage of the purchase price; usually this refund is a little less than the total VAT. The refund applies only to goods, not services. The procedures for refunding and the amounts eligible vary with each country. Most countries set a minimum that you must spend per store to be eligible for a VAT refund. If you're planning to buy several wool or cashmere sweaters in Great Britain, for instance, you will save money by grouping your purchases to meet the VAT refund requirements.

If you plan to buy much more than simple souvenirs, or to make any major purchase, call the tourist office of the countries you plan to visit and ask for specifics about the VAT refund program. You also can ask at major stores, which provide the refund forms, but it's better to know the rules before you go. For more information on VAT refunds, see Chapter 26, "Boosting Your Buying Power."

CHAPTER 21

Beating the High Cost Of Airfare

While your airfare to Europe may be one of the biggest expenses of your vacation, there are ways to trim costs. The more flexible you are about the timing of your trip, the greater your savings. Even a few days' difference in departure can net a major savings on airfare.

Travelers traditionally head to Europe in the summer when airfares are highest. By going between October and April, you will save money.

For example, a check of the lowest round-trip airfares at press time on major carriers between New York City and London showed that you could save about $200, or about 30 percent, by timing your trip in the off-season. Airfares are subject to constant fluctuation; the round-trip prices at the time were $438 in winter, $538 in spring or fall, and $638 in summer.

No-frills travel agencies or discount travel clubs sometimes can earn you extra savings on top of already-discounted airfares.

While most travelers choose a major U.S. or foreign airline when going to Europe, there are other flight alternatives. Charter flights, tickets from a consolidator and travel as a courier are low-cost options, but all involve more risk or limitations.

Here's a look at the different options.

Take note!
☞ **Reserve seats early.** Many airlines allow seat selection up to 30 days before departure. Mark your calendar and call to get the best seat possible so you don't have to spend 10 hours in the middle seat on a fully booked trans-Atlantic flight.

Airline Fares

More than half a dozen U.S. airlines and many European carriers fly from a number of U.S. gateways to cities all across Europe.

The lowest fare offered for an international flight is known as an APEX (advance purchase excursion) fare, which usually carries some restrictions. There may be a 14-, 21- or 30-day advance purchase requirement, a minimum-stay requirement of seven days and a maximum-stay limit of 90 days. These tickets usually carry penalties for scheduling changes, and they may be non-refundable.

The excursion fare varies by season. Fares are lowest in January or February, but there's a downside to visiting Europe then: colder weather. However, sites will not be crowded with tourists as they are in summer, and the theater and fine-arts events will be in full swing.

Fares are slightly higher during the spring shoulder season, mid-March through April, and the top fares come in high season, which starts in May or June (depending on the carrier). In September or October, fares drop for the fall shoulder season.

Exact dates of seasonal changes vary among the airlines. Be flexible when scheduling your trip and when choosing an airline. Call several airlines or a travel agent and ask when the lowest fares occur, rather than setting travel dates and trying to find the cheapest fare to fit your schedule. Adjusting your travel by a few days could save you a considerable amount of money.

You also will save on airfare by booking a midweek flight, rather than a more expensive weekend flight. Always include a Saturday-night stayover.

Be on the alert for occasional fare wars, when carriers announce extremely low ticket prices. Check your newspaper for ads promoting such fares, but read the fine print. These ads usually show a one-way fare in big numbers but require that you purchase a round-trip ticket.

Even though you've made a reservation, you haven't locked in your fare until you purchase the ticket. So it's best to buy the ticket (with a credit card) soon after booking a flight, but keep watching the ads to see if a lower fare is announced. If an airline runs a special promotion after you've bought your ticket, ask to have your ticket reissued. In many cases, the airlines will do so.

Besides the major U.S. and European airlines, some lesser-known carriers offer service to specific cities in Europe at competitive prices or reduced rates. Virgin Atlantic Airways flies to London from New York's Newark and JFK airports, Boston, Miami, Orlando, Los Angeles and San Francisco, and Tower Air goes from New York's JFK airport to Paris and Amsterdam; both operate year-round. Martinair flies from 10 U.S. cities to Amsterdam, with some flights operating only from spring through fall.

Other Options

If your timetable is loose, you might check into fares offered by charter operators and consolidators. Beware that these two options involve risks and could end up costing you more money.

Before looking into these options, be sure you know the lowest fares you can get to your destination on major scheduled airlines. Sometimes regular carriers have fares nearly as low as charters or consolidators, and regular carriers' tickets offer greater consumer protection.

A third option is to act as a courier; while the price may be right, the timing may not suit your needs.

Here's a look at these options:

Charters

Wholesalers lease planes from airlines to operate charter flights on which they sell the seats at a deep discount. You deal with the charter operator, not the airline. Normally, all the seats on a charter flight are sold at one price, but costs can vary according to departure date.

Charters often are seasonal, operating during popular travel periods; for instance, some European charters fly only in the summer. Flights frequently book up quickly.

There are risks to buying a charter ticket, as well as inconveniences in traveling by charter. Flights can be delayed — maybe a day or more — or even canceled if they don't sell well. Charter companies also can raise your fare up to 10 days before your departure.

Flying for Less

Check out these five ways to cut costs of airfare to Europe. Remember, each has drawbacks.
- Fly off-season with a major carrier. It's your safest bet. Trade-off is unpredictable weather, so pack a coat.
- Go with a charter. Service is limited, and you risk being stranded if the flight is canceled.
- Buy ticket through a consolidator. It's an option that nets savings for those who don't plan far ahead. But check out the carrier and its schedule before you buy; you could face major delays traveling if a flight is canceled.
- Act as a courier. This is for free spirits with carry-on bags only.
- Use a no-frills agency or discount travel club. Cash your rebate to buy a meal or two.

Charters fly less frequently than regular flights, often only once a week on a turn-around trip. For example, a charter flight may leave each Friday night from New York City to Paris and make the return trip each Saturday. You must plan your vacation around the limited number of flight days.

Most charters fly only from major cities, most frequently from New York City and Boston for European destinations. They also usually serve only selected cities, sometimes just one destination.

For travelers who live in or near metropolitan areas served by charters, such flights are viable cost-cutting options; but for travelers who must book connecting flights, charters are not good options, for two reasons. The cost of airfare to the gateway can negate savings on the charter compared to fares of scheduled carriers from your home city of nearby. If the charter flights aren't on time, you must foot any bills for hotels and meals, and you may face an increased fare on your connecting ticket if you miss a flight.

Charter tickets may carry a penalty fee for exchange or cancellation, although sometimes you can pay a small additional charge at purchase for a refundable ticket. Ask about refund policies and trip insurance when looking into a charter.

At the airport, check-in lines for charter flights generally are long and slow-moving. The flights may be on aircraft that squeeze as many passengers in as possible; since the flights are frequently fully booked, you're left with little legroom and storage space.

With all their caveats, charters can provide significant savings. For instance, Homeric Tours had charters from New York City to Athens (summer only) for

$549 compared to a $756 discounted fare from a consolidator and a $978 advance-purchase fare from a scheduled carrier; applicable taxes were extra.

If you're willing to take the risks of charter travel, look for a travel agent who's knowledgeable in charters and willing to book one. This may require some calling around because charter flights aren't listed in the agents' computer reservations systems. Some charter operators to Europe are Homeric Tours, (800) 223-5570; Balair, (800) 322-5247; and Fantasy Holidays, (800) 645-2555. Council Charter, (800) 800-8222 or (212) 661-0311, sometimes has charter tickets but acts mainly as a consolidator (see following section).

Consolidators

Consolidators are volume ticket brokers who purchase excess seating from the airlines at deeply discounted prices. They mark up the prices slightly and sell them to the public, but usually still manage to undercut the airlines' lowest fares.

The consolidator tickets with the greatest discounts are to destinations in the Far East, although you can find numerous consolidator tickets to Europe.

At press time, a round-trip consolidator ticket between New York City and London was quoted at $474 (plus taxes) in the high season (a savings of $164 over the lowest fare from an airline) and $353 (plus taxes) in the shoulder and off-season (a savings of $85).

The major advantage of consolidator tickets is that you usually get a low price without having to meet the advance-purchase restrictions. Thus, if you decide to go to Europe next week, a consolidator ticket can be a major savings over the regular fare — but you can't be guaranteed a consolidator fare will be available.

Take note!
☞ **The highest airfares to Europe are during the summer.** You'll save money and still have fair weather by going in the spring or fall. True bargain hunters will wait for winter, when fares are lowest — but so are temperatures.

There are drawbacks. Consolidators may use lesser-known carriers, which do not have as frequent service as major carriers do. Tickets normally can't be used on other airlines, so if you miss your flight, or if it is canceled, you must wait until that airline's next service to your destination. This could mean the next day, or longer. Although flights usually are direct — no change of plane — they may have several stops.

You may not receive your ticket until a day or two before your trip, or you may have to pick it up at the airport just prior to departure. Penalties for cancellations can be high, and customer service from the consolidator is minimal.

Before buying a consolidator ticket, know the name of the carrier you would be flying, the kind of aircraft used, the frequency of service and the number of stops to your destination. Inquire about cancellation and refund policies. Be sure you're comfortable with the arrangements. If possible, pay for the ticket with a credit card; if something goes wrong, you can dispute the charge. Beware: Some consolidators may charge a fee for using a credit card.

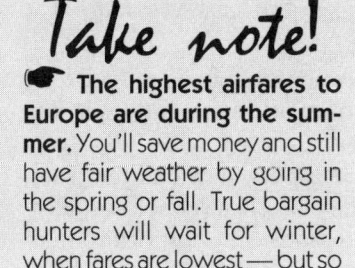

After purchasing the ticket, call the airline directly, if you have time, to confirm that you are on the passenger list. (Consolidators must report passenger names to the carrier; if the carrier doesn't have your name, you may have trouble boarding the flight.)

To find consolidator tickets, check with a large travel agency and ask if it works with, or acts as, a consolidator. Major city newspapers often have ads for consolidator tickets in their travel sections, but it's wise to check out the company with the Better Business Bureau before buying a ticket, particularly if you are paying cash.

Hidden Charges

International flights are subject to departure taxes, U.S. customs fees and other "hidden" charges, so called because they usually are not included in advertised airfares but are mentioned in the fine print. Always ask if taxes are included in fare quotes. In addition to these standard extra fees, most U.S. airports impose an airport facilities tax, commonly $3. Your country of arrival also may add a tax to the ticket. Always ask for the final cost when checking airfares.

The following chart shows the standard U.S. fees that are added to an airline ticket between the United States and Europe; there may be some variation by airline and departure city.

Fees	Amount
U.S. departure tax	$ 6.00
Customs fee	$ 6.50
Immigration fee	$ 6.00
Agriculture inspection fee	$ 1.45
Security fee	$10.00
Airport facilities tax	$ 6.00
TOTAL	$35.95

Uniglobe, a nationwide network of travel agencies, is one source for consolidators that is available in many cities. Major national consolidators are UniTravel, (800) 325-2222; Council Charter, (800) 800-8222; and Jet Vacations, (800) JET-0999.

Couriers

Many shipping companies use personal couriers to accompany important parcels or business papers such as legal and financial documents. Couriers give up their baggage space and in return receive deeply discounted tickets.

The shipping company will purchase a ticket at the regular fare. The company then uses the allotted baggage space to transport the documents and parcels of their customers, charging them accordingly. This generates enough profit that the shipping company can sell the ticket, at a greatly reduced rate, to an individual willing to act as a courier. With couriers, companies speed deliveries by shipping materials as baggage that can be claimed quickly upon arrival, rather than sitting in a warehouse awaiting clearance.

Courier travel is not as clandestine as it may sound. You're not transporting illegal goods. Couriers meet with a representative of the shipping company several hours before the flight. The representative will deliver the shipment to the airport and check it in as baggage, then give you the airline ticket and a manifest pouch that describes the contents of the shipment. At your destination, another representative will meet you to receive the baggage claim checks and the shipment. Return tickets are held by the shipping company and distributed at the airport.

Courier travel is so popular that there are now companies matching shipping firms with potential couriers. The savings for travelers are substantial, ranging from 30 to 75 percent off a full-fare coach ticket; the cheapest tickets are available to those who can fly at a moment's notice. Stays range from one week to 30 days.

Because you forfeit your baggage space to the shipping company, you can take only carry-on luggage aboard. International tickets are usually non-refundable. You may be required to pay for your ticket with a money order or certified check; payment by credit card or personal check is not widely accepted.

> *Take note!*
> ☞ **What time is it?** The 24-hour clock dominates transportation schedules in Europe. Get accustomed to translating p.m. hours to 1300-2400.

If you want to be a courier, you must be able to travel on short notice. While you sometimes can book up to five months in advance, courier companies usually receive last-minute flight assignments and have to provide escorts within hours. Typically, couriers travel alone. A companion who wanted to fly as a courier would have to take the next flight to that destination, usually the next day. It's not difficult for the courier broker to find two consecutive flights to the same destination. Courier companies expect their couriers to look professional, and they may ask you to wear business attire. They may also prohibit drinking during your flight.

If you can comply with the time and baggage restraints, courier flights can yield excellent savings. For instance, a New York-Paris courier flight in summer was priced at $399 compared to a $598 consolidator fare and an $868 advance-purchase fare with a regular carrier; prices excluded taxes.

To check into a courier flight, contact a courier broker. Some companies charge a yearly registration fee and may require a deposit. Courier brokers include Now Voyager, (212) 431-1616, and Discount Travel International, (212) 362-8113.

No-Frills Agencies

Discount travel agencies or clubs offer rebates to customers who purchase airline tickets from them. They do not assist you in the planning of the trip, hence the "no-frills" description. You do most of the groundwork, such as searching for the best fare, finding a flight and perhaps making the reservations.

Typically, you call the discount agency with the flight information and a credit card number. The agency writes the ticket and mails it to you along with a rebate check. The rebate normally is a percentage of the purchase price. There may be an annual fee to join a club or a service charge.

A major benefit of such agencies or clubs is the added savings you get on already-discounted airfares. Such agencies or clubs usually can pay off in savings if you travel several times a year or know you're going to buy higher-priced tickets, such as for a European trip. When considering such agencies or clubs, check both the fees and the benefits. Higher fees may not net any more savings or perks.

Discount agencies include Travel Avenue, (800) 333-3335; Pennsylvania Travel, (800) 331-0947; and Smart Traveller, (800) 448-3338.

Air Travel Within Europe

Airfares within Europe traditionally have been high. Several airlines now are offering coupons that reduce the cost of intra-European travel. Usually, the coupons must be purchased with a round-trip trans-Atlantic ticket at a published fare to and from the same European gateway. Other restrictions also may apply.

Coupons are a good buy if you plan to travel longer distances or need to go to several cities across Europe. Before buying coupons, though, compare the cost with standard one-way airfares to your destinations and with the costs of rail travel and rental cars.

Air France, in cooperation with Air Inter, Sabena and Czechoslovak Airlines, offers the Euro Flyer Pass. This is available to passengers who purchase a round-trip ticket from the United States to Paris for a stay of seven days to two months. The coupons cost $120 each; you must buy at least three coupons but no more than nine. A single coupon is good for a flight between any two cities in Europe.

British Airways offers the Europe Air Pass; you must purchase at least three coupons but no more than 12. Each is good for one flight. Fares are governed by zone and range from $78 to $156 per flight. The pass is available with a round-trip ticket from the United States to Europe via the United Kingdom.

Ask your travel agent about other airlines offering intra-European specials.

CHAPTER 22

Choosing a Tour

If you've been putting off that European trip because it's too costly, consider a tour package, which could save you 30 percent — or more — over arrangements made on your own.

With any type of tour package, you benefit from low group rates, which tour operators can negotiate because they deal in a high volume of traffic. Because operators buy blocks of hotel rooms, they're able to get prices much lower than discounts available to individual buyers.

Most tour packages combine several elements of travel in one price, allowing the traveler to know ahead of time what costs will be and better control expenditures.

Generally, tours are divided into two types: escorted and independent. Escorted group tours long have been a popular way to see Europe, particularly for first-timers, but independent travelers in the '90s have learned they can find both freedom and savings in unescorted tour packages. Here's a look at the two types of tours:

Take note!

☞ **Save some free time.** Don't rush to sign up for all the optional excursions on a tour. After several days, you may want some free time for yourself. Also, the cost of organized side trips can add up. You often can do the same or a similar activity/excursion on your own for considerably less money and at your own pace.

● Escorted tours follow prearranged itineraries led by a tour guide who accompanies the group. Most tour groups move around Europe by motor coach — but don't expect the old-fashioned buses once used for sightseeing. Most motor coaches have roomy, comfortable seats and picture windows; many coaches even have VCRs. Tour leaders see that passengers rotate seat assignments so everyone gets good views — and a chance to know others on the tour.

The elements covered in the price of an escorted tour vary. Budget tours include the basics but few meals and extras, while luxury tours will be more inclusive. Generally, all tours include at least lodging, transportation, daily breakfast and basic sightseeing. Many tour prices also include most dinners, but they frequently exclude lunches, allowing travelers to sample local food on their own.

● Independent tours offer travelers the opportunity to choose their own destinations and sightsee at their own pace. Tour hosts often are available to offer sightseeing tips or even book local tours, but flexibility is the main feature of independent tours. If you decide to go to the theater one evening, you can select your own show to attend, rather than take what's prearranged on a designated night. Or you can linger longer at a museum or shop.

Besides lodging and airport transfers, an independent package might include daily breakfast, car rental or local transportation, a welcome reception and one city sightseeing excursion.

Several airlines offer money-saving packages that are ideal for the independent traveler who wants the cost-cutting benefits of group travel — without the group. These packages typically include round-trip airfare and hotel stays, with perhaps some sightseeing.

For example, here are some independent tour packages offered by British Airways at press time; prices will change. The six-night packages are a better

Tour Brochure Lingo

When deciding on a tour, it's important to read the brochures carefully — and to understand the language used. For instance, eight cities may be listed on the tour — but when you scrutinize the itinerary, you may notice that you're simply passing through one or two of the cities. If you don't understand some of the tour descriptions, ask your travel agent. Here are some terms and phrases often found in tour brochures.

Accommodations
Single room — A room with one bed for one person.
Twin room — A room with two beds for two people.
Double room — A room with a double bed for two people.
Pension — A European guest house or inn.

Extra Costs
High-season supplement — Additional charge imposed during the busiest times of the year.
Add-on fare — Additional airfare for travel between your home city and the domestic gateway from which the tour originates.

Possible Snags
Force majeure — An event or effect that cannot be reasonably anticipated or controlled.

Meals
Continental breakfast — Usually consists of bread, rolls, butter, jam and tea or coffee.
AP (American Plan) — Includes breakfast, lunch and dinner.
MAP (Modified American Plan) — Includes two meals.
EP (European Plan) — No meals.

Tour Prices
All-inclusive — Tour price includes everything (or nearly so) — usually all land arrangements and round-trip airfare and/or other transportation. All-inclusive rarely includes tips and excludes purchases of a personal nature.
Land price — The cost for land arrangements only.
Fly/drive holiday — An independent tour with rental car.

value than the three-night ones, reducing your per-night cost considerably. "A Taste of London" tour, including trans-Atlantic airfare from New York City, round-trip transportation between airport and hotel, hotel room with bath, continental breakfast and trip-planning materials, starts at $649 for three nights/$769 for six nights in summer, and $489 for three nights/$589 for six nights Oct. 1-Dec. 31. "Treasures of London" offers the same basic package plus a $25 sightseeing voucher, a London Visitor Travelcard for unlimited transportation on the city's transit system, the Royal Pass good for admission to five palaces and a theater pass for one performance; it starts at $749 for three nights/$889 for six nights in summer, and a similar offering drops to $569/$689 Oct. 1-Dec. 31. Packages vary in price according to the hotel chosen; expect to pay about $80 more than the lowest rate for a midpriced hotel. All prices noted are per person, double occupancy.

Take note!
☛ **Dine on your own.** You may get tired of eating with the tour group every night. Plan a couple of nights out on the town on your own.

Similar packages are available from other U.S. gateways, with other airlines and to various European capitals.

Tour packages have both advantages and disadvantages. On the pro side:

● Good value in low per-diem costs is one of the major selling points both for escorted and independent tours.

● Escorted tours cut a lot of the hassle of traveling since you don't have to handle your luggage or find your way on a road map.

● A tour leader eases the language barrier, and a guide acquaints you with the customs and history of each area.

● Independent tours provide access to popular hotels that might not be available otherwise.

Among the drawbacks:

● Free-spirited travelers may dislike the mandatory schedule of escorted tours — getting your luggage outside your room early in the morning, sitting down to meals at predetermined times.

● Escorted tours require that the group moves together most of the time, and that closeness can be wearing on those who like privacy.

● Some tours have long stretches of time on motor coaches.

● Visits to attractions may be shorter than you would like because you're in a group.

The key to a good trip, either on an escorted or independent tour, is finding the right package for your budget and travel interests. Start by doing some homework and asking key questions of a travel agent before you book. The following is a list of questions to keep in mind when you're looking at brochures and talking with a travel agent:

1. What kind of tour do I want?

Do you want a panoramic tour of Europe that takes you through several countries, hitting the highlights in the major cities? This is often the choice of first-timers. Or would you prefer a regional tour that focuses on the major attractions in one or two countries? Do you want to venture out on your own, or would you feel more comfortable having a tour guide with you at all times?

2. Where will I be staying?

While tour operators may not specify hotels booked in each city, they tell what class hotel the tour uses. European hotel classifications differ from those we're accustomed to in the United States. Tour brochures often mention tourist class, superior tourist class, first class and deluxe hotels. (For more information on hotel classifications, see Chapter 23, "Picking a Hotel." Tour brochures also usually say if you're guaranteed a room with a bath every night. Ask a travel agent for information about the hotels the tour operator lists as typical choices and determine if they're what you want.

3. How many meals are included?

Check to see which meals and how many are included so you will know how much to budget for extra food. Usually lunches are not included; tour operators have found that travelers prefer to experiment on their own. Some travelers find that breakfast and dinner are enough; they may skip lunch or buy a snack only. When booking an escorted tour, be aware that tour operators select preset menus, usually served at the hotel restaurant. If you want to try local restaurants, look for a tour that includes fewer meals or specifies that you may order a la carte. For travelers who are a little less adventurous, it's wise to pick a tour that includes as many meals as possible.

Cost Comparison of Tours Vs. Do-It-Yourself Trip

The following chart compares the cost of taking a 10-day escorted package tour of Ireland with Collette Tours to the cost of doing the same trip on your own. Prices are per person, double occupancy.

Ireland tour features	Collette Tours	On your own
8 nights of hotel accommodations	Included	$960
6 dinners, 8 breakfasts, including gratuities	Included	$306
6 full-day sightseeing excursions, including admissions	Included	$300
3 evenings of local entertainment	Included	$80
Rental car and gas	Transportation included	$263
Total cost:	**$1,199**	**$1,909**

You save $710 per person with a package tour

Source: Collette Tours, (800) 248-8986. The tour visits Dublin, Limerick, Dingle Peninsula, Killarney, Ring of Kerry, Blarney Castle, Waterford and the Cliffs of Moher.

4. Does the itinerary suit my travel style?

Look over the itinerary carefully. Determine if the important things you would like to see are included. If you've decided on an escorted tour, how much free time will you have to do your own sightseeing or shopping? See if you're spending the most time in the cities that are of the greatest interest to you. Does the tour move too fast or too slow for your tastes? Is there too much walking or too much time spent on the road?

> *Take note!*
>
> ☛ **Take a map.** You'll add to the enjoyment out of a coach tour if you track your progress on a road map. Ask your driver to show you the planned route each day. You'll become more knowledgeable about your trip — and learn the particularly scenic areas and appealing towns for a return trip.

5. What are the terms and conditions of the tour?

The conditions and policies regarding any trip can be found somewhere in your travel brochure — usually in fine print at the back — and they deserve careful attention. Check the reservation, cancellation and refund policies. This section also should specify what is not included in the tour price. If you don't understand the meaning of some terms, ask your travel agent.

6. How stable is the tour operator?

Check the reputation of the tour operator. Ask the travel agent how long an operator has been in business, if the agent has had any complaints about the company and how the operator solves problems that might arise. Ask what kind of protection you have if the tour operator goes out of business or cancels tours after you have paid part or all of the trip costs.

After all your questions have been answered and you've narrowed your choices, it's time to compare tours that you like. Make a list of the pros and cons of each tour. Compare what's included in the price of each and estimate your extra costs. Then, calculate the total cost on a per-diem basis so you can compare shorter and longer tours and determine which is the best deal for you.

CHAPTER 23

Picking a Hotel

Contrary to what many travelers fear, you don't have to pay $250 a night for a hotel room in Europe. There's a wide variety of lodging choices to suit nearly any budget.

Accommodations range from small, simple inns that dot the countryside to cosmopolitan hotels with all the amenities. Hundreds of hostels offer inexpensive, no-frills lodging, and many European families turn their homes into comfortable guest houses. You can stay on a working farm or play like royalty in a chateau.

One of the best ways to cut lodging costs is to buy a tour package, either an escorted tour or a simpler package that covers transportation and accommodations only. Because tour operators book large volumes of rooms, they can get lower rates than are available to the general public. (For more information on packages, see Chapter 22, "Choosing a Tour.")

Independent travelers who want to explore on their own can do so easily in Europe, with or without advance hotel reservations — if they do some homework to become familiar with the lodging scene.

A Guide for Independent Travelers

The following is a primer for independent travelers to European accommodations, how to find them at a lower cost and how to book them.

Before leaving for Europe, contact the tourism office for each country you plan to visit. Almost all these offices offer free hotel guides, and many have information geared to budget travel. Several countries have guides for young tourists that focus on inexpensive lodging ideas, but travelers of all ages can use these.

Later in this chapter, you will find a country-by-country guide to lodging costs and information available.

Be prepared for widely varying accommodations; Europe does not have the many chain hotels with standardized rooms that are common in the United States. Many hotels are very old, which may — or may not — translate to charming. Rooms range from tiny to enormous, and bathrooms can be antiquated or high-tech.

Smaller hotels and inns may have only a breakfast room, and you may tote your own luggage up the stairs. Other lodging is more traditional, with elevators and bellboys, restaurants and gift shops.

Take note!

☞ **Know your floor.** Floors of European hotels and other buildings are marked differently from their American counterparts. In Europe, the ground floor is called just that. The next level up is referred to as the first floor, and the rest follow numerically.

DISCOUNT TRAVEL HANDBOOK   141

Unlike the United States, most European countries have a defined rating system for hotels, although it is not standardized across Europe. Generally, the rating is based on the hotel's size, the level of luxury and the type of services provided. In standardized ratings, ambiance usually doesn't come into consideration but it may in subjective ratings given by guidebooks.

For example, hotels in France are classified by the French Ministry of Tourism. Ratings start at one star for a budget hotel, while two stars indicate a quality tourist hotel. The highest rating, for luxury hotels, is four stars plus the letter "L."

Other countries have similar classification systems, but the quality of hotels at each star level varies from country to country. Also, some countries go up to five stars for the most luxurious hotels.

For the most affordable accommodations, look at establishments with three or fewer stars. Guest rooms may be quite similar in two-star and three-star lodgings; the differences usually are in hotel size and whether there's a full-service restaurant.

You also will encounter the terms "tourist class," "first class" and "deluxe" hotels. Tourist class frequently indicates an older hotel that will have some rooms without baths; you will see both "standard" and "superior" tourist class, with the latter being more updated or offering more amenities.

While many Americans think of first class as being the best, that is not the case in European hotels. First class usually means larger, full-service lodgings. What is considered first class in the United States is deluxe or luxury class in Europe.

There are two major differences to watch in booking rooms. There's often a distinction among single, twin and double accommodations in Europe, whereas in U.S. lodging, the same room may be rented as a single or double. Single rooms (for one person) are likely to be quite small and may be tucked into some remote part of the hotel. A twin room has two single beds, and a double has a double (or larger) bed. When two travel together, you need to specify twin or double in Europe.

Also, rooms don't always have private baths, particularly in less costly hotels, but guest rooms typically have a wash basin with running hot and cold water. For a shower or bath, you go down the hall to a bathroom. The toilet usually is located in a separate room, often marked W.C. (water closet). In some inexpensive lodging, you may pay a fee to use the shower or bath.

Although most U.S. travelers are accustomed to having private baths, the

---

Take note!

☞ **Phone home — NOT.** Before making an international call from your hotel room, always ask what the fees are. Many hotels attach a high surcharge when you make long-distance calls through their switchboards and bill them to your room. Even when you use a calling card or call collect, you likely will pay a fee for using the phone in your room.

If you plan to call home on your trip, check with your designated long-distance phone company about how to call home at lower rates. The larger phone companies have numbers that will let you access their operators from overseas.

bed-and-breakfast craze has introduced many to shared baths. Many Americans traveling in Europe alternate between spending more money to get a bathroom some of the time and opting for a shared bath other times.

Making Reservations

The task of finding accommodations and making hotel reservations in Europe might seem overwhelming, especially if there's a language barrier. There's also the expense of making overseas calls or the time element of corresponding by letter.

You could use a travel agent and let someone else do the research and communicating for you. Travel agents usually work with the larger hotel chains, though, and aren't always tapped into the independent inns and guest houses. Agents may, however, know of cost-cutting discounts at the larger, better-known hotels.

> **Take note!**
> ☞ **Know which room is cheaper.** A room with a double bed usually costs less than a room with twin beds, and a room with a shower is sometimes cheaper than one with a bathtub.

It's wise to have advance reservations for your first two nights or so, then you can make other arrangements once you're in Europe. For your reservations, you can either use a travel agent or, with hotel guides from tourist offices, book your own room. When working with an agent, identify your budget range and your preference in type of accommodations — such as whether you want to be close to the sights, have a private bath or desire a restaurant in the hotel.

If you want to deal directly with a hotel, it's best to make contact by letter or fax. Indicate the number of people in your party, the type of room you desire (single, twin or double, with or without bath) and the dates of your arrival and departure. Ask for confirmation by return letter.

Using Tourist Information Centers

It's easy to find lodging on your own in most parts of Europe, thanks to tourist information centers located in cities, towns and even villages. Marked with an "i" sign, these usually are found in train stations, airports and at central locations, often near tourist sites.

These centers keep an inventory of hotel space in their areas and can match you with lodging to fit your budget. Besides telling you what's available, the centers usually can book a room. Many independent travelers, using rail passes or driving on their own, rely on these centers to find lodging at each new destination. You must make inquiries in person. Checking early in the day assures a better choice. During special events or conventions, a city's lodging may be totally booked, but the center can direct you to suburban areas or nearby towns.

While European tourism boards in the United States can provide lodging information, they cannot make reservations for you, but they can advise where tourist information centers are located.

Cheaper in the Country

Lodging is less expensive in smaller towns and rural areas than in the big cities. If you want to concentrate on city sightseeing, you can cut costs by staying in suburban areas, but choose lodging that is easily accessible to a rail line or subway route into the city.

If you want to tour a region or several countries, you can cut costs — lodging and food — by spending more nights in smaller towns and villages than in cities.

Outside the cities, you'll find many bed-and-breakfast inns and family-run guest houses, often called pensions (pronounced *pahn-see-ōn* in Europe). Pensions usually are simple, comfortable and clean establishments. While the less-expensive inns won't have extra amenities, the staff usually is congenial and helpful. Some places do not have rooms with private baths.

In smaller lodgings, you usually do not need a reservation; in fact, some do not accept reservations. When you see an appealing bed-and-breakfast inn or guest house, inquire about availability and ask to see the room before agreeing to take it. Most innkeepers will be happy to oblige. Smaller accommodations frequently don't take credit cards, so be prepared to pay in cash.

Renting a Vacation Home

If you are staying a week or more in one location, or if several people are traveling together, consider renting a cottage or apartment. These are private homes rented out during the vacation season; sometimes the owner resides in another building on the property.

In some countries, rental cottages are called holiday homes or "self-catering vacations." The homes are furnished, although some require you to bring your own bed linens and bath towels.

If you want to rent a home, reserve as early as possible. Renting houses is popular among European travelers who often book places for monthlong vacations. (August is the big summer vacation month in Europe.)

Depending on the type of place, renting can cut your lodging costs, particularly if several travelers share expenses. For instance, the catalog for Interhome, a company that offers more than 22,000 European houses and apartments for rent, lists a farmhouse in Provence, in southern France, for as low as $668 per week. The house can accommodate up to six people, bringing the daily cost to about $16 per person. In Paris near the Eiffel Tower, a studio apartment for two people costs $658 per week, or $47 per person per day; the most central locations cost $800 and up.

For information, contact Interhome, 124 Little Falls Road, Fairfield, NJ 07004, (201) 882-6864. Other European home/apartment rental agencies include Barclay International Group, 150 E. 52nd St., New York, NY 10022,

> *Take note!*
>
> ☞ **Know how to flush.** Figuring out how to flush European toilets can become a game — all seem to have different flushing mechanisms in varying places. You may yank a chain, push a button, pull a knob, step on a pedal — or do nothing because it flushes automatically.

(800) 845-6636 or (212) 832-3777, and Hometours International, P.O. Box 11503, Knoxville, TN 37939, (800) 367-4668.

Stay on a Farm

For a change of pace — and a chance to get to know local people and their customs — consider a stay at a working farm. Many European farming families welcome visitors who want a rural vacation. Guests can help with chores, or they can relax and tour the scenic countryside. Typically, your fee would include breakfast, but some farms offer half-board (two meals) or full-board (three meals) plans.

At a Finnish farm, for example, you can stay in a guest room for $34-$65 per person per day, including three meals. Usually, hosts accept cash only and may ask for payment upfront.

Tourism offices can provide information on farm vacations.

Hostels

For really inexpensive lodging, consider a hostel. Although these cater mostly to budget-conscious students backpacking their way through Europe, hostels are open to all ages. The buildings they occupy range from a chalet in Switzerland to a castle in Germany.

The rates vary according to the season and location. There are seven hostels in London, ranging in price from 7.9 to 19.10 pounds ($12-$29)a night. In France, one night in a rustic, rural hostel can be as low as 29 francs (about $6), while a night in Paris will cost 108 francs ($22), including breakfast.

These are no-frills operations. Hostels have dormitory-style accommodations with bunk beds; sleeping quarters and bathrooms are segregated according to sex. A bunk comes with mattress, pillow or blanket, but guests need to bring their own bedsheets. Hostels have dining and common rooms for socializing and fully equipped self-service kitchens. Many European hostels have cafeterias. Guests may be asked to perform a small chore, such as sweeping a room, to contribute to the hostel's upkeep.

Smaller hostels in rural areas may close during the day. If staying more than one night, you would need to leave in the morning and return that evening, but

Card Can Halve Room Cost

The Entertainment Europe directory lists more than 750 hotels that give a 50 percent discount — sometimes. If the hotel is already running a promotion, then the discount is less.

A caveat: Participating hotels allot a limited number of rooms available at the discount. Even if the hotel has vacancies, you may not be able to get a room at the reduced rate, especially during peak seasons.

The directory, covering 400 destinations, comes with a membership card that qualifies the buyer for the discounts. The directory costs $48. For information, contact Entertainment Publications, (800) 445-4137.

your luggage can be stored at the hostel during the day.

It's a good idea to arrive early in the day to make sure you get a bed. You can reserve your room in advance, although the hostels do keep a block of beds available for walk-ins. To reserve a bed, contact the international booking network at Hostelling International/American Youth Hostels. There is a $5 charge per international booking.

If you plan to stay at a number of hostels throughout your trip, consider joining HI/AYH, the main hostel organization. Non-members can stay in the hostels, but when space is limited during the busy seasons, members get priority. Non-members pay an extra $3 per night.

An annual membership costs $10 for ages 17 and under, $25 for ages 18-54, and $15 for ages 55 and beyond. A family membership costs $35.

HI/AYH also offers two types of accommodations packages in Europe that include transportation and sightseeing passes. Prices are guaranteed because they're prepaid. The first night's lodging is confirmed, but it's up to you to reserve or find hostel lodging for the remaining nights.

> **Take note!**
>
> ☞ **Bring some essentials.** Many hotels in Europe do not supply washcloths. Pack your own. Take a bar of soap, as well, since it's not always provided in smaller places. In low-cost bed-and-breakfast inns and pensions, towels may be thin.

Currently, City Stay weekend packages are offered in Amsterdam, London, Luxembourg, Paris and Vienna. At press time, a three-night/four-day "City Stay" in Paris that included hostel accommodations, a three-day metro/bus pass, a three-day museum pass and a Seine cruise cost $160 (plus applicable fee).

HI/AYH also offers the weeklong Go As You Please program. Participants receive seven overnight vouchers, as well as discounts for local sightseeing and transportation. At press time, this package was available in England, Wales, Ireland, Northern Ireland, Luxembourg, the Netherlands, Norway and Sweden, with prices starting at $135 (plus fee).

You must be a member of HI/AYH to take part in the City Stay and Go As You Please programs. For information on the two programs, or to find out more about hostel locations or memberships and request brochures, contact HI/AYH, 733 15th St. N.W., Suite 840, Washington, DC 20005, (202) 783-6161.

Country-by-Country Guide to Lodging

The following gives an idea of popular lodging options in Europe; if available, we have given some price examples. We also have listed some of the guides and brochures provided by tourism offices. For the addresses and phone numbers of tourism offices, see Chapter 31, "Getting Information."

Austria: Moderately priced hotels run about 475-635 schillings ($50-$67) per person per night for a double room with bath. Beware: Austrian hotels usually quote prices per person.

Two chains of midpriced hotels with individualized decor are Best Western

Austria, (800) 528-1234, and MinOtels Europe, (800) 336-4668. Both offer voucher programs that allow you to stay at any of the participating properties for a prepaid price. Private homes provide guest rooms also. They display a sign saying "*Zimmer Frei*" ("room available") or showing a white bed on a green background. At these guest houses, rates run $25-$55 in rural areas and $45-$85 in cities for a double room. Taxes and breakfast usually are included.

Tourism offices in Vienna, including locations at the airport and major rail stations, can provide hotel information and make reservations.

The Austrian National Tourist Office offers the following:
- "Affordable Austria" — moderately priced lodging in major cities.

Belgium: Hotels in Belgium are rated by the Benelux Hotel Classification System, which also applies to accommodations in Holland and Luxembourg. Ratings are based on price, facilities and number of rooms.

Pensions and bed-and-breakfast inns are $25-$70 per person per night. Many hotels throughout the country offer weekend discounts year-round and all week during July and August.

The Belgian Tourist Office can provide a list of U.S. representatives of Belgian hotels, and the following brochures:
- "Hotel Guide."
- "Budget Holidays" — farm vacations.

Britain: Lodgings are inspected regularly by local tourist boards and classified according to the range of facilities and services provided.

Double rooms in London, with bathroom and including breakfast, run 80-230 pounds ($120-$345) per night. Rates at a bed-and-breakfast inn outside London are 30-55 pounds ($45-$83) per night.

If you visit between October and March, you sometimes can save as much as 50 percent, especially if you book for two or more nights.

The following brochures are available from the British Tourist Authority:
- "London Accommodation for Budget Travelers" — establishments with

Club France

This association for Francophiles is especially good for anyone planning to spend a week or more in France. The annual membership fee is $65 per person, $35 for each additional family member. Club France members receive room upgrades and VIP treatment at more than 500 hotels across France. Other benefits include: three-day pass to 65 museums in Paris; discounts on admissions to museums, monuments, concerts and summer festivals; 10 percent off purchases at two major department stores in Paris; the "France Discovery Guide"; a quarterly newsletter; free subscriptions to several French publications; and access to a toll-free information line in both the United States and France. Club France members receive a membership card and a directory of all discounts and privileges. Hotel discounts range up to 40 percent. For information and a free brochure, call (800) 881-5060.

double-room rates of less than 50 pounds ($75) per night.
- "City Apartments" and "Britain: Self-Catering Holiday Homes" — information on renting apartments or cottages.
- "First Stop Britain: A Guide for Young Travellers."
- "Britain: Bed & Breakfast."
- "Britain: Stay on a Farm."
- "Britain: Stay in a British Home."
- "Britain: Stay at an Inn."

Denmark: A Danish *kro* is the equivalent of our bed-and-breakfast inn. These accommodations range from simple to luxurious. Rates are $80-$120 a night for a double room; vouchers are available in the United States. Check with the tourist office for sources, and shop the prices. Also ask about Copenhagen Card hotel packages.

The Danish Tourist Board offers the following brochures:
- "Hotels in Denmark."
- "Inns and Hotels in Denmark."
- "Bed-and-Breakfasts in Denmark."

Finland: Midpriced hotels run 420-880 markkaa ($97-$202) or from 320 markkaa ($74) off-season for a double room with bath. Nightly rates at guest houses and bed-and-breakfast inns run $17-$42 per person. Rooms typically do not include a private bath.

The following brochures are available from the Finnish Tourist Board:
- "Finland Hotels."
- "Finland Budget Accommodation and Holiday Villages."

France: Lodging in France ranges from small family-run hotels to grand old castles. You can save money by staying in the lesser-known regions of the French countryside, minimizing time in Paris and the seaside resort areas.

For more economical lodging, check three-star hotels, where double rooms average 800 francs ($160), or two-star hotels, where doubles average 450 francs ($90) a night. Rates may be higher in major cities and lower in villages.

In other parts of France, travelers should look for the small inns marked by the yellow and green Logis de France sign. These inexpensive lodgings offer local charm and regional cuisine and adhere to high standards of comfort. There are more than 4,000 Logis de France inns, typically located in or near small towns. Nightly rates average 300 francs ($60).

It's possible to spend a night in royal luxury, too. Relais & Chateaux is a chain of independently owned hotels and restaurants, each known for distinctive character. Relais & Chateaux has more than 400 properties in 41 countries, including about 150 places in France. Many are former castles, abbeys and manors that have been converted to deluxe hotels. While most of their hotels are priced in the high end, Relais & Chateaux does have first-class lodging at moderate

---

Take note!
☞ **Lock your door.** Many older hotels and smaller inns do not have automatic-lock doors on rooms. You must lock the door with your key. To be safe, always check the knob when you exit your room.

Hotel Vouchers

Hotel vouchers are available for accommodations in Austria, Germany, Hungary and the Scandinavian countries of Denmark, Finland, Norway and Sweden. These typically must be purchased before your trip. A voucher can be redeemed for one night in a participating hotel. Sometimes voucher prices are per person, based on double occupancy, so a couple traveling together would need two vouchers for one night. Breakfast and taxes usually are included. Vouchers do not guarantee a room; you should make reservations for your first night, at least.

A caveat: The voucher prices typically are based on the average nightly rate at all participating hotels. Posted room rates can be higher — or lower — than the prepaid rate. Try to get your money's worth and stay at hotels where you know you'll be saving money. Note that some top-class hotels add a surcharge.

The tourism offices can give you a list of travel agents who sell the vouchers. The agent may charge a handling fee and require that you purchase a minimum number of vouchers.

Austria, Germany and Hungary: Danube Valley HotelChecks are redeemable at hotels along the Danube River in these three countries. They cost $56 per person per night, based on double occupancy, and include breakfast and sometimes dinner. A surcharge applies at the top-category hotels.

Denmark: Danish Inn Cheques cost from $95 to $121 per couple per night, including breakfast and taxes. Valid all year at more than 85 establishments.

Finland: Finncheques cost $39 per person per night. At some hotels, the voucher includes breakfast and lunch. Valid May-September at more than 250 hotels.

Germany: WunderChecks cost $56 per person per night, based on double occupancy. Breakfast is included, and in some cases, dinner also is included. They're accepted at more than 190 German hotels. Vouchers are accompanied by the WunderCard, which provides discounts for sightseeing, dining and shopping.

Sweden: Sweden Hotel Cheques cost $102 per night for a double room, including breakfast and taxes. Valid all year.

Other Scandinavian vouchers and passes (good in Denmark, Finland, Norway and Sweden): Best Western Hotel Cheques cost $50 per person per night, including breakfast and taxes. Valid May 15-Sept. 15.

The Scandinavian Bonus Pass is a discount card that provides savings of up to 50 percent at 180 participating hotels throughout Scandinavia. The card costs $25 and can be used by two adults and accompanying children. Valid early May to late September and weekends all year. Contact the Scandinavian Tourist Board, (212) 949-2333, for a list of representatives selling Scandinavian hotel vouchers and discount passes.

rates. For example, the Chateau de Trigance, a hillside fortress in the south of France northwest of Nice, has nightly rates starting at 520 francs ($104). The Georges Blanc, an estate and gourmet restaurant in Burgundy that has received the highest Relais & Chateaux rating, has prices starting at 1,280 francs ($256). These rates are for a double room and include tax. Relais & Chateaux can provide information and brochures on hotels, but reservations must be made with the individual property or through a travel agent. For information, contact Relais & Chateaux, 11 E. 44th St., Suite 704, New York, NY 10017, (212) 856-0115.

Take note!
☞ **Eat on the cheap.** Don't eat breakfast at your hotel if it is not included in your room rate. It's much cheaper to go down the street to a cafe or bakery, plus it gives you a chance to observe the local ambiance.

France also has a well-organized network of 38,000 rural homes available for rent. Called *gites ruraux*, they range from small cottages to medieval chateaux. Prices vary according to the region and season. In the off-season, you can find a rural *gite* for as low as $400 a week; regular season prices start at about $450 a week. Most require a one-week stay but allow weekend bookings during off-peak periods. *Gite* owners must meet government standards.

In the United States, a company called The French Experience can book *gites*. For a $20 registration fee plus service charges, this company will communicate your lodging desires to the proper regional tourist office in France, then contact you with descriptions of available sites. Determine if properties have all the basic amenities you want, and ask if pictures are available before making a decision. Ask what the procedures are if the property does not meet your expectations when you arrive.

For information and a free brochure, contact The French Experience, 370 Lexington Avenue, Suite 812, New York, NY 10017, (212) 986-1115.

The French Government Tourist Office provides the following:

● Regional hotel listings, hotel association guides and lists of U.S. representatives of French hotels.

● "French Discovery Guide" — general travel tips.

Germany: Hotel prices can vary widely within a star category, but the more economical choices are two-star and one-star hotels. Midrange prices for two-star hotels are about 200-300 marks ($143-$214) and for one-star hotels about 160-200 marks ($114-$143) for a double room, with city properties usually higher.

The "*Zimmer Frei*" ("room available") signs mark the modestly priced guest houses in Germany's provinces. Many of these cost 40-80 marks ($29-$57) per night for a double room.

The German National Tourist Office provides the following:

● "Bed & Breakfast in Germany" — addresses of local tourist offices and booking services in about 500 towns. It gives a price range for lodging in each town but does not list individual accommodations.

Italy: The most economical lodging choices are: three-star hotels, where double rooms in the major cities run 125,000-270,000 lire ($85-$175) a night; two-star hotels, 90,000-175,000 lire ($58-$113); and one-star hotels, 60,000-130,000 lire ($39-$84). These three categories previously were called pensions. Smaller hotels may be B&Bs.

The Italian Government Tourist Board can supply lists of hotels for most cities or areas of Italy, as well as a list of U.S. representatives of Italian hotels.

Luxembourg: The Luxembourg National Tourist Office offers "Luxembourg Hotels and Restaurants." Some hotels in this brochure have three-day, all-inclusive packages including some or all meals.

The Netherlands: Three-star hotels provide economical lodging, with a double room running 75-200 guilders ($45-$120) a night.

The Netherlands Board of Tourism offers the following:
- "Tourist and Budget Hotels" — 250 one- to three-star hotels.
- "Amsterdam: City of Many Faces" — includes a hotel supplement.

Norway: Tourist-class hotels offer double rooms with bath for 550-900 kroner ($83-$135) a night. Pensions run 300-700 kroner ($45-$105) a night for a double room. Holiday homes and cottages run as low as $28-$47 per person per night.

The Norway Fjord Pass provides discounts at about 250 hotels, pensions and mountain lodges, where breakfast is included. It costs $11 and can be used by two adults. Valid May 1-Sept. 30.

Spain: Midpriced hotels run 6,000-9,000 pesetas ($50-$80) a night for a double room with bath.

The Spanish government operates a network of more than 80 *paradores*, often former castles, monasteries and manor homes that have been converted to hotels. They too are rated by the local governments; most fall into the three- and four-star categories. Nightly rates in *paradores* range from $80-$250.

Sweden: Average-priced hotels run $160 a night for a double room with bath ($137 in Stockholm) and budget hotels run $132 a night ($100 in Stockholm). Rates are lower mid-June to mid-August.

The Swedish Travel and Tourism Council offers the following:
- "Hotels in Sweden," — lodging and discount information.
- *Sweden Traveler* — a magazine with travel information.

Switzerland: Midpriced lodging options are three-star hotels, where a double room with bath runs 170-350 francs ($136-$280) a night, and two-star hotels, with rooms for 130-180 francs ($104-$144) a night. Prices may be lower in villages.

The Swiss National Tourist Office provides the following:
- "Swiss Hotel Guide" — Swiss Hotel Association publication with hotels, pensions and *garni* hotels, which offer lodging, breakfast and beverages.
- "Hotels Specially Suitable for Families" — more than 100 hotels.
- "Season for Seniors" — hotels and resorts that offer special off-season rates for senior citizens (women over 62, men over 65).
- "Swiss Farm Holidays."
- "Swiss Hotel Representatives in the U.S.A."
- Regional and local hotel lists.

CHAPTER 24

Renting a Car

Renting a car gives you the ultimate flexibility for travel in Europe — but planning ahead is important, not only to save money but also to avoid surprises when you pick up your car.

Overseas car rental can be expensive, and you may be shocked at the price of gasoline, which can run more than $4 a gallon. Also, you will encounter differences in cars available for rent in Europe vs. in the United States.

Shopping around is important because prices can vary widely. Among the major U.S.-based rental companies offering cars in Europe are Alamo, Avis, Budget, Hertz, Payless and Thrifty. National Interrent operates in Europe as European Interrent.

While you may feel more comfortable dealing with a known name, there also are European-based rental companies that offer competitive rates and similar

European Road Signs

Every country in Europe uses the same system of road signs. There are three basic categories of signs, indicated by shape. A triangular sign signals danger, such as a steep hill or narrow road. A circular sign provides instruction, such as displaying the speed limit. Square signs give information, such as where to park or find repair service.

The following examples illustrate some commonly seen road signs in Europe.

INTERSECTION	DANGER	DANGEROUS CURVE	ALL VEHICLES PROHIBITED
CUSTOMS	SPEED LIMIT	END OF SPEED LIMIT	PARKING

cars. Most have offices in this country. Among the better-known are Kemwel and Auto Europe, which have toll-free numbers. To find other European firms, check with a travel agent or an airline that flies to Europe.

It's best to reserve a rental car several weeks before your trip, which you can do through a travel agent or directly with a rental company. Booking in advance helps ensure that you get the car you need at the best price.

There are several key elements to consider when shopping for the best deal. The following information will help you find a good value when renting a car.

Choosing a Car Size

Small cars are popular in Europe, and you will find a wide variety of them, including some with unfamiliar names. When looking at the lowest-priced cars, the subcompacts, though, you need to be careful that you're not getting one too tiny and cramped.

Take note! **Know the names of towns along your route.** On European highways, you will see town names more often than route numbers to identify direction.

Consider the number of people traveling together, the luggage you're carrying and the distance you're driving.

When talking to car-rental agents, ask about the various models and sizes available and how many people each type of car comfortably accommodates. While the least-expensive car may not suit you, you usually can find a comfortable smaller car at a low price.

If you want or need a larger car, though, it may hike your costs considerably. For instance, although prices change depending on the season, a subcompact car comparable in size to a Geo Metro offered through Avis in Switzerland cost $166 a week, but a midsize car similar to a Pontiac Grand Prix cost $244.

Traveling light will save you money on a car — and cut the hassle of toting a lot of big bags.

Always ask about the car's luggage stowage. It is safer to rent a car with a trunk in which you can store luggage out of sight. If you rent a hatchback-style car without a trunk, ask for one with a cover for the luggage area so bags will be

Gas Prices

The following list shows the lowest prices available in unleaded, self-serve gas, which is sold by the liter in Europe but converted to gallons here for comparison to U.S. costs.

City	Price per gallon	City	Price per gallon
Amsterdam	$4.85	Paris	$4.33
London	$3.40	Stockholm	$4.00
Milan	$4.03	Zurich	$4.10

Source: Runzheimer International, which tracks travel costs worldwide; above costs based on '95 prices.

hidden. If you stow luggage in sight in your car — in the back seat or in a hatchback with no cover — you run a higher risk of a break-in and theft.

Automatic vs. Manual Transmission

Most European cars have manual transmissions. You may have difficulty finding some classes of rental cars with automatic transmission. In some cases, you will pay so dearly for the difference that you may want to brush up on your gear-shifting skills.

For instance, at press time, Avis quoted the following examples to show the cost differences in cars with manual vs. automatic transmissions. In France, an Opel Corsa, a small car similar to a Geo Metro, cost $201 for a week; it's available with manual transmission only. A Renault Laguna, similar to a Pontiac Grand Prix, cost $289 a week with manual transmission, or $440 a week with automatic transmission.

In most cases, you will have to rent a midsize or larger car to get one with automatic transmission.

If you're not accustomed to shifting gears and the difference in cost for an automatic transmission is low, it's probably worth the extra money not to have that added challenge in a strange country. Also, if you're renting in England or any other country where traffic moves on the left instead of the right, remember that the steering wheel and gear shift will be on the opposite side of the car than is customary in the United States.

> *Take note!*
>
> ☛ **Time rentals right.** You don't need a car for sightseeing in your arrival city. City parking is scarce and expensive, and city driving is more difficult. Local transportation is cheaper and more convenient. If possible, give yourself a few days to observe driving habits and become comfortable in the country before getting a car.

Taxes and Insurance

When checking prices, always ask about all applicable taxes with each company so that you can compare total costs.

In particular, check about the value-added tax, similar to a national sales tax, which is assessed in most European countries. Many car-rental quotes don't include the VAT, which can add a hefty amount to your total rental price.

The VAT is highest in Denmark, Hungary and Sweden, where it is 25 percent. France tacks on 20.6 percent, and England charges 17.5 percent. Switzerland has a low 7 percent.

To save money, try to plan an itinerary that allows you to rent a car where the VAT is lower. If you will be visiting both France and Switzerland, renting your car in the latter country will save you considerable money. For example, after adding the 20.6 percent VAT, a one-week rental of a midsize manual-shift car in France cost about $349 at press time. In Switzerland, where the VAT is only 7 percent, a similar car cost about $261 for a week.

Keep in mind that as a foreign visitor, in some countries you may be eligible for a refund of a percentage of the VAT. Contact the tourism board for the

Car-Rental VATs

The following shows the value-added tax (VAT) assessed on car rentals in Europe. The VAT is similar to a national sales tax and can increase your total car-rental cost substantially. Foreign visitors may be eligible for a refund of part of the VAT.

Country	VAT	Country	VAT	Country	VAT
Austria	20%*	Great Britain	17.5%	Poland	22%
Belgium	20.5%	Greece	18%	Portugal	16%
Denmark	25%	Ireland	10%	Spain	16%
Finland	22%	Italy	19%	Sweden	25%
France	20.6%	Luxembourg	15%	Switzerland	7%
Germany	15%	Norway	22%		

*Plus a separate 1.2% tax.

applicable country for information on the refund process. Also, see Chapter 26, "Boosting Your Buying Power," in this section.

You need some kind of insurance in case you have a wreck. You can rely on your own personal insurance, coverage by the credit card you use for the rental or coverage sold by the car-rental firm.

First check with your insurance company and your credit-card companies to determine what coverage you have on car rentals in the foreign countries you plan to visit. Most personal insurance policies do not cover driving overseas. Some credit cards provide coverage for damage to or loss of the car but not for personal injury, and some may specify countries where they won't cover you at all.

Car-rental firms sell collision or loss damage waivers, commonly called CDW or LDW. This is a form of insurance that relieves you of responsibility if the car is damaged or stolen while you have it. The CDW does not provide coverage for personal injury, though; car-rental firms sell separate personal accident insurance.

The CDW and personal injury coverage from a car-rental firm can be costly, in some cases adding $20 or more a day. A few companies quote a rental rate that includes the CDW fee, and such rentals are usually more economical than if you have to buy the CDW separately.

While most people decline the CDW when renting cars in the United States, you may want to consider it more seriously overseas, even if your personal policy and/or credit card will cover you. Ask yourself: Would you really want to deal with the hassle of settling a claim in a foreign country? Also, would you have enough money or a high enough limit on

Take note!

☞ **Familiarize yourself with road signs.** Before you leave home, get a European road atlas or maps of the specific areas where you plan to drive. Large bookstores should have maps, or check with Forsyth Travel Library in Shawnee Mission, KS, (800) 367-7984, which stocks a large selection of European road maps. In Europe, ask the car-rental agent for any literature that identifies road signs and keep it handy in your car.

your credit card to cover the cost that a car-rental firm might assess for damage or loss?

If you buy the CDW, the car-rental firm will cover the cost of damages to the car. While you have to fill out forms, you don't get bogged down in appraisals of damage and settlements. If you are relying on your own coverage, you usually will have to pay assessed damages on site and get reimbursed by your credit card or insurance company later. Also, you may encounter problems upfront if you have a set limit on your credit card. The car-rental firm may "clamp" a part of the total value of the car — which could be several thousand dollars — on your credit card in case there is damage or loss. That clamp is not removed until the car is returned, thereby limiting your use of the card while you travel unless you have a high charge limit.

> *Take note!*
> ☞ **Check the driving customs.** Ask the car-rental agent about local driving habits, such as whether you can turn on a red light, what blinkers are used to signal that a car should or should not pass and whether the inside lane is restricted to passing only. Also inquire about making cross-traffic turns, such as a left-hand turn. In some places, you cannot turn across traffic when on the main road; you exit to a side lane, then go across the highway.

Costs and Form of Payment

While you will need to show a major credit card to rent a car, you usually can pay either in cash or with the credit card at the end of your rental.

Car-rental rates are based on the local currency, thus the dollar equivalent is subject to change. While the rate in Britain may be set at 100 pounds sterling, for instance, what you pay in dollars can fluctuate. The final charge can be slightly different from when you rented the car and from what you were quoted on the phone.

When booking, inquire about ways to minimize your cost. Some companies

---

Safety First

Conduct a quick safety inspection of any vehicle before agreeing to rent. If your car does not pass the following test, ask the company for another automobile.

● Check for tire defects. Look for bald or bulging tires — they could be warning signs of an impending blowout.

● See that your car has a spare tire and jack.

● Check that the car has a first-aid kit and a red triangle (the European sign for "danger").

● Make certain that turn signals, all lights, seat belts and windshield wipers function properly.

Always be sure you have a phone number that you can call for emergency road service.

offer advance-payment rates at a guaranteed U.S. dollar rate.

If you charge your rental on a credit card, the local currency is converted to U.S. dollars when the paperwork passes through a European bank. Thus, your final charge could be more or less than what you had figured when you returned the car.

It's wise to stay aware of the economy in Europe and whether currencies are fluctuating much. Normally there would be only slight differences in the value of the dollar from the day you charge the rental to your card to the day it is processed by the bank. But if currencies are showing considerable fluctuation at the time you rent, you should gauge whether it's better to pay cash or to charge the rental and take your chances on the final rate.

Hidden Costs

Some companies have recently added a mandatory "theft" charge that can cost up to $15 a day in some countries.

Airport surcharges have become common in Europe. Some are a set amount, such as 10 deutsche marks (estimated $6) in Germany and 54 francs (estimated $10) in France. Other surcharges are a percentage of your total rental bill, which can be more costly. For instance, Italy tacks on a 10 percent surcharge; that's on top of its 19 percent VAT. When surcharges are high, avoid them by renting your car at a non-airport location.

Numerous highway tolls in Austria, France, Italy and Spain can add an extra $5-$15 daily.

Beware of Good Deals Too Good to Be True

Some airlines promote free or discounted car rentals in travel packages they sell. While the deal may sound good, it may require a premium airfare purchase. Compare the package to an independent airfare and car rental to decide on the best bargain. If a package is cheaper, ask what model and size car is included and determine if that's what you want.

> **Take note!**
>
> ☞ **Have identification.** Driver's licenses issued in the United States are valid in Europe, but have your passport handy at all times. Some companies suggest that you purchase an international driving permit, available at American Automobile Association offices. The permit is $20 for non-AAA members and $17 for members. Two passport photos are required; these can be done at AAA offices for a fee.

CHAPTER 25

Riding the Rails

Traveling by train is a safe, comfortable and fun way to explore Europe. It's also a cost-cutting way to combine sightseeing with transportation.

The extensive rail network spreads 100,000 miles over the continent, encompassing everything from the world's fastest, most modern trains to classic old cog railroads that still chug up mountain slopes. Service between cities is quick and frequent.

Trains are popular with Europeans for both business and leisure travel, often providing the most efficient means of transportation for short hauls or even longer runs.

For visiting Americans, the trains provide not only transportation but also an opportunity to see the countryside and mingle with the people.

Riding a train in Europe is a different experience for many Americans, particularly those who live where there's little, if any, train service.

The first surprise to many visiting Americans is that large European cities often have several train stations, which are as busy as major airports. Each has a number of tracks and large automated billboards listing train departures and arrivals along with track assignments. Many of the stations have cafes or restaurants, some renowned for good food.

Train travel is made easy for Americans with European rail passes, which provide a convenient, flexible and economical way to tour independently. A number of European rail systems have joined together to offer the Eurailpass, good for travel in all of the member countries, now up to 17. In addition, neighboring countries have joined to offer regional passes, and some individual countries have cost-cutting passes to use within their borders.

The 17 countries participating in the Eurailpass program are: Austria, Belgium, Denmark, Finland, France, Germany, Greece, Hungary, Ireland, Italy, Luxembourg, The Netherlands, Norway, Portugal, Spain, Sweden and Switzerland.

Note that Great Britain — England, Scotland and Wales — a popular destination on European itineraries, is not included. There are passes for rail travel within Great Britain.

> *Take note!*
> ☛ **Get to the track on time.** Many trains, particularly the long-distance ones, make few and only brief stops, two minutes often, so passengers must board or disembark quickly. By the track, look for a chart showing the order of coaches on long-distance trains. See whether first-class cars, for example, are toward the front or rear and position yourself accordingly along the track. A big 1 or 2 on the side of the car tells you whether it's first- or second-class.

158   DISCOUNT TRAVEL HANDBOOK

The greatest advantage of a rail pass is convenience, the ability to hop on and off trains and go nearly anywhere you want without having to stand in line to buy a ticket or communicate in a foreign language. After you validate the pass, it's your ticket to ride. Simply show it to the conductor when your ticket is requested.

Today's traveler will find a choice of rail passes to fit a variety of travel plans. While most passes are for rail travel only, some passes combine rail travel and car rental, while a couple add air transportation.

European rail passes are available through a foreign rail representative such as Rail Europe, (800) TGV-RAIL, or DER Rail, (800) 421-2929, or through travel agents. See accompanying box listing rail representatives and the passes they handle.

Eurail Passes

There are five types of European rail-only passes. All are valid in the 17 countries listed above, but all must be purchased in North America prior to departure. See box for details on choices and prices.

Eurailpass: Five choices, allowing unlimited first-class travel for periods of

Eurail Passes

The length of validity and latest available prices for these passes are outlined below. Children under age 12 pay half the adult fare; kids under 4 travel free.

Pass type	Validity	Cost per person
Eurailpass (first class)	15 days	$522
	21 days	$678
	1 month	$838
	2 months	$1,148
	3 months	$1,468
Eurail Flexipass (first class)	Any 10 days in 2 months	$616
	Any 15 days in 2 months	$812
Eurail Saverpass* (first class)	15 days	$452
	21 days	$578
	1 month	$712
Eurail Youthpass (second class)	15 days	$418
	1 month	$598
	2 months	$798
Eurail Youth Flexipass (second class)	Any 10 days in 2 months	$438
	Any 15 days in 2 months	$588

*Price per person for two or more people traveling together; three or more required April 1-Sept. 30.

DISCOUNT TRAVEL HANDBOOK

15 days to three months.

Eurail Flexipass: Two choices, allowing unlimited first-class travel for 10 or 15 days within two months.

Eurail Saverpass: Three choices allowing unlimited first-class travel for a minimum of two people for 15 days, 21 days or one month. For April 1-Sept. 30, a minimum of three people is required.

Eurail Youthpass: Three choices, allowing unlimited second-class travel for

Europasses

The following passes allow unlimited travel within three to five participating countries: France, Germany, Italy, Spain and Switzerland. Choices of three or four of the countries can vary, but the countries must border each other. Passes can be extended to countries listed in footnote. Children under age 12 pay half the adult fare; kids under 4 travel free.

Pass	Type	Validity	Cost per person Single adult	2 adults together
Europass (first class)	3 countries	5 days in 2 months	$316	$237
		6 days in 2 months	$358	$269[1]
		7 days in 2 months	$400	$300
	4 countries	8 days in 2 months	$442	$332[1]
		9 days in 2 months	$484	$363
		10 days in 2 months	$526	$395[1]
	5 countries	11 days in 2 months	$568	$426
		12 days in 2 months	$610	$458[1]
		13 days in 2 months	$652	$489
		14 days in 2 months	$694	$521[1]
		15 days in 2 months	$736	$552
Europass Youth* (second class)	4 countries	5 days in 2 months	$210	
		6 days in 2 months	$239	
		7 days in 2 months	$268	
		8 days in 2 months	$297	
		9 days in 2 months	$326	
		10 days in 2 months	$355	
	5 countries	11 days in 2 months	$384	
		12 days in 2 months	$413	
		13 days in 2 months	$442	
		14 days in 2 months	$471	
		15 days in 2 months	$500	

*Europass Youth is restricted to those age 25 and younger on first date of travel; two-traveling-together plan not available. [1]Fares have been rounded off to the next highest dollar.
Passes can be extended as follows: Austria, $45 Europass, $32 Europass Youth; Benelux countries, $42 or $28; Greece, $90 or $70; Portugal, $29 or $22.

those age 25 and younger for 15 days, one month or two months.

Eurail Youth Flexipass: Two choices, allowing unlimited second-class travel for those age 25 and younger for 10 or 15 days within two months.

The **EurailDrive Pass** combines train travel with car rental. It's a good option for those who want to go between metropolitan areas by train but leisurely explore some of the surrounding countryside by car. Passes are valid for any seven days (four by rail, three by car) within a two-month period. Additional car days and up to five additional rail days can be purchased for an extra fee.

You must buy the pass and the additional days prior to your trip. Travelers can choose to rent from either Hertz or Avis, but only cars with manual transmission are offered. Reservations must be made at least seven days before departure for Europe. Prices are per person, per car. Economy-size car: $339, 2 adults; $419, 1 adult. Small-size car: $379, 2 adults; $479, 1 adult. Medium-size car: $389, 2 adults; $509, 1 adult. For a third or fourth person sharing the car, the cost is $269 per person. Additional car days are available for $55-$85, depending on the car size, while additional rail days (a maximum of five) cost $55 per person.

Best Buys

While rail passes are a wise buy for many travelers, they're not always the best deal. Before purchasing a pass, evaluate your vacation itinerary. Look at the distances you plan to travel and the number of cities you want to visit to see if you would be better off buying individual point-to-point tickets.

Take note!
☛ **Buy a rail pass early.** A pass is good for six months from purchase. Since prices usually go up each year, you can save money by buying one in December if you know you want to travel in Europe in late spring or early summer of the next year. Passes aren't validated until your first train trip.

According to Rail Europe, the general rule of thumb is this: If you plan to travel more than 700 miles within two weeks, a rail pass is the best buy.

Here are some comparisons of prices. Individual first-class tickets from Paris to Rome to Vienna and back to Paris add up to $673 per person. If you purchase the 15-day Eurailpass for $522, you'll save $151. The Saverpass at $452 each for two or more people traveling together would save $221 per person. A Europass for three or four countries with an extension for Austria is another money-saving option, cutting the cost to as low as $282 each for two traveling together, or a savings of $391 over the point-to-point fares. Europasses vary in the length of validity and number of countries in which the holder may travel; the pass must be valid in all countries on your route, whether you make a stop or not.

Sometimes it is slightly cheaper to travel point-to-point by second class than it is to buy the Eurailpass, which is available only for first-class seating except for youth passes. Individual second-class tickets following the same Paris-Rome-Vienna-Paris route cost $447, less than the Eurailpass or Saverpass but not less than some Europass options for travel in limited countries. (First class has slightly roomier, more plush seats.) When the cost differential is small, the rail pass is the better choice. It allows more freedom and flexibility, letting you get off the train, explore and reboard the next train, change your itinerary or add other cities and towns at the last minute. As well, it saves time and cuts the hassle of buying individual tickets — unless you do this before you leave home.

For shorter trips, such as excursions while basing yourself in a major city, single tickets, particularly in second class, may be the better deal, depending on the distance traveled.

For instance, two short round trips, from Paris to Rouen and from Paris to Chartres, cost $142 first class, $104 second class. A France Railpass is $198 or $160, and $148.50 or $120 each when two travel together. However, a ticket from Paris to Nice, in southern France, costs $398 for a round trip first class and

When Should You Buy a Rail Pass?

As a rule, for longer trips in Europe, you will save money buying some kind of rail pass; for shorter ones, you will do better with individual tickets. Here are examples to show the differences in costs. Individual ticket costs shown are for first-class travel.

Multi-country sightseeing

Paris-Rome-Vienna-Paris

	Cost	Savings
Individual tickets	$673	–
Eurailpass (15-day)	$522	$151
Saverpass	$452	$221

Paris-Brussels-Amsterdam-Paris

	Cost	Savings
Individual tickets	$284	$32-$238
Eurailpass	$522	–
Saverpass	$452	–
Europass	$358/$279*	–/$5

*Includes pass extension to Benelux countries; lower price for each when two travel together.

Single-country sightseeing

Paris-Nice-Paris

	Cost	Savings
Individual tickets	$398	–
1st Class France Railpass	$198[1]	$200
2nd Class France Railpass	$160[1]	$238

Paris-Rouen-Paris and Paris-Chartres-Paris

	Cost	Savings
Individual tickets (first/second class)	$142/$104	$56
1st Class France Railpass	$198[1]	–
2nd Class France Railpass	$160[1]	–

[1] Two can travel together for $148.50 each first class, $120 second class.

$230 second class. Using a France Railpass would save up to $200 first class ($250 when two travel together) and up to $70 second class ($110 when two travel together).

Basically, the more you travel, the more you save, but before buying a pass, compare prices.

Regional Passes

If your travel focus is limited to a specific area, a regional or individual country pass may fit your agenda. In the following lists of these passes, all prices are per person. While most passes should be purchased before you leave home, some can be bought in Europe. Check with a foreign rail representative, such as Rail Europe or DER Rail, for the latest information.

Europass: Three to five choices, allowing unlimited first-class travel for periods of five to 15 days within two months in three, four or five bordering countries. The five participating countries are France, Germany, Italy, Spain and Switzerland. Two adults traveling together qualify for lower per-person rates. See box for details on choices and prices.

Europass Youth: Five and six choices, allowing unlimited second-class travel by those age 25 and younger for periods of five to 15 days in two months in four or five bordering countries. Participating countries are France, Germany, Italy, Spain and Switzerland. See box for details on choices and prices.

Europass Drive: Valid for any eight days (five by rail, three by car) within two months; additional car days and up to 15 more rail days can be purchased. Good for travel in three of five Europass countries: France, Germany, Italy, Spain and Switzerland. Rentals are through Hertz or Avis; only cars with manual transmission are offered. Rates start at $305 per person for two traveling together or $465 for one person. Additional car days are $55-$85 and rail days $31.50 each for two or $42 for one.

Benelux Tourrail Pass: Unlimited travel on state railways of Belgium, Luxembourg and the Netherlands. Five days of travel within one month, $217 first class, $155 second class, and for passengers 25 and younger, $104 (second class only).

European East Pass: Good for first-class rail travel in Austria, Hungary, Poland, the Czech Republic and Slovakia. Five days within 15 days, $195; 10 days within one month, $299.

ScanRail pass: Unlimited travel in Denmark, Finland, Norway and Sweden. Five days within 15 days, $222 first class, $176 second class; 10 days within one month, $346 or $278; one month, $504 or $404. Youth passes for similar time frames are available.

ScanRail 'n' Drive: Combines a five-day ScanRail pass with three days of car

---

Take note!

☛ **Go to the right station.** In major cities, trains depart from different stations according to their destinations. Trains going north will depart from one station, while those going south leave from another. Hotel concierges or taxi drivers can direct you to the right station if you tell them your destination.

rental. Valid any eight days within 15 days. Rates start at $289 first class, $249 second class per person for two traveling together and $365 or $325 for one adult. Additional car days are $55-$85; supplement charged on car rental in Finland.

Country Passes

(Those age 25 or younger should inquire about youth passes and reduced fares for children. Those age 60 and older should ask about senior discounts.)

Austrian Railpass: Four days of travel within 10 days, $165 first class, $111 second class.

BritRail Pass: Good for unlimited travel in England, Scotland and Wales. Eight days, $325 first class, $235 second class; 15 days, $525 or $365; 22 days, $665 or $465; one month, $765 or $545.

BritRail Flexipass: Unlimited travel in England, Scotland and Wales. Four days of travel within one month, $289 first class, $199 second class; eight days in one month, $399 or $290; 15 days in one month, $615 or $425.

Finnrail Pass: Three days within one month, $179 first class, $119 second class; five days within one month, $249 or $169; 10 days within one month, $339 or $229.

France Railpass: Three days within one month, $198 first class, $160 second

> **Take note!**
> ☛ **Travel light.** Many stations have several tracks, and you often have to use stairs to change tracks. It's better to carry two small bags than one large one that's too heavy to tote comfortably up and down stairs. Don't count on porters being anywhere.

Where to Buy Rail Passes

Most European rail passes must be bought outside the country of origin, or in the case of Eurailpasses, outside Europe. Most rail passes covered in this chapter can be bought in the United States from a travel agent or through a foreign rail representative, such as the companies listed below.

Rail representative	Reservations number	Passes offered
Rail Pass Express	800-722-7151	BritRail and Eurail
Rail Europe	800-848-7245	Europass, Eurailpass, European East, Benelux, ScanRail, Austria, Bulgaria, Finland, France, Hungary, Norway, Portugal, Romania, Spain, Switzerland
DER Rail	800-421-2929	Europass, Eurailpass, Benelux, ScanRail, Austria, Germany, Greece, Holland, Italy, Norway, Spain
CIE Tours	800-243-8687	Ireland and Great Britain

class. Two adults may travel together for $148.50 each first class, $120 second class. Up to six additional rail days are available for $30 each.

France Rail 'n' Drive: Three days of rail travel and two days of car rental within one month. Rates start at $189 first class, $159 second class per person for two traveling together and $279 or $239 for one adult. Additional car days are $44-$74 and rail days $30.

France Rail 'n' Fly: Combines France Railpass with one day of air travel on Air Inter. Must be used within one month, $245 first class, $215 second class per person for two traveling together and $295 or $255 for one. Additional rail days are $30 and additional flights $99.

France Fly Rail 'n' Drive: Combines France Rail 'n' Drive pass with one day of travel on Air Inter. Must be used within one month. Rates start at $289 first class, $259 second class per person for two traveling together and $379 or $339 for one. Additional car days are $44-$74, rail days $30 and air flights $99. Cars with automatic transmissions are available.

German Railpass: Five days of unlimited rail travel within one month, $260 first class, $178 second class; 10 days within one month, $410 or $286; 15 days within one month, $530 or $386.

German Rail Twin Pass: Allows two passengers to travel on one pass. Five days within one month, $390 first class, $267 second class; 10 days within one month, $615 or $429; 15 days within one month $795 or $579. Prices are for two people.

Greek Flexipass: Three days within one month, $86 first class; five days within one month, $120.

Greek Flexipass Rail 'n' Fly: Three days of rail travel within one month and one one-way flight coupon, $163 first class, $142 second class. Extra flight coupons $63.

Holland Railpass: Three days of travel within one month, $88 first class, $68 second; five days within one month, $140 or $104; 10 days within one month, $260 or $184.

Hungarian Flexipass: Five days of first-class travel within 15 days, $55; 10 days of travel within one month, $69.

Norway Rail Pass: Seven days, $250 first class, $190 second class; 14 days, $330 or $255. Prices lower for travel October through April.

Norway Flexipass: Three days of travel within one month, $190 first class, $135 second class. Prices lower for travel October through April.

Portuguese Railpass: Four days of travel within 15 days, $99.

Romania Railpass: Three days within 15 days, $60.

Spain Flexipass: Three days of travel within two months, $180 first class,

> *Take note!*
> ☞ **Board the right car.** Coaches will have a panel on the outside designating their origination city and destination, along with names of major stops. Be sure you get onto a car going to your destination; some cars don't go the full route. If you have a reservation, find your designated car number and seat assignment. Otherwise sit anywhere that's not a reserved seat. If a train is about to leave, hop on any car, then find the right one as it's moving.

$140 second class; up to seven additional rail days are available for $40 or $32 each day.

Spain Rail 'n' Drive: Three days of rail travel and three days of car rental within two months. Rates start at $249 first class, $219 second class per person for two traveling together and $329 or $299 for one. Additional car days are $49-$99 and rail days $40 or $32. Cars with automatic transmissions are available.

Swiss Pass: Four days, $264 first class, $176 second class; eight days, $316 or $220; 15 days, $368 or $256; one month, $508 or $350. Passes for the same time periods for two traveling together start at $198 or $132.

Swiss Flexipass: Any three days within 15 days, $264 first class, $176 second class and $198 or $132 per person for two traveling together.

Swiss Card: Provides two single-journey trips between any Swiss airport or border town to any destination in Switzerland. Valid for one month for one round trip, $142 first class, $116 second class. Pass also includes a 50 percent discount on all Swiss railways, as well as discounts on buses and steamers.

Swiss Rail 'n' Drive: Three days of rail travel and three days of car rental within 15 days. Rates start at $275 first class, $205 second class per person for two traveling together and $415 or $325 for one person. Additional car days are $55-$85.

Know the Rules

Keep in mind the following conditions when considering rail passes:

1. You normally must buy your pass before departing for Europe.

This is true for all Eurailpasses and most regional or country passes, though some individual country passes can be purchased after arrival. Ask before you leave home.

2. A pass does not guarantee a seat on a train.

Seat reservations are optional for most trains, but required by a few. They are mandatory for the high-speed TGV trains in France. Reservations also are necessary for sleepers (first-class bedrooms for one or two passengers) and couchettes (second-class open bunks grouped six to a compartment).

You can make reservations in advance through a foreign rail representative (listed in box accompanying this chapter) or a travel agent when you buy your pass. There may be a reservations fee.

Rail Europe, a major supplier of passes, suggests making only limited advance seat reservations, such as when your schedule demands you be at a destination at a certain time, during holidays or at peak travel times. Additional reservations can be made as necessary when you're in Europe. You want to avoid spending money for reservations that you are unable to keep or that may prove unnecessary. While you may plan your itinerary ahead, you don't need reservations for each leg.

3. Most passes must be validated in Europe.

Just prior to starting your train travel, present your pass and passport to a railway official at a train station ticket window. The agent will inscribe your pass with the start date (that day) and the stop date, as well as your passport number. Validation must be within six months of issue. To get the most use of the pass, don't validate it until you plan to start using it.

An exception: the EurailDrive Pass is validated at the time of purchase, so know your first date of rail or car travel.

4. Protect your rail pass.

Safeguard your rail pass like you do your passport. Once passes could not be reissued if lost or stolen, but now pass-protection programs provide insurance against loss or theft, although you still will be out extra money. The insurance can be bought with the pass for $10 and repays 100 percent of the cost of the valid days remaining when the pass is lost or stolen. To recoup your loss, you must take these steps: File a report of the loss with the local police in Europe and get a copy of the report. Purchase a rail ticket or replacement pass for a validity as close as possible to the unused travel days on the lost pass. After returning home, submit proof of all rail purchases, the police report and a notarized statement to the appropriate provider as noted on your policy.

To help in planning a train trip, request brochures from Rail Europe of White Plains, NY, (800) TGV-RAIL, or DER Rail of Rosemont, IL, (800) 421-2929.

CHAPTER 26

Boosting Your Buying Power

Stretching your vacation dollars in Europe takes on an added challenge since you must deal with different currencies and fluctuating values. Doing some homework before your trip will pay off in savings.

Start by becoming familiar with the exchange rates in the countries you plan to visit. You will find a listing of current rates in the travel and/or business sections of metropolitan newspapers. Or, check with the largest bank in your city. It's wise to track the exchange rate for several weeks and see whether there is much fluctuation and whether the dollar is gaining or losing against other currencies.

Acquaint yourself with the names and denominations, both paper and coins, of the foreign currencies, such as pounds and pence in Britain and francs and centimes in France. Estimate the dollar value of the foreign money and mentally calculate the equivalent of $10, $20, $50 and $100 (or higher) so that you become familiar with amounts you will be handling in Europe. For instance, with French currency trading at about five francs to the U.S. dollar, $10 would be 50 francs, $20 would be 100 francs, $50 would be 250 francs and $100 would be 500 francs.

Take note!
☛ **Know your numeric PIN.** Not all European ATMs display letters on their keyboards, so if your personal identification number has letters, know it in numbers. Also check with your bank to be sure your PIN will work in overseas machines; you may need another PIN.

Next, think about items you might want to buy other than usual souvenirs. Check out prices in your own home area so you know whether you're getting a good deal in similar items abroad. For instance, if you like the Benetton or Laura Ashley brands of clothing or Ferragamo, Bruno Magli or Bally shoes, know what some items of those brands cost at home so you can tell if the European prices are bargains. Also know the specialties of various countries so you can shop for good buys. For instance, Britain is known for its woolens, so you may want to look for men's and women's sweaters. If you like French brands of perfumes, know what the various sizes of bottles cost at home so you can sniff out a good deal abroad.

The following tips on money matters will help you get the most for your dollar.

Exchanging Money

Most vacationers travel with a combination of cash and traveler's checks and convert dollars to the local currency as needed. Today many travelers also use debit cards in automated teller machines.

You should plan to have some local currency when you arrive in a foreign country or exchange some dollars at the airport. If the exchange rate upon arrival (at an airport or train station) is close to what you've been tracking, then convert the amount of money you estimate you'll need for a day or two. If the rate is not as good as expected, exchange only what you need until you can find a better place to do transactions. Sometimes airports and train stations have good rates, but usually not.

You often can get the best exchange rate using your bank debit card or other cards that allow you to withdraw money from your checking account. The ATM networks use the bank exchange rate, which is more favorable than the rate for individuals. However, there usually is a service fee, and ATMs may be hard to find outside major cities. Check with your home bank for the names and locations of banks abroad that are linked into the same network.

> *Take note!*
>
> ☞ **Bring U.S. $1 bills.** Although the dollar doesn't have quite the cachet it used to, it is acceptable to tip using $1 bills. Also, when paying for something, if you run short of local currency you often can add $1 bills as needed to make up the difference; most merchants and taxi drivers are familiar with $1 bills but may not know larger bills.

A caveat: Some credit cards allow you to get cash advances, which are billed to your account, but you are subject to interest charges on the advance and pay a fee per advance, which can be hefty. You also pay an ATM fee.

Banks are usually your next best choice for exchanging money, but the rate can vary from bank to bank. Rates normally are posted next to the foreign exchange window or on a placard in front of the bank.

Although many travel guides warn vacationers to avoid exchanging money at hotels, their rates may be competitive — and you have the convenience factor.

You'll probably find the least attractive rates at exchange booths called "bureaux de change." These private companies often charge a high commission.

Some restaurants will take your traveler's checks and give change in local currency — but always ask what the conversion rate is. You may do better putting your meal on a credit card.

When looking for the best deal, always ask how much you actually get for your dollar, after all fees and commissions. That's really the bottom line.

Stay alert to fluctuations in the exchange rate as you travel, but remember that you nearly always will get slightly varying rates. In seeking the best exchange rates, look at the differences in dollars rather than local currency and balance your savings against your time spent chasing the best rates. For instance, a difference of 25 lire between rates at your hotel and a bank translates to less than $2 when exchanging $100, with lire at about 1,500 to the dollar. If you're exchanging a small amount, it may not be worth your time to go to the bank; but if you're exchanging a large amount, it could be time well spent.

When cashing traveler's checks, save on fees by converting larger amounts at one time. By cashing $200 worth at once, you'll save three commission charges and other fees over what you'd pay if you cashed $50 at a time. You usually will get a better exchange rate for your traveler's checks than for cash.

Making Purchases

Use a credit card whenever possible. You'll save exchange transaction fees and may get a better exchange rate. The amount on your statement will reflect the exchange rate on the day that the transaction is posted, not on the day the item was bought. You may end up paying slightly less — or more — but there's usually not much difference.

A caveat: Know your credit card limit before leaving home and keep track of what you're spending.

Credit cards are not as widely accepted in Europe as they are in the United States. In some countries, merchants prefer traveler's checks because they have to pay a commission on credit card purchases.

VAT Refunds

Most European countries have a value-added tax on goods, similar to sales tax in the United States except the VAT usually is included in the price of the item. Although the VAT averages 15 percent, it sometimes is a hefty 25 percent.

Foreigners may be able to get a refund of a percentage of the purchase price; usually this refund is a little less than the total value-added tax. The refund applies only to goods, not services. Most countries require a minimum purchase, either per store or per item, for a buyer to qualify for the refund. The minimum purchase requirement ranges from a low of about $15 in Sweden to a high of about $405 in Switzerland.

Stores that give VAT refunds usually display a sign or sticker in the window; if you don't see one, ask. Merchants usually do not initiate the VAT refund process unless requested. Carry your passport when shopping, as you will need to show it in order to be eligible for the refund. At the store, the merchant will fill out the necessary forms or will ask you to do so.

Procedures for obtaining the refund vary from country to country. Generally, you present your purchases and forms to a customs official or VAT desk as you leave the country. With the new European Union, which encompasses most European countries, U.S. visitors get the VAT form validated when they leave

---

Take note!

☞ **Spend all foreign coins.** At the end of your trip, any foreign paper currency you have left can be exchanged for dollars at an airport or international bank, but many exchange sites will not take coins. Try to use up most of your foreign coins in their country of origin. The rest will become souvenirs.

Toward the end of your trip, convert only the dollars you think you will spend before you leave. Try to avoid paying two exchange fees — dollars into francs and francs back to dollars. You always get less when selling back local currency than when buying it. For instance, you may get 5.13 francs for your dollar, but it may take 5.8 francs to buy back your dollar.

the union, rather than when exiting each individual country. While goods are subject to inspection, it's rarely done. You may get the refund on the spot, or you may need to mail the paperwork back to the merchant, who will send you the refund. Refunds may come in cash, a check issued in local currency or, if you pay by charge card, as a credit to your account.

More than 90,000 stores in 20 European countries participate in Europe Tax-free Shopping, a VAT refund service that has streamlined the process for the consumer. Participating merchants display a "Tax-Free for Tourists" sticker in the store window. The merchant will issue a refund check, which you present to a customs official for validation upon departure.

Value-Added Tax Refunds

Most European countries have a value-added tax (VAT) on goods, similar to a sales tax except the VAT usually is included in the price of the item. U.S. visitors to Europe may qualify for a refund of part of the VAT. This chart shows each country's required minimum purchase amount to qualify for a refund and the amount of the VAT refunded, in percentage of the purchase price. For inexpensive purchases, your refund could be so small that it is eaten up by a service fee, which sometimes is assessed.

Country	Required minimum purchase[1] Local currency	Estimated dollars	VAT refund[2]
Austria	1,000 schillings	$95	16.7%
Belgium	7,001 B. francs	$230	17%
Denmark	301 D. kroner	$50	20%
Finland	100 markkaa	$25	18%
France	1,200 F. francs	$240	17.1%
Germany	50 marks	$35	13%
Great Britain	50 pounds[3]	$75	14.9%
Greece	40,001 drachmas	$170	11.5-15.3%
Holland	301 guilders	$180	14.9%
Hungary	25,000 forint	$190	9.1-20%
Ireland	no minimum		17.4%
Italy	300,000 lire[4]	$185	13-16%
Luxembourg	3,000 L. francs	$100	13%
Norway	300 N. kroner	$45	18.7%
Portugal	10,000 escudos[4]	$65	14.5%
Spain	15,000 pesetas[5]	$120	13.8%
Sweden	100 kronor	$15	20%
Switzerland	500 S. francs	$405	6.1%

[1]All purchase requirements are per store, except as noted. Dollar amounts are rounded off and based on late '95 exchange rates. [2]Percentage of purchase price refunded; actual VAT may be higher. [3]No official limit; individual stores may set amount, which varies from 50 pounds upward. [4]Plus VAT. [5]Per item.

At an ETS refund desk (located at major airports and train stations and at many border crossings), you will be reimbursed for the VAT, minus a service fee of about 20 percent. The refund is available in three ways: in cash, as a check mailed to your home, or as a credit to your charge card. Many desks also can reimburse you in U.S. dollars.

Tipping

In most European countries, restaurants and hotels include a service charge in the bill. Look for such words as *service compris* or *servicio incluido* on the menu or at the bottom of your bill. Most Europeans leave an additional tip, such as the small-denomination coins received as change. If a service charge is not included, it is customary to leave a 10 to 15 percent gratuity.

Taxi drivers usually get a 10 to 15 percent tip, but there are exceptions. For example, in Switzerland, Belgium, Denmark and Finland, it is not customary to tip taxi drivers unless special service is given. Check with your hotel concierge if you're unsure about local customs.

Duty-Free Shops

Articles sold in airport duty-free shops are free of duty and taxes only for the country in which the shop is located. Purchases still are subject to U.S. customs duty.

In countries that have the value-added tax, the prices on items in the duty-free shop will lack this tariff. Buying something duty-free will save you the hassle

Duty Rates

U.S. citizens returning from Europe can bring home up to $400 in purchases without paying any customs fees. The next $1,000 in purchases is subject to a flat fee of 10 percent. Above that, specific duties are assessed according to the articles. Here are examples of rates on popular items.

Item	Duty
China (tableware)	8-26%
Clocks (valued over $5 each)	6.4% plus 45 cents
Clothing	3-34.6%
Jewelry	6.5-27.5%
Leather shoes	2.5-20%
Leather wallets	4.7-8%
Paintings (done entirely by hand)	None
Perfume*	5%
Watches	3.9-14%
Wine (one liter)*	8.3-30.9 cents
Wool sweaters	7.5-17%

*Subject to federal excise taxes.

of going through the VAT-refund procedure, but don't save all your shopping for the airport. You run the risk of a desired item being unavailable — or not at as good a price as you saw during your travels within the country.

The most commonly bought duty-free items are liquor, cigarettes and perfume. At one time these goods were true bargains at duty-free shops, but they aren't anymore, with the proliferation of discount merchandise in the States. Use the duty-free shops to look for unusual or hard-to-find liquors or perfumes or special products of the country.

U.S. Customs, Duties

You can bring up to $400 in purchases back into the United States from Europe without paying any customs fees under two conditions: You were abroad at least 48 hours, and you have not used the $400 exemption within the preceding 30 days. Above $400, a flat 10 percent rate is applied to the next $1,000 worth of purchases; after $1,400, the duty varies according to the article. But certain items — such as antiques more than 100 years old, drawings, paintings and some loose gems — are not subject to U.S. duties. Therefore, you may not have to pay as much duty as you might expect.

If you cannot claim the $400 exemption because of the 48-hour or 30-day restrictions, you are eligible for a $25 exemption.

When you return to the United States, if you have exceeded the duty-free limit, the customs official will question you about specific purchases. The inspector will place the items having the highest rate of duty under your exemption and assess the flat 10 percent duty on the items taxed at lower rates. For items that are not subject to a flat rate of duty, the customs official will determine the appropriate rate per article.

A gift shipped from abroad is exempt from duty if less than $50 in value. Items that you ship home to yourself cannot be included in your customs exemption and are subject to duty when received.

Free Information

● "Know Before You Go," published by the U.S. Customs Service, details the allowable exemptions and duty rates, lists prohibited and restricted articles, and provides information on duty-free shops, shipping goods home and packing baggage for easy inspection. "Know Before You Go" and other informational literature are included in a traveler's packet available from customs offices across the country. Or request them from U.S. Customs Service, 1301 Constitution Ave. NW, Washington, DC 20229.

● "Shopping in Europe" outlines the VAT-refund services provided by Europe Tax-free Shopping. Europe Tax-free Shopping, 233 S. Wacker Drive, Suite 9700, Chicago, IL 60606-6502.

CHAPTER 27

Getting Around Town

You can move about almost any major European city easily and inexpensively if you do as most residents do — use public transportation and walk. Forget driving a car in the cities. Traffic is heavy, European driving habits are different and parking is a hassle.

Navigating European cities can be a fun adventure, often leading to discoveries that yield highlights of a trip. A stroll down a narrow cobblestone street or along a tree-shaded river walk brings you closer to a city's culture and history. Walking is a good way to see local color and find some little cafes or boutiques that are popular with residents.

If distances are too great for walking, or if you're in a hurry, the local mass transit system provides an inexpensive, swift and efficient way to get around, often faster than taking a taxi. Most European cities have a network of subway and bus and/or streetcar routes that will take you nearly anywhere within the area.

Methods for purchasing mass-transit tickets vary across Europe; you usually can buy them from ticket windows, vending machines, bus drivers or streetcar operators, tobacco shops and newsstands. Most transit systems offer discounted multiple tickets and passes good for unlimited travel over several days. Multiuse tickets often are good on all types of transportation.

In most cities you have a choice of taking the bus or riding the subway.

From a bus, you have the advantage of seeing the sights. For instance, riding on the top level of a double-decker bus in London is a great way to see the city. But it's more difficult to know the exact route and stops of a bus, whereas a subway's route is readily identified on easy-to-find maps. Buses also run slower than subways and can get stuck in traffic. And, methods for boarding, deboarding and validating tickets on buses can vary from city to city and be more confusing than using a subway.

Many tourists are more comfortable navigating city subways, often known as

> ## *Take note!*
> ☞ **Go second class.** Subways in some countries have first- and second-class seating, designated by numbers 1 and 2 on the side of the subway car. Seats are nicer in first class, but you're usually not going to be on the subway long, so why pay more? Beware: You're subject to a fine if you sit in first class with a second-class ticket, although the ticket-checkers are lenient with tourists.

the metro. Paris and London have excellent underground rail systems. Stations are clearly marked, and you usually don't have to walk far to find one.

You can pick up a subway map at a ticket window, information office or hotel. Maps showing routes and stops also are displayed both in the stations and on the trains.

With all their crisscrossing routes marked in different colors, subway maps may bewilder some tourists at first glance, but the rail systems are easily mastered. You need to know three simple elements to navigate a system:

1) the name of the stop closest to where you are now.

2) the name of the stop closest to your destination.

3) the name of the destination at the end of line in the direction you want to go.

To board the train headed in the right direction, follow signs for its final destination at the metro station. If you're making a transfer from one route to another, know the end destination of each train and follow the signs. Trains run frequently during business hours and early evening.

If you want to use the metro during a day of sightseeing, ask your hotel concierge to show you the best route to get to your destination; he or she can direct you to the nearest stop and tell you which metro line to take.

Although taxis are a more expensive means of transport, you might feel safer using one during late hours. Be aware that various surcharges may apply. There may be a handling charge for any luggage (for instance, when transferring to your hotel upon arrival); this may be assessed per bag or by weight. Fares can go up after midnight, or on weekends and holidays. You may need to tip 10-15 percent, if it is not included in the fare.

Below are examples of rates and discount passes for the mass transit systems in some major European cities. When prices are listed in local currency, the approximate dollar amount follows in parentheses. These dollar amounts reflect exchange rates at press time and are subject to change.

London

The London bus and subway network is divided into zones, and fares vary according to the number of zones you cross.

A short bus ride costs about 50-70 pence (75 cents-$1.05), depending on the time of day you travel — bus fare is cheaper after 9:30 a.m. After midnight, special night buses marked with an "N" operate throughout London and into the suburbs until 6 a.m.

Tickets for the London subway, known as the Underground or the Tube, start at 90 pence ($1.35). Keep your ticket when riding the Tube; you'll need to give

---

Take note!

☞ **Hang on to your city transit ticket.** Don't throw out your stub until you've completed your journey. In some cities, buses and streetcars run on the honor system; tickets are not collected regularly, but transit inspectors may make random checks. Also, some metro stations require you to show a ticket upon exiting.

it to the ticket collector at the end of your journey.

Underground service from Heathrow Airport into central London runs about 3.10 pounds ($4.65), while special "airbus" service for the same route costs about 5 pounds ($7.50). A taxi ride from Heathrow to Piccadilly Circus (centrally located) would cost about 40 pounds ($60). If you arrive at Gatwick Airport, farther away than Heathrow, your best choice in transportation is a BritRail train into Victoria Station; a round-trip ticket costs about 18 pounds ($27) standard class or about 26 pounds ($39) first class. Trains are easily accessible from the airport.

There are two types of passes available for London train and bus travel:

Visitor Travelcard: Provides unlimited travel on almost the entire London bus and Tube system. The card also comes with discount vouchers for some of the city's top attractions. The card cannot be purchased in Britain; you must buy it prior to departure. It is available from some travel agents and BritRail Travel International offices in North America.

Prices are: 3 days, $25 adult, $11 child; 4 days, $32 adult, $13 child; 7 days, $49 adult, $21 child. Contact the British Tourist Authority, (800) 462-2748, or BritRail, (800) 677-8585, for information on the closest agent to your hometown.

London Travelcard: Provides unlimited travel on buses and the subway. This card can be used only after 9:30 a.m., Monday-Friday, but all day on weekends and public holidays. It is not valid on night buses. You can purchase the card at subway and bus stations; prices vary according to the number of fare zones crossed. Cards are available for different lengths of time; check locally to see if any serves your needs. Cards valid for a week or more require a passport-size photo of the user.

Frankfurt

Tickets and passes are valid on Frankfurt's buses, streetcars, commuter trains and subway. A single ticket costs 2.70 marks (about $1.90) or 3.20 marks ($2.25) during rush hours (6-9 a.m. and 4-6:30 p.m.). Short-distance tickets are 1.80 marks ($1.25).

A 24-hour ticket good for unlimited travel within the city costs 8.50 marks ($5.95). All tickets can be purchased from the blue vending machines at stops and stations; bus tickets can be bought from the driver upon boarding.

Munich

Munich's public transit system consists of buses, streetcars, commuter trains and the subway. You can purchase a ticket for use on any of these from a ticket

---

Take note!

☞ **Be alert.** Watch for pickpockets when riding any public transportation system, especially during crowded peak hours. Women should hold a purse in front of them with a hand over it. Men should not carry a wallet in a back pants pocket where a thief can easily reach it. Instead, keep it in the front pocket or inside jacket pocket. Better yet, use a money belt concealed under clothing.

counter or ticket vending machine in train stations. A single ticket covering the inner city zone costs 3.30 marks ($2.30). A day pass covering central Munich costs 12 marks ($8.40). This is an excellent buy; up to two adults and three children traveling together can ride on one pass from 9 a.m. until the end of the day's service.

Rome

Rome's public transportation system consists of buses, streetcars and the subway. Although the subway is limited to two lines, and buses are often overcrowded, they do serve major tourist sights and are a bargain. Single tickets for the underground and for buses/streetcars cost 1,500 lire (about $1). A ticket valid for 75 minutes on the underground, bus and streetcar costs 1,500 lire ($1); it can be used only once on the underground but on as many buses and streetcars as desired. A monthly transportation pass is available for 50,000 lire ($33).

Remember that when riding the bus in Rome, enter through the rear doors and exit through the middle doors.

Paris

The Paris subway, called the Metro, is a very efficient and economical way to travel. One ticket for 7.50 francs (about $1.50) will take you as far as you need to go, and you can make as many connections as necessary. Hang on to your ticket throughout your ride, as transit officials do make random ticket checks on Metro cars.

For a good value, purchase a *carnet* (a book of 10 tickets) for 44 francs (slightly less than $9), which cuts the per-ticket cost to slightly less than $1.

The *Paris-Visite* Card, marketed to tourists, is good for unlimited public transportation within the city limits. Prices are $10 for one day, $18 for two days, $25 for three days and $37 for five days. You'd have to do quite a bit of Metro travel for this to be worth it, though. For the one-day *Paris-Visite* Card at $10, you'd have to make about seven Metro trips to break even.

The *Paris-Visite* Card is available in the United States from Marketing Challenges International, (212) 529-8484.

Vienna

Vienna's transit system consists of buses, streetcars, the metropolitan railway and the subway. Tickets and passes are valid for all modes of transport.

The Vienna Card is a combination transit pass-discount card, offering three days of unlimited travel on the transit system and four days of discounts for sightseeing, concerts, events, shopping and some dining. It costs 180 schillings (about $18) and is available at tourist information offices and hotels.

A single ticket costs 17 schillings ($1.70) at tobacco shops/newsstands and from vending machines at subway stations, or 20 schillings ($2) if bought after boarding a bus or streetcar. A pass good for 24 hours costs 50 schillings ($5); a pass for 72 hours costs 130 schillings ($13). You can use these as often as you want within the valid time frame.

An eight-day strip ticket costs 265 schillings ($26.50) and can be used by more than one person. One strip per person is stamped on the day's first trip; one validated strip gives one traveler access to the whole public transport system for the rest of the day. A person traveling alone could use the pass for eight days, or two people could use it for four days.

Scandinavia

The Scandinavian countries — Denmark, Finland, Norway and Sweden — offer tourist passes for unlimited travel on public transit systems. These passes also include free or discounted access to museums and attractions, as well as discounts for theaters, restaurants and sightseeing tours (see Chapter 28, "Seeing the Sights"). In some cases, cards are valid for a set number of hours — 24, 48 or 72. A 24-hour card can be used over two days; for example, from noon on Friday until noon on Saturday.

You can purchase these passes at hotels and tourist offices in the city that you're planning to visit, or at some travel agencies in the United States. To find out where to purchase a pass, contact the applicable country's tourism office here in the United States (see list of offices and phone numbers in Chapter 31, "Getting Information").

Because these passes include extra benefits and discounts, they're pricier than transit-only passes. If you're not planning to visit a lot of attractions in one or two days, look for a local transit-only pass or discount card.

The following cards allow unlimited travel on public transportation systems, free or discounted access to sights and other travel discounts.

Copenhagen Card: Valid on the city's buses and trains. Prices: 24 hours, 140 kroner (about $24); 48 hours, 230 kroner ($40); 72 hours, 295 kroner ($51).

Helsinki Card: Valid on city subway, buses, streetcars and local trains. Prices: 24 hours, 95 markkaa (about $20); 48 hours, 135 markkaa ($28); 72 hours, 165 markkaa ($35).

Oslo Card: Valid on the city's trains, subway, streetcars, buses and boats. Prices: one day, 130 kroner (about $19); two days, 200 kroner ($30); three days, 240 kroner ($38).

Stockholm City Card: Valid on city's subway and streetcar systems. Prices: 175 kronor (about $23) per day, with 24-hour, 48-hour and 72-hour passes available for $23, $46 and $69 respectively.

CHAPTER 28

Seeing the Sights

You'll probably want to see as much as possible of Europe's impressive art collections, stately castles and many historic landmarks. To gain the most from your trip, read about your destination before you leave home and arrive with an idea of what you want to see.

In any city, make your first stop the local tourism office (marked with an "i"). Besides having staffers who can answer questions and orient you to the city, these centers offer current literature about local sights and attractions, as well as upcoming cultural events and festivals.

While admission fees to individual attractions are nominal, these costs quickly add up. Here are ways to cut your sightseeing expenses:

● Take advantage of free days at museums. Nearly all designate one day a week that's free, and if your schedule permits, set that day for your museum visits. (Also, check what day the museums are closed.)

● Ask about special discounts — for seniors and students, for instance.

● Plan your own sightseeing. Some travelers like to take an introductory tour in major cities so they get an overview of the sights, then return on their own to areas of particular interest.

● Cut down on entry fees to museums and other attractions by purchasing a pass that allows unlimited access to many sights.

Take note!

☞ **Dress appropriately.** When touring in major cities and when you expect to go into noted cathedrals, wear conservative clothing. Some churches or cathedrals do not allow shorts, cut-off T-shirts or any other skimpy tops. For cathedral visits, pants and skirts with tops that have sleeves are appropriate. Some landmark homes or castles don't allow high heels or hard-sole shoes on highly polished wood or marble floors. They may loan you soft felt covers to slip over such footwear.

The following is a sample of passes offered. Most are available at tourist information offices in the applicable city; some can be purchased in the states. To find out about purchasing these passes and to check on ones available in other cities, call the applicable tourism office in the United States (see Chapter 31, "Getting Information"). Prices are given in local currency, with dollar estimates at current exchange rates; for the latest dollar cost, check exchange rates at time of travel. Local prices are subject to change.

Amsterdam Culture and Leisure Pass: Offers free admission to five top museums, including Rijksmuseum and the Van Gogh Museum, free casino admission and discounts on boat tours, attractions and at restaurants. The pass costs 29.90 guilders (about $19.50) and provides one-time access or discounts at sites.

Great British Heritage Pass: Allows access to nearly 600 homes, castles, monuments, ruins and gardens in Great Britain, including Stone Age villages, Winston Churchill's birthplace and the ancestral home of George Washington. A seven-day pass costs $39, 15-day pass $58 and a one-month pass $85; these are available in the States from travel agents. The passes are available in Britain at the British Travel Centre near London's Piccadilly Circus. When bought in Britain, passes cost similar to the U.S. amount, though can vary with the exchange rate. A pass will save you money if you plan to see several attractions.

Madrid Paseo del Arte: Provides admission to three top museums, El Prado, Reina Sofia and Thyssen. Costs 1,050 pesetas (about $9) and is valid for one-time admission to each museum.

Paris Carte-Musee: Covers admission to 65 museums and monuments in Paris, including the Louvre, the Arc de Triomphe and the Musee d'Orsay (known for its superb collection of Impressionist art). A one-day pass costs 70 francs (about $14), three-day pass 140 francs ($28) and five-day pass 200 francs ($40).

Rome Museidon Card: Allows access to a number of specified museums but not all the largest ones. Check the list before buying to see if it serves your interests. A two-day blue card for limited museums costs 13,000 lire (about $8), two-day yellow card for additional museums 23,000 lire ($14.50), four-day orange card 30,000 lire ($19) and seven-day green card 48,000 lire ($30).

Take note!

☞ **Look both ways.** As you're walking about town, make it a rule to look both left and right for oncoming traffic before crossing a street. Be especially careful in Britain, where drivers keep to the left. For pedestrians, that means when crossing a street with two-way traffic, you first must look right — not left as we do in the United States. Elsewhere, such as in Vienna, watch out for streetcars that move in opposite direction to auto traffic, even on one-way streets.

Transport and Touring

The following cards provide admission to attractions and unlimited travel on local public transportation systems (see Chapter 27, "Getting Around Town"). Some cards are valid for a specified number of hours such as 24 or 48; a 24-hour card can be used over a two-day period if bought in the afternoon, for instance.

Copenhagen Card: Allows entry to more than 50 museums and other attractions, provides travel discounts and includes a 128-page tourist guide. A 24-hour pass costs 140 kroner (about $24), 48-hour pass 230 kroner ($40) and 72-hour pass 295 kroner ($51).

Helsinki Card: Good for admission to more than 50 museums and galleries. Includes a free sightseeing coach tour. A 24-hour pass costs 95 markkaa (about $20), 48-hour pass 135 markkaa ($28) and 72-hour pass 165 markkaa ($35).

Oslo Card: Provides entry to most museums, a free sightseeing cruise and various discounts. A one-day pass costs 130 kroner (about $19), two-day pass 200 kroner ($30) and three-day pass 240 kroner ($38).

Stockholm City Card(Sweden): Provides free or reduced admission to museums and attractions, as well as a free sightseeing boat tour. Passes cost 175 kronor (about $23) per day, with 24-hour, 48-hour and 72-hour passes available.

Vienna Card: Provides unlimited travel on public transit system for three days and discounts for four days at museums, attractions, concerts, shops and some restaurants and coffeehouses. Costs 180 schillings (about $18).

Made for Walking

The best way to take in the sights and observe the local daily life is by walking. At city tourism centers, ask about maps for do-it-yourself walking tours or low-cost organized walking tours you can join.

For instance, the Austrian National Tourist Office in New York has a map that shows four walks through Vienna's historic areas. London offers numerous organized walking tours that suit all kinds of interests — such as neighborhoods associated with the writings of Sherlock Holmes and Dickens.

Remember that sightseeing in Europe isn't just touring ancient castles or roaming the galleries of a famous museum. It's also exploring a quiet cobblestone road, browsing at a colorful street market or talking with new-found friends in a cafe or coffeehouse.

There are many ways to enjoy yourself in Europe that won't cost a cent. In London, watch the Changing of the Guard in front of Buckingham Palace. In Paris along the Seine, wander among the vendor stands with their collections of old books, magazines, postcards and prints. Window shop on the fashionable streets of Rome, or people-watch in one of Europe's beautifully landscaped gardens.

Don't over-plan your day's sightseeing. Leave time for unexpected discoveries.

CHAPTER 29

Dining Out For Less

Europeans are proud of their culinary heritage and it shows, from the small corner cafe to the most fashionable five-star restaurant.

If your budget allows, you may want to splurge on a few elegant dining experiences, but you can enjoy many gastronomic delights without having to shell out big bucks at fancy restaurants.

Avoid establishments that look like they attract a lot of tourists. Go to popular neighborhood restaurants — pubs, bistros, *trattorias* and *tavernas*. At these, you'll find local specialties at the most reasonable prices.

Check for a listing of restaurants at the local tourist office and ask for recommendations from residents or other travelers.

You also can "window shop" for restaurants — most of them display their menus in a window or on a placard just outside the entrance. See which ones have menus — and prices — that appeal to you and which places seem to be attracting a local crowd.

While *bifteck* and *pommes frites* (steak and french fries) are popular fare in Europe, you should try the regional dishes. Ask about local specialties and order what most appeals to you. Also, when drinking beers and wines, the regional ones will be less expensive. A good bet is the house wine, which can be ordered in carafes of several sizes, some serving only two glasses.

You'll save money if you order from the *prix-fixe* (fixed price) menu, sometimes called the *table d'hote* or tourist menu. The menu offers a three-course (or more) dinner at a set price, which is less than ordering each item a la carte. You usually select an appetizer, entree and dessert from two or three choices in each category. Coffee often is included. Many restaurants feature a choice of *prix-fixe* menus at different prices.

Here are some insights into dining in Europe.

Breakfast

With a few exceptions, continental breakfast is standard. It consists of plain rolls and sometimes croissants, jams and jellies, juice and coffee or tea.

In England, full breakfasts of eggs and bacon are common, and in Holland and

> *Take note!*
>
> ☞ **Share a table.**
> It's common for diners to share their table when space is tight. Europeans may simply nod at you to take the vacant chairs, or you may ask. There's no obligation to converse with others at the table, but you may if you wish.

the Scandinavian countries, you may be served cheeses and cold cuts along with rolls and coffee or tea. In Austria and Switzerland, muesli (granola) may be added.

If you're staying at a hotel that doesn't include breakfast in the room rate, scout the neighborhood for a small cafe, bakery or other food shop that serves breakfast. These will be cheaper than your hotel restaurant, and you have more local ambiance.

Lunch

Lunch frequently is the big meal of the day, especially in France and southern Europe where it can be a long, leisurely affair rather than the short, rushed break that most Americans know.

Ask about local dining hours, because continuous service is not as common as in the States. In some areas, restaurants may be open only during specific hours for lunch and dinner. When you're traveling, particularly driving and sightseeing, watch that you don't accidentally miss the lunch hour. Carry some snacks in case you find everything closed.

Save money at lunch by stopping at a bakery, where you can find sandwiches prepared on bread fresh out of the oven — and choose from divine pastries for dessert.

Many European train stations have excellent restaurants with inexpensive menus and fast service. Some even have elegant, upscale restaurants. Major department stores in European cities also have good lunch counters.

Take note!

☛ **When's dinner?**
Early evening in central and northern Europe, later as you move south. It's hard to find full meal service past 10 p.m. in England, but restaurants in southern Spain are barely cooking before 10 p.m.

If you want to sample the fare at a fine restaurant, go at lunch and order from the *prix-fixe* menu. It will be much less expensive than the dinner menu. Call ahead and make reservations though, especially if you want to go to a well-known restaurant.

Dinner

Dinner in southern Europe is served quite late, after 8 p.m. in Italy and France and after 10 p.m. in Spain. In the late afternoon or early evening, the Spaniards take a break for *tapas*, snacks accompanied by wine or beer, served in bars. In England and northern Europe, dinner is served earlier in the evening, and it may be difficult to find restaurants open past 10 p.m.

Dining Habits

Some items that we take for granted in the United States aren't automatically served in Europe.

If you want water with your meal, you'll need to request it. The waiter may ask if you want bottled mineral water (for which you'll be charged). If you don't want to pay, ask for tap (or ordinary) water. If you do want mineral water, specify whether you want the fizzy carbonated kind ("with gas") or plain water ("without gas").

With the exception of France, bread isn't always served with a meal. You may need to request it — and pay a nominal sum for it.

In some countries, the order in which courses are served is different. In Italy, for example, pasta often is one course and may be served before the meat dish. In some countries, the salad comes after the main dish; if you want it earlier, tell your waiter. Coffee often comes after dessert; if you want it with your meal or with dessert, ask. If you want a refill on your coffee, you'll be charged for it.

CHAPTER 30

A Sampler Of Dollar-Wise Travels

Now that we've given you the planning tools for thrifty travel in Europe, let's see how to put the tips to work. In this chapter, three travel journalists show how to stretch your dollars in specific destinations.

London — More per Pound

It was a costly Sunday morning, thanks to a few high-priced blunders.

First, I rushed out of the hotel without my compact umbrella — an error that should never be committed in London. I headed for the Underground station to catch "the Tube," as Londoners call their subway, but the skies opened on me.

Alas, the station was closed on Sundays, so I hurried toward another one as the rain became blinding. Giving in, I hailed a cab, which cost 10 pounds (about $15) to reach the Underground station at Kings Cross. There I caught the quickest Tube to Hampstead to join a tour. Finally I broke down and bought a little umbrella — for 9.50 pounds (about $14.25).

If I'd planned just a bit, I'd have remembered my umbrella and found out earlier which stations are closed on Sundays. My only expense would have been 90 pence (about $1.35) for the Tube to Hampstead.

"Planning" is the key word here — both before and during a trip. In advance, you'll discover the best deals to London by traveling in the off-season (fall through late spring) or looking for an air-hotel package. From January through March, you will find the lowest airfares and packages. The weather may be a bit nippy — take a raincoat with warm lining — but the city brims with activities then.

There are many ways to make your money go further while you have a great London experience. Here are eight great budget builders.

In lodgings, think small. The grand hotels charge proportionate rates, often $300 a night or more. Less costly alternatives are the small "boutique" hotels, ideally located and often luxurious in decor but costing about half the price of their baronial neighbors. The number of these

Take note!

☞ **Help in London.** The British Travel Centre, near London's Piccadilly Circus, can take care of a number of travel needs. The staff books rail and air travel, reserves sightseeing tours and theater tickets and helps visitors find suitable accommodations. The bookshop has a wide selection of guidebooks and maps.

hotels is swelling, but for most travelers they're still a splurge since many will cost more than $150 a night.

My personal favorite is the Franklin Hotel, at 28 Egerton Gardens in Knightsbridge (800-473-9487 in the United States), a 37-bedroom townhouse overlooking a tree-filled garden square. Impeccably decorated, the hotel is furnished with antiques and has big windows that lend an airy ambiance.

All guests enjoy the downstairs drawing and sitting rooms and cozy bar, and room service is available 24 hours. Breakfast is either in guest rooms or in the hotel dining room, and a butler and valet, secretarial and concierge services are offered. Rooms start at 145 pounds ($217.50) a night; rates occasionally drop to 120 pounds ($180).

> **Take note!**
>
> ☞ **Lunch at the pub.** In London, many pubs serve hearty, inexpensive lunches. Typical fare includes sandwiches, salad and such specialties as shepherd's pie (minced meat topped with a crispy potato crust) and bangers and mash (sausages and mashed potatoes).

Expect to pay $100 and higher per night for a hotel within the main part of London. Prices often will include a hearty breakfast, though, that can help cut your food tabs. To find lower-cost hotels, call the British Tourist Authority, (800) 462-2748, and request its "London Accommodation for Budget Travelers" guide. Browse through the booklet and target hotels that best suit your budget. The BTA can answer questions you may have about specific hotels.

Another source of information is the London Tourist Board's central reservations service, 011-44-171-824-8848 (when dialing from the United States), which also can book hotels.

Also, check hotel chains. Best Western is one of the largest chains, with more upscale properties in Europe than its customary motels in the United States. Its least expensive hotel in London is the Phoenix, where rates sometimes are slightly below $100 a night, including continental breakfast. Forte is another major chain with varying classes of hotels, many offering a 30 percent savings when you book 30 days ahead. Always ask about specials.

Often the best rates for a hotel are through packages offered by airlines that include your airfare, lodging and often transfers between the airport and hotel. Airlines offer varying classes of hotels in their packages, from budget to luxury, all at discounts.

Shop smart for meals. If you've chosen a hotel that includes breakfast in its rates, it's just a matter of spending wisely on the day's other two meals. Ask your concierge where some good *prix fixe* menus can be found in the neighborhood, or look for them while shopping or museum-hopping. Quite a few restaurants post these menus in windows or outside on blackboards.

Alastair Little's, a trendy Soho spot at 49 Frith St., has a wonderful lunch special for about $15 in the downstairs bar. Restaurants in Covent Garden offer pre-theater dinner menus set at 20 pounds ($30). Pubs from Chelsea to Hampstead post traditional pub lunches of roast beef or lamb with potatoes and

Yorkshire pudding for about 5 pounds ($7.50).

Two of my favorite ways to stretch dining dollars concern creative lunching. I plan my morning outing to wind up around the Knightsbridge area, home to Harrods and Harvey Nichols — stores with outstanding food halls. A sack lunch for picnicking in Hyde Park might include quiche or a cold salad plate (each about $5.25), deli sandwich (about $3), or pita bread with eggplant dip and dolmas, stuffed grape leaves (about $5).

There's also the delightful English indulgence, afternoon tea, which makes a perfect late lunch or early dinner. This ritual typically begins by 3:30 p.m. at most hotels and some stores (even Giorgio Armani). At the Goring Hotel in Grosvenor Gardens, not far from Buckingham Palace, you'll be served a generous assortment of little but not-too-prissy sandwiches, huge scones, plenty of thick clotted cream, fine strawberry jam and, of course, pots of excellent English tea. The price is 9.50 pounds (about $14.25).

Buy a Travelcard. Skip the taxis and use London's Underground, a marvelous, practical system. The trademark red, double-decker buses are ready people-movers, as well. The most economical way to use both is with a pass called a travelcard.

One of the best buys for tourists is the London Visitor Travelcard, available from travel agents in the United States. A three-day card is $25 for adults and allows unlimited use of the London transit system. It also provides discount vouchers for attractions. The card must be bought before leaving home. Four- and seven-day cards are available also.

A London Travelcard — good for covering central London — affords unlimited transportation on the bus and Tube after 9:30 a.m. on weekdays or all day on Saturdays and Sundays. This type of card is for sale in London at subway and bus stations. A one-day Travelcard that covers London's central transit zones costs only 3.50 pounds (about $5.25). If you're doing a good bit of sightseeing, this makes more sense than buying 90-pence ($1.35) tickets every trip. Check locally about passes valid for longer periods; these usually require a passport-size photograph.

Another tip for travelers using Gatwick Airport: You can take the Gatwick Express train between the airport and Victoria Station, paying about 18 pounds ($27) round-trip, instead of a much more expensive cab ride.

> *Take note!*
> ☛ **Know your size.** Manufacturers in the United States, Britain and continental Europe use different sizing systems for clothes and shoes. For example, a dress that's a size 10 in the States is a 12 in Britain and a 40 in the rest of Europe. Literature from tourism offices typically has sizing conversion charts.

Hit the streets. The most economical and personal way to become acquainted with London and its myriad wonders is to hoof it around town.

Those who enjoy a good trek will be glad to find no less than 60 different walking tours offered weekly in London. These are scheduled morning, afternoon and evening, and varied themes meet the interests of even the pickiest traveler. Among the tour titles are Sherlock Holmes and the Baker Street Beat, Beatles Magical Mystery Tour, Jack the Ripper Haunts, and Shakespeare's and Dickens' London.

Tours generally cost no more than 4 pounds ($6) per person. Among those offering walks are The Original London Walks (in England call 0171-624-3978) and Londoner Pub Walks (0181-883-2656). Check your hotel or the British Travel Centre near Piccadilly Circus for information and brochures on walks, which can be booked with a day's notice or less.

Deals and steals. Shopping in London doesn't have to be expensive. Sales are never better than the big one at Harrods every July, when practically everything is marked down 50 percent or more. Department stores usually discount merchandise 25 to 75 percent at sales in January and June.

Some of the best finds, however, are at markets. Portobello Road's renowned Saturday morning market still has a scattering of good antique deals, but touristy junk has cluttered it somewhat. Pewter flasks, old lithographs and the odd china piece are among finds.

Camden Lock, open daily, is an indoor-outdoor extravaganza with affordable street fashions, artsy African prints, Central American crafts, housewares and pottery. New Caledonian is a huge outdoor antiques market held early on Fridays, attracting many antique dealers. For a listing of markets, check a current issue of *Time Out*, the weekly guide to London.

The London stage. When buying theater tickets, bear in mind that those ticket agencies all over town are quite handy, but service charges are about 10 percent and up. You can skip surcharges by going directly to theater box offices.

Fifty percent savings are found at the Half-Price Ticket Booth on Leicester Square, open noon-2 p.m. for same-day matinees and 2:30-6:30 p.m. for that evening's performances. When I went on a Friday, I was able to buy a 10th-row ticket for that night's "Separate Tables" for about $20, plus a $3.15 service charge. It was my third choice, however. Don't count on getting half-price tickets to hot shows like "Miss Saigon" or "Sunset Boulevard."

And don't buy from "ticket touts" (scalpers). They operate outside the law and may sell counterfeit tickets or overcharge you for seats available at the box office for a better price.

Some of the best things *are* free. Peruse your favorite guidebook or *Time Out* to find free attractions to balance your sightseeing budget.

A fun freebie is Speakers' Corner, a spot in Hyde Park near Marble Arch where Sunday mornings are alive with the entertaining antics of anyone who wishes to take the floor. There's also an endless array of street shows by freewheeling performers in Covent Garden Piazza, where market stalls and sidewalk cafes provide superb people-watching opportunities.

There's no charge, either, to tour the extraordinary British Museum, Museum of Mankind, Victoria & Albert Museum and some other museums.

Hang on to your money. Wear a money belt just under your waistband or sweater for easy access — pickpockets are active. Ask retailers for value-added tax (VAT) return forms. As a tourist, you should be able to get back 14.9 percent of the tax on goods you purchase.

For more help in planning a London vacation, contact the British Tourist Authority, 551 Fifth Ave., Suite 701, New York, NY 10176, (800) 462-2748.
— *June Naylor Rodriguez*

(Prices were calculated at an exchange rate of 1 pound to $1.50. Rates will fluctuate.)

Paris — Franc Facts

Paris can be a pricey city, no doubt, with $50 lunches and $300-a-night hotel rooms not uncommon. Yet a vacationer doesn't have to have a fat pocketbook to enjoy the City of Lights.

You will find good value if you do your homework and develop a money-saving travel style. Staying in smaller hotels, using the subway, walking, and dining in neighborhood bistros can cut your costs while also giving you a closer look at the real city.

Here are franc tips for saving in Paris.

Homework: Start your research by reading budget guidebooks and talking to friends who've recently been to Paris. From the French Government Tourist Office (address at end of this article), request the "French Discovery Guide," which offers general tips, and its listing of Paris hotels.

Also check airline-hotel packages, which often offer accommodations at significant discounts. But be sure to cross-check prices and features to make certain you aren't getting more (or less) than you want. For example, the lowest-priced room on one airline's list of hotel packages is $94 a night, double occupancy, including continental breakfast. It has a private bathroom but no closet; you'll hang your clothes on hooks on the wall.

Getting there: Pack light so you can avoid taking a taxi from the airport to your hotel, a trip that will cost you about 200 francs ($40) from Charles de Gaulle Airport or 150 francs ($30) from Orly Airport. You can cut that cost by more than 50 percent by taking the Air France bus from either Orly (34 francs, about $7) or Charles de Gaulle (51 francs, about $10) airports to a downtown Paris terminal, from which you can get a taxi or subway to your hotel. Or, you can take trains that connect both Paris airports to the city's outstanding public transportation system of subway lines (the Metro) and buses.

Take note!

☛ **Getting around Paris.** Paris is divided into 20 neighborhoods called *arrondissements*; most guidebooks and city maps show their locations. Addresses and directions commonly refer to the *arrondissements*. The last two digits of an establishment's postal code identifies the neighborhood; for example, an address ending in 75008 is in the eighth *arrondissement*.

Lodgings: The French government rates hotels from one to four stars, and all establishments must post room rates. One- and two-star spots are your best budget bets; expect to pay at least 200 francs (about $40) and up for a double room. The average nightly rate for a double room in two-star hotels is 450 francs ($90).

Be specific about what you want, and remember that amenities may not be what you expect at hotels in the United States. A double bed costs less than twin beds, and rooms with showers are cheaper than those with bathtubs. Cheaper yet are those in which the bathroom is down the hall.

The Sorbonne neighborhood is known for its budget accommodations. Students live at some of the hotels during the school year, but during the summer these hotels are looking for guests. Don't hesitate to ask to see a room before you agree to take it.

Some youth hostels accept travelers of all ages, and a few have rooms for couples or families. Contact Hostelling International/American Youth Hostel, 733 15th St. N.W., Suite 840, Washington, DC 20005, (202) 783-6161.

Take note!

☛ **Discount couture.** For haute couture at discounted prices, visit the consignment shops in Paris' tony 16th *arrondissement*, where the wealthy drop off their rarely worn designer duds — Chanel, Valentino and Hermes, to name a few. It's not bargain basement — a $2,000 suit might be priced at $500 — but it's the place to go if you want to splurge on Paris fashion.

Food: When you book your room, ask what the rate is if you exclude breakfast. You often will save money by eating a continental breakfast of coffee and croissant in a small cafe or bakery rather than paying for it with your room at your hotel. If you stand at the bar in a cafe rather than sit at a table, you will save even more on the cost of a meal.

You'll pay less if you eat your main meal at midday rather than in the evening; luncheon menus are lower-priced. Also, a restaurant's set menu is cheaper than ordering a la carte. Dining spots post menus outside, so you can shop for one that delights your palate as well as your wallet. Ethnic cuisine, such as Vietnamese or North African, often costs considerably less.

For a splurge, seek out bistros operated by the city's finest chefs. At these, you can dine well for $40-$50, considerably less than at better-known restaurants operated by the same chefs. For example, Tour d'Argent chef Claude Terrail also runs La Petite Rotisserie du Beaujolais.

Carry-out lunches or dinners offer another way to save. Paris is awash in delicatessens, bakeries and specialty food stores, and you can picnic alfresco with such glorious backdrops as the Tuileries Gardens.

Transportation and sightseeing: Use the city's efficient network of public transportation. An individual ticket on the Metro or bus costs 7.5 francs ($1.50); a *carnet* of 10 tickets at 44 francs (about $9) cuts your per-trip fare — and saves time since you don't have to buy tickets for each trip. Also check about money-saving passes at local tourist offices.

A few museums have "free days," and some reduce prices for students and seniors. One-, three- and five-day *Carte-Musee* passes to 65 museums and monuments cost 70 francs ($14), 140 francs ($28) and 200 francs ($40) respectively; they're available at museums and monuments, tourist offices and main Metro stations. They offer a real bargain if you plan museum-hopping days.

Shopping: If you're a budget traveler planning to upgrade your wardrobe in Paris, you may be disappointed. Streets like Saint-Placide and Alcide are lined with discount stores, but the styles aren't what you'll see in the neighborhoods where Kenzo or Ted Lapidus have set up shop.

As you wander through department stores, prices may stifle your desire to buy. Yet Paris' fabulous street markets and specialty stores are entertaining even if you don't spend a *sou*. If you do spend 1,200 francs ($240) or more at a single store (and have your passport on hand), you're entitled to a value-added tax (VAT) refund of 17.1 percent. Ask a store clerk for the paperwork and details about how to get the refund.

Free sights: Paris offers great people-watching and free sightseeing, including Notre Dame Cathedral and the exquisite plazas outside. You'll find the graves of composer Chopin, chanteuse Edith Piaf, rock star Jim Morrison and dozens of other historic figures at Pere-Lachaise Cemetery. Strolling along the Champs-Elysees, circling the Arc de Triomphe, walking through the Luxembourg Gardens and marveling at the Eiffel Tower from across the Seine won't cost a cent.

Information: French Government Tourist Office, 444 Madison Ave., 16th Floor, New York, NY 10022, (900) 990-0040. (Phone calls cost 50 cents a minute.) — *Marcia Schnedler*

(Prices were calculated at an exchange rate of 5 French francs for $1. Rates will fluctuate.)

Switzerland — Getting Peak Value

It was a glorious day in May, and we were wandering through the Swiss Alps by train. Craggy peaks, like cathedrals of rock, towered overhead. Half-timber cottages dotted sun-dappled valleys. In the lake district near Italy, we picnicked and watched a flock of hang-gliders coasting like eagles on the breeze high above.

Ours was an easy way to enjoy Switzerland's stunning beauty, and it was surprisingly cheap. Rail passes let us forget about buying individual train tickets. Lunch was bread, cheese and fruit purchased at a grocery store before boarding. Even hotels were affordable, though we wandered by whim.

In Lugano, a view of church towers and rooftops descending the steep hillside charmed us into spending the night. For a $2 fee, the hotel service at the station found us a double room, with bath and breakfast. The Hotel Dischma, an unassuming place wedged into a row of modern apartment blocks, was an 80-cent bus ride away. May tourism was light, so we found ourselves in a prime top-floor room, whose balcony revealed a sweeping view of Lugano's shimmering lake and cool peaks — all for only $70 a night.

Switzerland has a reputation for being beautiful, charming, friendly — and expensive. But a few simple rules — and occasional luck — can help you enjoy the charm while spending fewer dollars than you expected to pay.

Getting around: By all means, use the trains. Switzerland's rail system is among the best in the world — clean, easy-to-use, punctual — and it's also the country's best tourist bargain.

Prepaid passes save money if you plan to ride the trains a lot; they also save time standing in ticket lines and changing money. Use Eurailpass if you expect to travel long distances and visit other countries. For Switzerland only, you're better off buying a Swiss Pass.

Second-class travel is the better deal, unless you particularly need the comfort of first-class cars. You can get eight continuous days of second-class travel for $220 (or $27.50 per day) vs. $316 ($39.50 per day) for a first-class pass. A 15-day second-class pass costs $256 (or $17.67 per day) vs. $368 ($24.53 a day) in first class. Four-day and one-month passes also are available. A Swiss Flexipass good for any three days of travel within a 15-day period is $176 for second class vs. $264 for first class.

> **Take note!**
> ☞ **Stay on a farm.** "Swiss Farm Holidays," a brochure from the Swiss National Tourist Office (212-757-5944), lists family-owned farms that welcome guests. You can help out with the chores or relax and enjoy the countryside.

A Swiss Pass covers travel on the entire national train system (including such scenic tours as the Glacier Express), most private railroads, lake steamers and postal buses, which go to smaller places that have no rail connections. You also get 25 percent off the price of mountaintop excursions. In addition, you'll ride free on buses and streetcars in 30 Swiss cities.

Buy a Swiss Pass from your travel agent or Rail Europe, (800) TGV-RAIL, before your departure. If you are traveling with children, ask about a Family Card, which lets parents using a Swiss Pass take children under age 16 on trains for free.

Trains are a good deal for more limited trips, too. A cab ride from the airport into Zurich can cost 35 Swiss francs (about $28) or more. Instead, go by rail to Zurich's main station for only 5 Swiss francs, (about $4).

Think small: No slight to the big cities, but Switzerland's beauty and charm are found in its smaller places.

Stein-am-Rhein, for example, lies only 30 minutes by train northeast from Zurich Airport, but the atmosphere is quiet and peaceful instead of big and bustling. At the Hotel Rheinfels (170 francs, $138, double, including breakfast and service charges), a charming 32-bed inn overlooking the Rhine River, the rooms were old-fashioned, with exposed beams and thick casement windows, and the floors creaked with age when we explored the antique-filled hallways. The hotel dining room featured fish at a pricey $20 per person, but the nearby Badstube restaurant had a hefty bratwurst plate for $12.

Sightseeing was only a few steps away — the St. George monastery, built in the Middle Ages; the city gates; and the town square, with half-timber houses whose facades are painted with scenes of medieval life.

Here, as in other small towns, you may pay 40 percent less for a room than in the big Swiss cities.

When you do visit the cities, you'll find that smaller, simpler lodgings give better value. For instance, in Basel, a charming and culturally rich old city, the five-star Basel Hilton with its many amenities charges 310-435 francs (about $252-$354) a night for a double room. Three-star alternatives average 280-290 francs ($228-$236) a night, and two-star hotels cost 210 francs ($171) or less a night — cheaper if you don't mind a bathroom down the hall. There is some overlapping of prices between categories.

If you're a plan-ahead traveler, question your travel agent about money-saving packages that are sometimes unadvertised. If you like to wing it, go to the hotel-booking office at the train station to find a room.

If you're staying a week or more, consider renting an apartment, chalet or villa (the Swiss National Tourist Office has listings of rental agencies). You can have the added fun of exploring shops and markets for fresh bread, produce and other foods to cook at "home." If you pick a central location, you can use it as a base for day-tripping all over the country on your Swiss Pass.

Short visits can be fun. We once made a two-hour visit to Lucerne — enjoying the views of city and mountains on a lakeside walk before lunch — then got back on the train and went elsewhere. It cost us $2 for a locker at the station, about $6 each for lunch. Brief as it was, the visit was a highlight of our trip — something we still fondly talk about years later.

Try to plan your trip outside the expensive and crowded July-August tourist season. Switzerland is pleasant, if cooler, up to late October — and you won't have to compete for bargain lodgings. The same is true in May and June.

Dining out: As anywhere, the fancier the restaurant, the higher the bill. The same goes for food served where tourists congregate. So seek out the small restaurants where locals go, and order local specialties. In German-speaking areas, that might be a bratwurst or *bauernwurst* platter for about $12; in the Italian canton, it could be spaghetti Bolognese or pesto for $8-$10.

Take note!

☛ **Swiss specialties.** Don't miss an opportunity to try popular Swiss dishes. These include fondue and *raclette* (melted cheese dishes), *rosti* (fried potatoes) and *bundnerfleisch* (air-dried beef sliced paper thin).

Skip expensive liquor and champagne in favor of local beer or wine, preferably from the tap.

In some restaurants, the best deal is the *prix fixe*, often referred to as the tourist menu, which may include appetizer, salad, main course and dessert. But why pay for all that food if you only want soup? Don't order what you won't eat.

Breakfast often is included in the price of a hotel room. You can lunch cheaply alfresco, with bread, cheese, sausage and fruit from a grocery store. Or try Migros, a chain of department/grocery stores with cafeterias that serve meals for $6-$12; these close at 6:30 p.m.

Shopping: After browsing the main shopping areas of Geneva and Basel, the Bahnhofstrasse in Zurich and the narrow, winding streets of Lucerne, I am convinced Switzerland is no place for bargain shopping. Prices on watches, clothing and antiques can be astronomical.

Still, there are some ways to save. Swiss Army knives are about 20 percent less than at home and much cheaper than in other European cities. Same for Swiss-made Bally shoes. U.S. discount outlets may have lower prices, but the selection may not be as good. If you really want that Rolex watch, shop at home first, then compare — you might save.

One thing you can expect is high-quality merchandise, especially on locally made goods. Visit the Swiss craft shops ("Schweizer Heimatwerk") to buy linen, embroidery, fine handkerchiefs, textiles, music boxes, wood carvings, ceramics, toys, dolls and other handmade items. For Swiss chocolates, drool over the fancy confectionery shops but buy at grocery stores.

For clothes, savvy shoppers avoid specialty shops and hit the department stores. Look for *Action* (sale) signs.

You can apply for a refund on the 6.1 percent value-added tax levied on items above 500 Swiss francs (about $407), but you must do so before leaving the country; ask how to obtain it at the time of purchase.

Tipping: "Don't overtip," a Swiss tourism official advises. Service charges are included in all hotel and restaurant bills as well as taxi fares and hairdresser fees. You're welcome to tip more, but it isn't necessary or expected. One exception: Tip the hotel porter up to 2 Swiss francs per bag.

Senior discounts: About 450 hotels offer lower rates to men age 65 or older and women above age 62, either all year or during specific "off-season" periods specified by each lodging. Many offer transfers from the train station and meal plans, too. Ask for the discount when reserving, then show your passport or ID card at check-in. Participating hotels are listed in the Swiss National Tourist Office publication "Season for Seniors."

Museums and other attractions have no official senior discounts, but it doesn't hurt to ask about reduced rates. Bring your AARP card or other ID and give it a try. Some museums offer free admission on Sundays.

Information: Swiss National Tourist Office, 608 Fifth Ave., New York, NY 10020, (212) 757-5944. — *Stephen Morgan*

(Prices were calculated at an exchange rate of 1.23 Swiss francs to $1. Rates will fluctuate.)

CHAPTER 31

Getting Information

European tourist offices in the United States offer numerous brochures to help plan a trip. Call or write these offices for free material on hotels, sightseeing, dining and shopping. Many also have guides geared specifically toward budget-oriented travel.

For one-stop information on 26 European countries, request the free, color guide "Planning Your Trip to Europe," from European Planner, P.O. Box 1754, New York, NY 10185.

Country	Information number	Address
Austria	212-944-6880	P.O. Box 1142, New York, NY 10108-1142
	310-477-3332	P.O. Box 491938, Los Angeles, CA 90049-5141
Belgium	212-758-8130	780 Third Ave., Suite 1501, New York, NY 10017
Britain	800-462-2748	551 Fifth Ave., Suite 701, New York, NY 10176-0799
	212-986-2200 (When in NYC)	625 N. Michigan Ave., Suite 1510, Chicago, IL 60611-1977
Cyprus	212-683-5280	13 E. 40th St., New York, NY 10016
Denmark	212-949-2333	655 Third Ave., Suite 1810, New York, NY 10017-5617
Finland	212-949-2333	655 Third Ave., Suite 1810, New York, NY 10017-5617
France	900-990-0040*	444 Madison Ave., 16th Floor, New York, NY 10022
		676 N. Michigan Ave., Chicago, IL 60611-2819
		9454 Wilshire Blvd., Suite 303, Beverly Hills, CA 90212
Germany	212-661-7200	122 E. 42nd St., 52nd Floor, New York, NY 10168-0072
	310-575-9799	11766 Wilshire Blvd., Suite 750, Los Angeles, CA 90025
Greece	212-421-5777	645 Fifth Ave., New York, NY 10022
	312-782-1084	168 N. Michigan Ave., Suite 600, Chicago, IL 60601
	213-626-6696	611 W. Sixth St., Suite 2198, Los Angeles, CA 90017

* 50 cents per minute, available weekdays.

Country	Information number	Address
Holland	312-819-0300	355 Lexington Ave., 21st Floor, New York, NY 10017
		225 N. Michigan Ave., Suite 326, Chicago, IL 60601
		9841 Airport Blvd., Los Angeles, CA 90045
Hungary	212-355-0240	150 E. 58th St., 33rd Floor, New York, NY 10155
Iceland	212-949-2333	655 Third Ave., Suite 1810, New York, NY 10017-5617
Ireland	212-418-0800	345 Park Ave., New York, NY 10154
Italy	212-245-4822	630 Fifth Ave., Suite 1565, New York, NY 10111
	312-644-0990	401 N. Michigan Ave., Suite 3030, Chicago, IL 60611
	310-820-0098	12400 Wilshire Blvd., Suite 550, Los Angeles, CA 90025
Luxembourg	212-935-8888	17 Beekman Place, New York, NY 10022
Malta	212-695-9520	350 Fifth Ave., Suite 4412, New York, NY 10118
Monaco	800-753-9696	845 Third Ave., 19th Floor, New York, NY 10022
Norway	212-949-2333	655 Third Ave., Suite 1810, New York, NY 10017-5617
Portugal	212-354-4403	590 Fifth Ave., New York, NY 10036
Spain	212-759-8822	665 Fifth Ave., New York, NY 10022
	312-642-1992	845 N. Michigan Ave., Suite 915 East, Chicago, IL 60611
	213-658-7188	8383 Wilshire Blvd., Suite 960, Beverly Hills, CA 90211
	305-358-1992	1221 Brickell Ave., Suite 1850, Miami, FL 33131
Sweden	212-949-2333	655 Third Ave., Suite 1810, New York, NY 10017-5617
Switzerland	212-757-5944	608 Fifth Ave., New York, NY 10020
	312-630-5840	150 N. Michigan Ave., Suite 2930, Chicago, IL 60601
	310-335-5980	222 N. Sepulveda Blvd., Suite 1570, El Segundo, CA 90245
Turkey	212-687-2194	821 U. N. Plaza, New York, NY 10017
	202-429-9844	1717 Massachusetts Ave. N.W., Suite 306, Washington, DC 20036

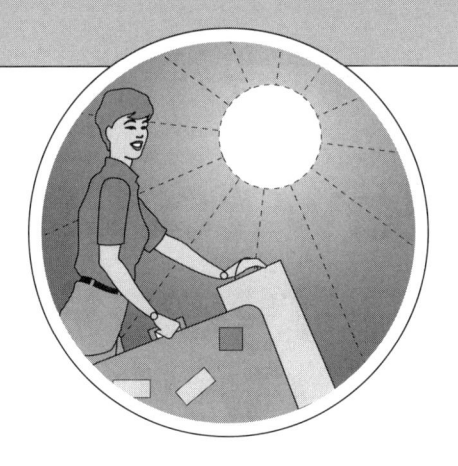

Savings For Singles

Most people accustomed to traveling alone are all too familiar with the dreaded single supplement. If you go solo, you pay a premium — the accepted standard for organized group travel. There are ways, however, to cut or even avoid these higher tabs, and the following chapter will put you on track for these savings.

CHAPTER 32

How to Cut Surcharges When You Go Solo

While the independent traveler who chooses to fly and/or drive solo on vacation rarely runs into any surcharge, those who want to take a tour or cruise almost always will be hit with a single supplement.

Most cruise lines and tour operators charge solo travelers 125 to 200 percent of the per-person, double-occupancy rate, on the theory that with a single occupant they're getting only half the normal amount of return.

Some lines and tour operators, however, offer money-saving, roommate-matching programs that pair individuals traveling alone with others of the same sex in order to eliminate the single supplement.

Cruising for Less

There are several ways to avoid a high single supplement on the seas.

A number of cruise lines offer to match you with a roommate. Some lines with room-share programs — Royal Caribbean Cruises Ltd., Princess Cruises, Holland America Line and Carnival Cruise Lines, for example — guarantee the per-person, double-occupancy fare if you sign up to share a cabin but they can't find a roommate. However, on the share program, you don't get a cabin assignment until the date of sailing. You could end up with the worst — or one of the best — cabins.

Some cruise lines have other alternatives. For example, in addition to a share program, Royal Caribbean Cruises Ltd. allows passengers to book a guaranteed single-occupancy fare. RCCL normally charges singles 150 percent of the per-person, double-occupancy rate but cuts that to 115 to 135 percent on the guaranteed single-occupancy rate. The kicker is that you won't know your cabin assignment until the sailing date. All discounted or guaranteed single rates are restricted to specific room categories.

> ### Take note!
> ☞ **Table for one.** Many solo travelers are more comfortable in a restaurant with a smaller, less formal dining room. Also look for cafes with outdoor terraces or small tables grouped closely together. In such settings, solo travelers can feel comfortable and often are drawn easily into conversations at adjoining tables.

Some ships also have single cabins at single rates. Royal Cruise Line and Cunard are among the lines with such cabins. Don't expect the single fare to be the lowest price on the ship, however. Single cabins often are in the midpriced to upper midpriced range. While the single-cabin rate usually runs more than the per-person, double-occupancy rate in the same category, it's not as much as a single supplement.

Another way for singles to save on cruises is through a singles' tour operator that organizes a group to sail. (See below.)

Singles Tours

For tours, solo travelers can check out a number of options. Some tour operators specialize in serving singles. Their pricing policies vary. Some do not charge any single supplement, but always ask if you will have a room by yourself or be sharing with someone. On many tours, particularly adventure trips, you may have to share a room because of the limited lodging available at some sites. Other companies may have a single supplement but offer to match those who want to share a room and guarantee the low rate even if they cannot find a roommate.

Take note!

☞ **Know your hotel's location.** In large, unfamiliar cities, write down the name and address of your hotel and mark the location on a street map to carry with you. If you get lost, the map will help others give you proper directions. Having a map is particularly helpful in foreign destinations where communication may be difficult.

Other tour options are companies that attract many singles and operators that target certain departures of their regular itineraries for singles.

Here's a sampling of tour operators that either specialize in singles trips or attract many solo vacationers:

One of the long-established organizers is **Solo Flights**, 10 Greenwood Lane, Westport, CT 06880, (800) 266-1566 or (203) 256-1235. This 22-year-old company works with other tour operators and also designs its own trips. Recent tours have included a jaunt to Costa Rica, a Delta Queen Steamboat Co. cruise on the Mississippi River and a New Year's vacation in London. The company also produces a free newsletter three to four times a year. **Mature Tours**, a new division of Solo Flights, specializes in single travel for "youthful spirits over 50."

For single travelers interested in a culinary theme, **Single Gourmet**, 133 E. 58th St., New York, NY 10022, (212) 980-8788, provides focused retreats on fine dining around the world. Destinations include England, France, Italy, Australia, California's Napa Valley and the Spoleto Festival in Charleston, SC.

Two large tour operators specializing in trips for travelers age 50 and beyond draw many singles. They are **Grand Circle Travel**, 347 Congress St., Boston, MA 02210, (800) 221-2610, which waives the single supplement on some trips on certain dates; and **Saga Holidays**, 222 Berkeley St., Boston, MA 02116, (800) 343-0273.

Finding a Travel Companion

If you're searching for a traveling companion who will share your travel interests and help you avoid the single supplement, look toward the following independent agencies whose business is pairing solo travelers. Each of these groups offers a newsletter for members to exchange profiles and correspondence.

Travel Companion Exchange, P.O. Box 833, Amityville, NY 11701, (800) 392-1256, is one of the largest and oldest in the business, with approximately 2,500 members. Six times a year it publishes *Travel Companions*, a thick newsletter that typically runs about 48 pages; half its content contains editorial about single travel, while the other half has listings of people seeking travel companions. A membership that includes the newsletter and the opportunity to place or answer ads is $99 for six months (plus two months free). Members automatically get six previous issues when they enroll. A one-year subscription to the newsletter without companion listings is $48, and a sample issue is $5.

> **Take note!**
> ☛ **Hotel safety.** At your hotel, never open your door to anyone without identifying them first, by looking through the peephole, by asking the name and, in the case of hotel personnel, by verifying the name with the front desk.

Another roommate matching service is **Travel in Two's**, 239 N. Broadway, North Tarrytown, NY 10591, (914) 631-8301. Its lifetime membership fee is $10 and a quarterly newsletter with updated tour listings costs $15 a year.

Partners-in-Travel, 11660 Chenault St., Suite 119, Los Angeles, CA 90049, (310) 476-4869, also pairs travel companions. For a $25 annual fee, members receive a packet that contains a directory profiling singles looking for travel companions, information on single travel and a list of tour operators that offer "singles-friendly" trips.

Tours for Women

Two services offer tours for women. They are: **Shared Adventures**, 420 W. 75th St., Downers Grove, IL 60516, (708) 852-5533; and **Rainbow Adventures**, 15033 Kelly Canyon Road, Bozeman, MT 59715, (800) 804-8686.

Both are run by travel agencies that specialize in women's tours and matching female companions. On Rainbow Adventures tours, roommates are rotated; each participant gets a new roommate at each stop on the trip.

Guide to Senior Discounts

If you're past age 50, don't be embarrassed to tell your age. It can earn you a wide array of travel discounts, which increase in number as you get older. The following guide will acquaint you with the savings available from airlines, hotels and others in the travel industry.

CHAPTER 33

Senior Airline Discounts

Beyond the ordinary airfare discounts available to all travelers, seniors have some special money-saving options when they fly.

Most major airlines and many regional carriers offer some form of senior discount — a set percentage off the fare, a special senior rate or coupon books, which reduce the cost of flights. Participating airlines usually offer no more than two of the options.

While each plan provides discounts, each also carries caveats for buyers. Travelers need to look carefully at all the programs to see which best serves their needs.

While seniors may earn other travel discounts as early as age 50, airlines are stricter about the minimum age. Some allow the discounts when travelers reach age 60, but most restrict the savings to those age 62 or older. Seniors should always travel with some proof of age, such as a driver's license or passport.

A recent survey of about 50 domestic and international airlines showed that about half offer senior discount programs and that U.S. carriers lead the way. Other than major airlines serving Canada, Mexico and Europe from the United States, few international carriers have senior discounts.

Here's a look at the pros and cons of each of the senior savings plans, starting with the most widespread program.

Take note!

☞ **Special meals.** If you have special dietary needs, most airlines can accommodate you if you give them at least 24 hours' notice. Many offer vegetarian, kosher, low-fat, low-salt and diabetic meals. Advise the reservations agent of your request at booking and reconfirm 48 hours ahead of flight.

Senior Rate Discounts

Most U.S. and some foreign airlines offer a 10 percent discount off their regularly available published fares — first class, business class, coach and excursion fares. Some also allow the discount off promotional fares, the super-low ones that are announced unexpectedly and are available only for a specific period of time. On some airlines, discounts may not be available on selected routes.

The discount provides a savings when lower fares aren't available or your travel plans don't qualify you for them. On international fares, the savings could be significant. In this age of airfare wars, though, there's frequently a promotion that will beat the 10 percent discount off a regular fare.

Many airlines allow a companion to fly at the same 10 percent discount. Required ages for companions may vary, but many airlines accept a second traveler of any age. Use the companion fare when it can cut costs for others traveling with you. For instance, if both spouses qualify for the senior discount, each can take along a companion, thereby cutting fares for two friends or additional family members making the trip.

You can request the senior discount or fare when you make reservations by phone. Simply advise the booking agent that you qualify for the discount. If tickets are purchased at the airport, proof of age — a driver's license for domestic travel or a passport for international travel — is required at time of ticketing. Otherwise, proof of age may be required at time of check-in or boarding.

> **Take note!**
> ☞ **Avoid jet lag.** To minimize jet lag, avoid caffeine and alcohol during the flight. Eat light upon arrival; heavy, greasy meals can overwork your digestive system and keep you awake. Don't try to sleep off jet lag at your destination; if you must nap, keep it to an hour or less.

Senior Fares

Though not as widely available as other discounts, senior fares do offer some excellent deals. Seven carriers — four of them international — have senior fares. America West Airlines, Hawaiian Air and Southwest Airlines offer such fares on domestic flights. Air France, Swissair and TAP Air Portugal offer reduced senior fares within Europe. Some are seasonal promotions while others are available year-round. When flying within Europe, be sure to ask about the fare when making reservations. El Al Israel offers senior fares on all flights from the United States to Israel and selected markets beyond.

Domestically, Southwest Airlines, a carrier that concentrates on the Southwest but serves 23 states from coast to coast, offers senior fares year-round. These are at an even greater savings than its regular fares, which are traditionally lower than those of major carriers. Plus, its senior fares come without restrictions. For example, a standard round-trip fare with Southwest from Houston to Phoenix is $488 on weekdays, $428 on weekends. A 21-day advance-purchase ticket is $238. The senior fare is only $198, a savings of $230-$290 over the lowest regular fares. Southwest's senior fare tickets are refundable and transferable.

Hawaiian Air, which flies mainly in the Hawaiian islands, offers senior fares seasonally.

If offered, the senior fares are usually the cheapest you can buy outside special promotions. However, the fares may not be available at all times or in all markets, and airlines may restrict the number of seats per flight.

Coupon Books

Nine airlines sell coupon books, all requiring seniors to be age 62 or older to qualify. Most books are sold with four or sometimes eight coupons, each for a one-way flight. A round trip usually requires two coupons, but some airlines require two coupons each way on longer flights, such as to Hawaii or Alaska.

Airline Senior Discounts

For those who meet the age requirements, many airlines offer a 10 percent discount off regularly available published fares and sometimes off special promotional fares. Some airlines have specific senior fares, which may not be as low as other

Airline	Minimum age	Discount off fares
Aerolineas Argentinas	60	10%
Aeromexico	62	10%
Air Canada	60	10%
Air France	62	10%/Senior fares[2]
Alaska	62	10%
America West	62	10%/Senior fares
American	62	10%
British Airways	60	10%
BWIA	62	10%[3]
Canadian	60	10%
Cayman	62	10%[4]
Continental	62	10%
Delta	62	10%
El Al Israel	60	Senior fares
Hawaiian Air	60	10%/20%/Senior fares
KIWI	62	10%
Lufthansa	62	10%[7]
Mexicana	62	10%
Northwest	62	10%
Southwest	65	Senior fares
Swissair	62/60	10%/Senior fares[8]
TAP Air Portugal	62	10%/Senior fares[10]
TWA	62	10%
United	62	10%
USAir	62	10%
Virgin Atlantic	60	10%

[1]Houston residents dial 939-0077. [2]10% discount from U.S. to Europe; senior fares in Europe, with minimum age 60 or 65, depending on destination. [3]Discount on flights from U.S. and Canada only. [4]Discount not valid on connecting flights with other carriers. [5]10% discount to Hawaii; 20% discount to South Pacific; no discount on inter-island fares; senior fares available at some times. [6]Companion program not available on South Pacific flights

discounted fares. Some carriers allow a companion to fly at the discount also; N/A in the chart means a companion program is not available from that airline. For more information about the individual air carriers and their programs, see "Senior Discount Carriers" in text.

Companion age	International availability	Reservations
N/A	Yes	800-333-0276
N/A	Yes	800-237-6639[1]
Any age	Yes	800-776-3000
N/A	Yes	800-237-2747
Any age	Yes	800-426-0333
Any age	Yes	800-235-9292
Any age	Yes	800-433-7300
Any age	Yes	800-247-9297
Any age	Yes	800-327-7401
Any age	Yes	800-426-7000
Any age	Yes	800-441-3003
Any age	Yes	800-525-0280
Any age	Yes	800-221-1212
55	Yes	800-223-6700
Any age[6]	Yes	800-367-5320
Any age	Yes	800-538-5494
Any age	Yes	800-645-3880
Any age	Yes	800-531-7921
Any age	Yes	800-225-2525
N/A	No	800-435-9792
Any age[9]	Yes	800-221-4750
Any age	Yes	800-221-7370
Any age	Yes	800-221-2000
Any age	Yes	800-241-6522
Any age	Yes	800-428-4322
Any age	Yes	800-862-8621

[7]Discount on flights to Europe only. [8]10% discount at age 62 from U.S. to Europe; 10-15% discount or senior fares in Europe, some at age 60. [9]Companion program not available on flights in Europe. [10]10% discount from U.S. to Europe.

The coupons are good for one year from issue date and may be used only by the purchaser.

Coupons are a hedge against rising airfares since they lock in a rate for one year. Also, they can provide dramatic savings to travelers who take longer flights, such as from coast to coast.

Currently, prices for the four-coupon books range from $495 to $596 (the latter the most common price). Three carriers also have books of eight coupons, ranging from $920 to $1,032. The four-coupon books yield a round trip on the Mainland for $248 to $298, while eight-coupon books cut the round-trip cost to $230 to $258. The eight-coupon book always has netted the lower round-trip cost to the consumer, though it's a more costly outlay and is only for those who know they will use all the coupons within a year. Kiwi offers six coupons for $660, making one round trip $220, the lowest fare for all the coupon books. Kiwi has limited service in the eastern half of the country.

While a good buy, the coupon books aren't always the best bargain. Frequent airfare wars sometimes offer tickets for less than the average fare using coupons,

Airline Coupons

The following airlines sell books of one-way flight coupons to passengers age 62 and beyond. Coupons are valid for one year from issue and, in most cases, for U.S. travel only. America West and TWA restrict travel times. America West, Continental and TWA have blackout dates. United has blackout dates for Hawaii only. Most airlines require reservations 14 days in advance, and some may limit the number of seats available per flight. Direct senior reservations phone number, if available, or regular reservations number is provided. Prices are subject to change.

Airline	Coupons	Information
America West	4 for $495	800-235-9292
	8 for $920	
American[1]	4 for $596	800-237-7981
Continental[2]	4 for $579	800-248-8996
	8 for $999	
Delta[3]	4 for $596	800-221-1212
KIWI[4]	6 for $660	800-538-5494
Northwest[3]	4 for $596	800-225-2525
TWA[1]	4 for $548[5]	800-221-2000
	8 for $1,032	
United[1]	4 for $596	800-633-6563
USAir	4 for $596	800-428-4322

[1] Two coupons each way to Hawaii. [2] Two coupons each way to Hawaii, Alaska, Mexico and the Caribbean. [3] Two coupons each way to Hawaii and Alaska. [4] Requires seven-day advance reservations. [5] TWA offers a four-coupon book for companions of any age who travel with a qualifying senior; the cost is $648.

particularly for shorter flights.

There are some drawbacks with the coupons. Getting the books and exchanging coupons for tickets can be time-consuming. You must be flexible with travel plans because some airlines restrict the number of seats available using the coupons. In some cases, you may have to travel earlier or later than you wish, thus incurring more lodging and meal expenses and negating some of your airfare savings.

When is a coupon book worth buying? It serves you best when you want to make long-distance trips. The longer distance you go on each trip, the greater your savings off regular fares. Short hops offer less of a savings with coupon books but still can be a good value.

Here are examples of the savings with coupons:

At press time, using a Continental coupon book, you could fly between Los Angeles and New York for a savings up to 38 percent off the lowest available fare. The least expensive fare was $404 round-trip for a 14-day advance-purchase ticket. The round trip was only $250 with an eight-coupon book, or $290 with a four-coupon book, a savings of $154 or $114 respectively.

But the savings dropped for a shorter trip. Between Dallas and Denver, for instance, the fare was $373 round-trip on a 14-day advance purchase ticket. The savings was $123 with an eight-coupon book, $83 with a four-coupon book.

You can order a coupon book through a travel agent or specific airline. While airlines may mail the coupon books to you, agents may send a voucher, which you must present at an airline ticketing office or an airport ticket counter to receive the coupons. Allow time for issuance — coupons are similar to traveler's checks, requiring your signature on each one and carrying identifying numbers.

Make reservations by the required number of days ahead of flight. Exchange coupon(s) for tickets via mail (risky) or at an airline ticket counter. It's safer to arrange ticketing a day or more before flying. You can exchange your coupon(s) for a ticket just prior to a flight, but if doing this, plan to arrive at the airport at least two hours early to allow needed time. If you are late, you run the risk of being bumped because you are not ticketed.

How do you decide which coupon book to buy? Here are some tips to help make a decision:

● Consider where you want to travel within the next year and how many trips you are likely to make.

Seniors frequently use the coupon books for both vacations and visiting friends and family — elderly parents, children or grandchildren — around the country.

If you live in the Midwest or along the East Coast and are planning a trip to Hawaii, consider buying a four-coupon book for that one trip. In most cases, you'll have to use two coupons each way, but the price of a four-coupon book likely will beat the lowest excursion fares available to the islands.

● See which airline coupon book best serves you.

Once you have a list of desired destinations, check the airlines that serve your local airport to see which flies to all of those destinations. If no single carrier has service from your airport to all of the spots, then you may be wasting money buying the coupon book.

● Ask about an airline's routing to your destinations. Be sure the routing is convenient, preferably without time-consuming layovers or connections that take you out of your way. For instance, to fly from Los Angeles to Seattle on Continental Airlines, you have to fly via a connection in Houston, making your trip more than twice as long as necessary.

● Determine all the restrictions that apply before buying the coupons.

Don't count on using your coupons to fly to see family over the Christmas holidays. All the airlines have blackout dates, particularly during holidays. If you can be flexible about your flight dates, you might find a window to go sometime during the holidays, but you won't be able to fly at peak times. (Christmas Day itself sometimes is open.) Some airlines have only a few blackout dates, while others have an extensive list of dates. Some airlines also restrict the days of the week that you may travel and the flights you can book.

● Don't count on being able to use your coupons on flights timed to meet a South Florida cruise. Saturday and Sunday morning inbound flights to Miami and Fort Lauderdale and Saturday and Sunday afternoon outbound flights from those airports will likely be unavailable to coupon holders.

● Ask what protection you have if a carrier stops serving your home city. You might have to fly or drive hundreds of miles to another airport to start your trip using your coupons.

● Ask if a carrier is in bankruptcy proceedings and if so, determine what protection you have if the airline stops flying when you still have valid coupons. If a carrier is bought out, it's likely that valid coupons would be honored, at least for a period of time; but if a carrier goes out of business, there's no guarantee that other airlines would honor the coupons.

Once you've decided on a coupon plan, here are some tips to get the most for your money:

● Have trips planned when you buy the coupons.

The clock starts ticking on your yearlong validity when you purchase the coupons at the ticket counter, not with the first flight. When buying eight coupons, it's particularly important not to waste any time using them. You must have the coupon book before making your reservation, and reservations in most cases must be made 14 days in advance of your flight.

● Always watch for special promotional fares that may beat your coupon rate.

Check for the lowest available fare in the market before you decide to use your coupons. If there's a lower fare, don't waste your coupons unless you're afraid they will expire unused. Use them to reap the highest savings.

Other Programs

A few years ago, three airlines offered 12-month passes, good for as many as 52 flights a year. Today, only Continental Airlines still has passes, but with numerous restrictions.

The Freedom Passport, good for travel on the Mainland and to the U.S. Virgin Islands, costs $1,999 ($3,499 first class). A four-month Freedom

Passport is $999. The Global Passport, good on the Mainland and to the Caribbean, Hawaii, Alaska and Continental's international destinations, costs $4,499 ($6,999 first class).

You must be age 62, and travel is permitted only between noon Monday and noon Thursday and all day Saturday. A passport holder may take a one-way trip per calendar week; a Saturday stayover is required between trips. Travel to any specific destination (other than the home gateway) is allowed a maximum of three times.

There are numerous blackout dates spread over eight months, including all the major holidays. Seating is limited for passport holders and may not be available on every flight.

The Global Passport restricts the number of international flights (all round trips) to: two trips to Canada; two to Mexico; two to the Caribbean; one to Central America; one to Hawaii; one to Alaska; one to Europe; one to the South Pacific. Flights are also restricted to specific cities within those destinations.

If the international pass is more than you will use, you can buy the domestic pass and purchase international add-ons for $250-$600 per round trip, depending on location.

Continental also allows a travel companion of any age to buy a passport at the same price.

For frequent fliers, a passport can be a bargain, allowing as many as 26 round trips for only $77 each. You'd still be getting a good price if you flew one round trip a month, which would average out to $167 each trip.

However, their restrictions are extensive; it might be hard to take full advantage of your investment. If you purchase a first-class passport and there

Airline Passes

Continental Airlines offers four-month and 12-month passes to vacationers 62 and older and companions of any age. Travel times may be restricted, and seats are limited. Blackouts apply. Passes do not earn frequent-flier miles.

Airline	Cost	International destination	Information
Continental			
Freedom Passport[1]			
4-month	$999	No	800-441-1135
12-month	$1,999		
First class	$3,499		
Global Passport[2]	$4,499	Yes	800-441-1135
First class	$6,999		

[1] Mainland U.S. and U.S. Virgin Islands; low-cost international add-ons available. [2] Mainland U.S., plus Alaska, Hawaii, Mexico, Canada, Caribbean, Central America, Europe and the Pacific.

are no seats available in first class, you may fly in coach but there is no refund for the difference in pricing. Continental will provide a refund if service to your home gateway has been cancelled but not if service has been cancelled or suspended to any of your desired destination cities.

Senior Discount Carriers

Here is a roundup of U.S. and foreign carriers that have senior discount programs, with explanations and supplemental data for the chart and tables, as needed. The main reservations number is provided here. If airlines have special phone numbers for senior coupon books, these are listed in the coupon table. Restrictions and blackout dates apply only if noted. Refer to the chart and tables as noted for age criteria, costs and other specifics.

Aerolineas Argentinas: Flights to South America. Offers 10% discount. See discount chart. (800) 333-0276.

Aeromexico: Flights to Mexico. Offers 10% discount. See discount chart. (800) 237-6639 or, in Houston, 939-0077.

Air Canada: Flights to Canada. Offers 10% discount to both U.S. and Canadian citizens; no restrictions on travel during any day of the week or length of stay. See discount chart. (800) 776-3000.

Air France: Flights to Europe and beyond. Offers 10% discount on flights from U.S. to Europe and senior fares within Europe. See discount chart. (800) 237-2747.

Alaska: Flights to seven Western states, Canada and Mexico. Offers 10% discount. See discount chart. (800) 426-0333.

America West: Flights throughout North America. Offers 10% discount on most flights; check specific markets. See discount chart and coupon table. (800) 235-9292.

American: Flights throughout North America and internationally. Offers 10% discount and coupon books, good for flights between noon Monday and noon Thursday and all day Saturday. See discount chart and coupon table. (800) 433-7300.

British Airways: Flights from the United States to London, then to destinations worldwide. Offers 10% discount, and tickets are refundable for seniors. See discount chart. (800) 247-9297.

BWIA: (British West Indies Airways) Flights to and within the Caribbean. Offers 10% discount on flights originating from United States or Canada only. See discount chart. (800) 327-7401.

Canadian: Flights to Canada. Offers 10% discount. See discount chart. (800) 426-7000.

Cayman: Flights from Miami, Tampa, Atlanta and Houston to the Cayman Islands and Jamaica. Offers 10% discount (not good on connecting flights with other carriers). See discount chart. (800) 441-3003.

Continental: Flights throughout North America and internationally. Offers 10% discount, senior coupons and passes. Both coupons and passes have blackout dates over eight months, including major holidays and spring-break times. Extensive restrictions apply to use of passes; see text for more information. See discount chart, coupon table and pass table. (800) 525-0280.

Delta: Flights throughout North America and internationally. Offers 10% discount and has coupon books. Seating limited per flight with coupons. See discount chart and coupon table. (800) 221-1212.

El Al Israel: Flights to Israel and beyond. Offers senior fares to Israel and selected markets beyond. See discount chart. (800) 223-6700.

Hawaiian Air: Flights to Hawaii and South Pacific. Offers 10% discount on flights to Hawaii, 20% discount to South Pacific and senior fares sometimes. No senior discount available on inter-island travel. See discount chart. (800) 367-5320.

KIWI: Flights to scattered East Coast destinations, Chicago and Bermuda. Offers 10% discount and coupon books. See discount chart and coupon table. (800) 538-5494.

Lufthansa: Flights to Europe and beyond. Offers 10% discount only from U.S. to Europe. See discount chart. (800) 645-3880.

Mexicana: Flights to Mexico and beyond. Offers 10% discount off full coach fare only. See discount chart. (800) 531-7921.

Northwest: Flights throughout North America and internationally. Offers 10% discount and coupon books with limited seating per flight; standby travel permitted. See discount chart and coupon table. (800) 225-2525.

Southwest: Flights to 23 states mainly in the Southwest and West with limited destinations in the East. Offers senior fares. Tickets are refundable and transferable, but there is limited seating per flight. See discount chart. (800) 435-9792.

Swissair: Flights to Europe and beyond. Offers 10% discount from U.S. to Europe; various discounts and senior fares available within Europe. See discount chart. (800) 221-4750.

TAP Air Portugal: Flights to Portugal and beyond. Offers 10% discount only on trans-Atlantic flights; senior fares in Europe. See discount chart. (800) 221-7370.

TWA: Flights throughout North America and internationally. Offers 10% discount and coupon books. Coupons are good for flights between noon Monday and noon Thursday and all day Saturday; holiday blackout dates apply. See discount chart and coupon table. (800) 221-2000.

United: Flights throughout North America and internationally. Offers 10% discount and coupons. United's Silver Wings program, a special senior club, offers discounts on car rentals and hotels; membership is not required to obtain 10% senior air discount. Club fees: $75 for a three-year membership that earns three $25 flight certificates, or $150 lifetime membership with three $50 flight certificates. The airline restricts the number of seats per flight for use with the coupon books. See discount chart and coupon table. (800) 241-6522.

USAir: Flights throughout North America and internationally. Offers 10% discount and coupons. See discount chart and coupon table. (800) 428-4322.

Virgin Atlantic: Flights from New York area, Los Angeles, San Francisco, Boston, Miami and Orlando to London-Heathrow. Offers 10% discount. See discount chart. (800) 862-8621.

CHAPTER 34

Senior Lodging Discounts

The recent overbuilding of hotels has turned lodging into a buyer's market, with nearly as many different room rates today as airlines have fares. From club privileges to corporate and senior discounts, hotels offer a wide spectrum of savings in hopes of luring travelers and filling rooms that would otherwise remain empty.

In this competitive market, a senior traveler can benefit from planning ahead and rate shopping. Age-related discounts aren't always the greatest savings available. Special promotions and weekend packages available to everyone can offer considerable savings that usually beat any senior discount. Hotel discount plans, such as stay-at-half-price programs, also offer big savings (see Chapter 4, "Slashing Hotel Costs 50 Percent," in Cutting the Cost of Lodging section).

Most hotels do offer a senior discount, but few agree on a qualifying age. Some accept your membership in a senior organization as a key to discounts, allowing the savings to start as early as age 50. Others have set minimum ages from 55 to 65, and some hotels require membership in a club, some with fees, to earn the senior discount.

For the senior discount, many hotels cut only 10 percent off their rates, a small savings that usually can be beat by a package or special promotion in today's competitive market. A few hotels give as much as 50 percent off their rates on the senior discount. In most cases, the higher discounts carry more restrictions, requiring flexibility in travel plans.

Savvy seniors start their search for savings with senior programs but always ask if there's a better deal available.

Here's a look at several ways to get a discount on lodging.

Take note!
☛ **Bring I.D.** If you reserve the senior rate at a hotel, you may need to show proof of age, such as a driver's license, when you check in.

Senior Discounts

More than 30 hotel chains offer senior discounts ranging from 10 percent to 50 percent. Age requirements vary from 50 to 65, but many hotels waive their higher age minimums if you show membership in a senior organization, such as the American Association of Retired Persons (AARP), which has an entry age of 50.

Discounts may vary within the same hotel chain. Often the main hotel corporation cannot bind any independently owned locations to offer discounts promoted by the corporately owned locations.

Seniors will find discounts as high as 30 percent off rates at already low-cost lodgings, such as Econo Lodge, Friendship Inns and Sleep Inns, bringing a night's stay as low as $25 in some places. Those travelers who prefer more amenities in their accommodations will find 25 percent off at Hyatt, 30 percent at Radisson and up to 50 percent at Marriott.

Senior discounts are not as widespread at resorts as they are at other accommodations. However, it's always worth asking about senior specials because individual properties may offer a discount. For instance, the Grove Park Inn & Country Club in Asheville, NC, gives a 10 percent discount to AARP members with identification, as does the Sandestin Resort in Destin, FL. The Phoenician, a luxury resort in Scottsdale, AZ, had a senior rate of $265 for a single or double room at press time, $40 less than the regular rate.

> **Take note!**
>
> ☞ **Senior rooms.** Choice Hotels has special "Senior Rooms" in some of its Rodeway and Econo Lodge inns. These rooms feature brighter lighting, large-button telephones and TV remote controls, coffee-makers, large print on brochures, grab bars in bathtubs, lever-handles on doors and faucets and oversized, easy-to-read numbers on alarm clocks.

Senior Rates

Many hotel chains offer senior rates, but these special savings are rarely publicized outside the local area. The national reservations number may not have the information, and you may have to call specific hotels to learn about the programs. Often these discounted rates are used to entice senior travelers to stay at the hotel during off-season, midweek or weekends.

Some locations within a chain establish senior rates in place of the widely accepted discount. For instance, the Westin hotel in Boston offers AARP members a rate of $125 per night for double occupancy, based on availability. This is a major savings over the standard rate of $189.

Timing of special senior rates or programs will vary within the same hotel chain since peak seasons differ by region. The decision to offer senior rates rests with the individual locations. Rooms offered at the better senior rates may be limited, while lower standard senior discounts may be available so long as the hotel has accommodations.

Senior Hotel Clubs

Some of the highest senior discounts are available through a hotel's designated senior club. Several major chains have clubs; some charge fees, while others simply require proof of the qualifying age before issuing a membership identification card. For example, Days Inns offers only 10 percent off for those who belong to AARP but gives up to 50 percent off to members of its September Days Club, which charges a $14 annual fee.

Hilton gives up to 50 percent off to members of its Seniors HHonors Club. Members pay a $50 annual fee, which includes spouses. Ramada's Best Years

Hotel Senior Discounts

Below are major chains with senior discount programs. The number of rooms at a discount may be limited, and advance reservations may be required, particularly for the deeper

Hotel (seniors club)	Discount off rates	Minimum age	Reservations
Aston Hotels & Resorts (Sun Club)	25%	55	800-922-7866
Best Western	10%	55[1]	800-528-1234
Budgetel	10%	55[1]	800-428-3438
Clarion Hotels	30%	50	800-CLARION
Comfort Inns	30%	50	800-228-5150
Country Inns & Suites by Carlson	10%	55[1]	800-456-4000
Courtyard by Marriott	10%	50	800-321-2211
Days Inns (September Days Club)	15%-50%	50	800-329-7466
Doubletree	30%	50	800-528-0444
Econo Lodge	30%	50	800-55-ECONO
Embassy Suites	10%	55[1]	800-362-2779
Fairfield Inn	10%	50	800-228-2800
Friendship Inns	30%	50	800-453-4511
Hampton Inn	Senior rates	50	800-426-7866
Hilton (Senior HHonors[2])	Up to 50%	60	800-492-3232
Holiday Inn (Alumni Travel Program)	20%	50	800-465-4329
Howard Johnson (Golden Years Travel Club)	50%	50	800-634-3464
Hyatt	25%	62	800-233-1234
La Quinta	10%	65[1]	800-531-5900
Marriott	10%-50%	50	800-228-9290
Nendels Motor Inns	10%	55	800-547-0106
Park Inn	15%	50	800-437-7275
Quality Inn	30%	50	800-228-5151
Radisson	Up to 30%[3]	50	800-333-3333
Ramada Inn (Best Years Club)	25%	60	800-272-6232
Red Carpet Inns	10%	55[1]	800-251-1962
Red Roof Inns (Ready Card Plus 60)	10%	60	800-843-7663
Red Lion Inns (Prime Rate Program)	20%	50	800-547-8010
Residence Inn by Marriott	15%	50	800-331-3131
Rodeway Inn	30%	50	800-228-2000
Scottish Inns	10%	55[1]	800-251-1962
Sheraton	15%-25%	60[1]	800-325-3535
Shoney's Inns (Merit Club)	10%-15%	50	800-222-2222
Sleep Inns	30%	50	800-62-SLEEP
Super 8	10%	50[4]	800-800-8000
Travelodge (Classic Travel Club)	15%	50	800-255-3050
Vagabond Inns (Club 55)	5%-15%	55	800-522-1555
Westin (American Express Just For You/ United Airlines Silver Wings)	5%-30%/50%	55/60	800-228-3000

[1]Minimum age requirement waived for members of major senior organizations, such as AARP. [2]Discount available internationally through Conrad Hotels. [3]Guests age 65 and older at properties in Europe, the Middle East and Asia

discounts. Blackout dates may apply. Some hotels include discounts on other amenities. Some chains require membership in a club; clubs are free unless noted. Some hotels require membership in a senior organization, such as AARP, but many give discounts with proof of age. All discounts are subject to change.

Notes

Also receive $10 off daily rate or $50 off weekly rate of rental car.

Minimum age also waived for Mature Outlook members. Country Kitchen restaurants offer either special seniors menu or senior discount.
Discount is for AARP members; must show membership card at check-in.
Fee: $14 annually. Also receive car-rental discounts and 10% off meals and gift shop purchases. Non-club members who are in AARP get 10% discount.
Discount is for AARP members. Also receive 10% off food and non-alcoholic beverages.

Discount is for AARP members.

Seniors pay single-room rate for up to three people in room. (Only one person in room need be 50 or older.)
Fee: $50 annually, $285 lifetime; includes spouse. Also receive 20% off dinners.
No fee first year. $10 fee is waived for following year if member stays five nights at Holiday Inn properties during first year. Also receive 20% off food and non-alcoholic beverages, and complimentary continental breakfast.
Fee: $12.95 annually; includes spouse. Also receive 10% off meals, Alamo car-rental discounts, and savings on cruises and airfare.

Room discount is for AARP members. Anyone over age 50 receives 20% off food and non-alcoholic beverages and 10% off gift shop purchases.

AARP, United Airlines Silver Wings and Northwest Worldperks (frequent fliers club) members receive 15% discount on food and beverages.
Fee: $15 lifetime. Discounts on airfare, cruises and car rentals. Members are awarded points that are redeemable for free air tickets and Ramada weekends

Fee: $10 lifetime. Also receive three $5 coupons, each good toward one night's stay.
Discount is for members of AARP, Mature Outlook or Silver Pages. Also receive 10% off food and non-alcoholic beverages.
Discount is for AARP members.

Also receive car-rental discounts and free coffee or tea in room.

Members of American Express Just For You program get 10% off food and non-alchoholic beverages.

receive a discount equivalent to their age (a 65-year-old guest gets a 65% discount). [4]Minimum age set by individual properties; most set it at 50.

Club gives a 25 percent discount for a $15 lifetime fee.

Club membership may earn higher discounts plus additional travel savings. For example, the Days Inn September Days Club offers discounts on car rentals, meals and gift-shop purchases. Howard Johnson's Golden Years Travel Club members get discounts on cruises and airfares, as well as car rentals and on meals at the hotels. Some clubs offer such perks as extended check-out time, cash-checking privileges or free continental breakfast.

Some membership fees may not give a good return on your investment unless you're a frequent traveler. Sign up for free programs at chains you frequent, but be aware that some hotels in a chain may not participate. Before joining a program with a fee, be sure hotels where you are likely to stay offer the discount; evaluate whether the cost will save you money.

Blackout dates may apply; most hotels reserve the right to change these dates without notice, especially if there is a convention or other special event planned. Some clubs offer their higher discounts on rooms booked further in advance, but other advance-purchase programs or special promotions still may give better discounts.

Some hotel clubs, particularly those with a fee, require that you return an application before they grant membership privileges. Other hotels sign you for membership when you show proof of age at check-in. Members make reservations in advance and identify themselves as a club member — an identification number may be given to members.

CHAPTER 35

Senior Car-Rental Discounts

Finding senior discounts on car rentals is like navigating a maze — sometimes leading nowhere. Like airlines and hotels, car-rental agencies have numerous price variations and discounts. Adding to the confusion is a lack of consistency on senior discounts even within one company.

For seniors, most car-rental agencies offer 5 percent or 10 percent off standard daily and weekly rates, which usually are the highest rates charged. A few companies — Avis, for one — allow the discount off low-cost specials, but most do not, making the discounts rarely the best deal for car rentals.

The senior discounts usually are on par with the amount of savings gained through corporate or club membership discounts. In fact, the key to getting nearly any discount on car rentals is membership in or affiliation with a senior organization, a club (such as an auto club) or a corporation. In most cases, to get the discount you must identify yourself as a member of a group and often give a special qualifying code assigned to the group.

Checking out the discounts requires a "20 questions" approach to find the best rate for your travel plans. When we asked about a dozen companies what senior discounts were available, the general response from central reservations numbers was "From which city?" Even when a car-rental agency promotes a senior discount, not every location offers the savings.

'Senior Rate'

Reservationists sometimes are unaware of the discount but quote a "senior rate" instead, which turns out to be equivalent to what you'd pay with the allotted discount. For example, though AARP members may be told they get a 10 percent discount, a car-rental agent may not know the specific discount but will quote the company's "special rate" for AARP members. We were told by an agent that the AARP rate was $23.39 a day, which does calculate to 10 percent off the standard rate of $25.99.

If you're comparison shopping on discounts, don't expect agents to be too helpful if they're quoting senior rates. Overall, they seem to be uninformed about or unwilling to say the specific amount the company gives. So your best bet is to compare specific rates rather than the amount of the discounts.

The senior discount can save money at peak travel times or when your travel plans don't qualify you for any greater savings. Otherwise, you're better off seeking a low-cost package or special rate.

When booking a car rental, discuss your travel plans with a travel agent or car-rental agent and shop for the best rate possible during that time frame. Ask if extending or shortening the trip will lower the rate, and check if there is a special promotional rate on a smaller or larger car than you were considering.

For other money-saving tips on car rentals, see the Deals on Wheels section.

Agency Discounts

Here is a roundup of national car-rental agencies that have senior discount programs, with explanations, examples and supplemental data for the chart as needed.

Advantage — 10% discount for AARP members.

Alamo —10% discount off standard rates for anyone over 50.

Avis — 5%-25% off domestic rentals and 10% off international rentals for AARP members. Discounts can apply to lowest rates and packages.

Budget — 5%-15% discount, varying with location. Some sites require proof you're 55 or older; others honor AARP cards.

Dollar — Senior rates for AARP members or drivers over 65. Example: Weekend rate for a midsize car in Las Vegas, $37 a day with AARP card vs. $29.95 a day for the weekend rate and $49.99 standard weekday rate.

Enterprise — 10% discount off standard daily and weekly rates for AARP members.

Hertz — 5%-10% discount for members of AARP, Mature Outlook, the

Car-Rental Senior Discounts

Below are the major car-rental chains with discount programs for seniors. Discounts may vary depending on location; all sites may not participate. All discounts are subject to change without notice.

Company	Discount	Minimum age	Reservation number
Advantage[1]	10%	50	800-777-5500
Alamo	10%	50	800-327-9633
Avis[1]	5%-25%/10% Intl.	50	800-331-1212
Budget	5%-15%	55[2]	800-527-0700
Dollar	Senior rates	65[2]	800-800-4000
Enterprise[1]	10%	50	800-325-8007
Hertz[3]	5%-10%	50	800-654-3131
National[4]	10%-30%	50	800-227-7368
Payless	$3-$10	50	800-729-5377
Thrifty[1]	10%	55	800-367-2277
Value[1]	5%	50	800-468-2583

[1]Requires membership in AARP. [2]Age requirement waived with membership in AARP. [3]Requires membership in AARP, Mature Outlook, National Association of Federal Retired Employees, United Airlines Silver Wings program, Montgomery Ward's Years of Extended Savings program or retired military personnel. [4]Requires membership in AARP, Mature Outlook or Catholic Golden Age.

National Association of Retired Federal Employees, United Airlines Silver Wings program, Montgomery Wards' Years of Extended Savings program and for retired U.S. military personnel.

National — 10% off standard rates, 30% discount off business rates, and 10%-20% off selected international rates for AARP, Mature Outlook or Catholic Golden Age members.

Payless — $3 off the standard daily rate and $10 off the standard weekly rate for members of the Payless Nifty 50 program.

Thrifty — 10% discount off rates for drivers over 55. Discounts can apply to lowest rates and packages.

Value — 5% discount off standard rate on compact car or larger for AARP members.

CHAPTER 36

Senior Rail And Bus Discounts

When traveling by train, whether in the United States or abroad, age proves to be a valuable asset. Senior discounts are widely available and are generally easy to use with few restrictions.

These discounts can provide significant savings, particularly when combined with other discounted fares. When booking a trip through a travel agency or buying a ticket at the train or bus station, ask about the senior discount and whether it can be used with other specials or promotional discounts. Proof of age usually will be required when boarding and/or when tickets are validated during travel.

The following is a breakdown of senior discounts in North America and Europe. Other regions of the world have not been as quick to offer senior discounts, but when traveling in other countries always ask about possible senior savings.

North America

In the United States, Amtrak is the only national passenger rail system, serving 48 states and a few border points in Canada. The Alaska Railroad serves Alaska.

Amtrak has lowered the age limit from 65 to 62 for senior discounts and has simplified its program. It now offers a 15 percent discount good on the lowest available coach fare. In the past, it had a 25 percent discount restricted to the full one-way coach fares, not the round trips.

Rail Discounts in North America

Company	Discount	Minimum age	Reservations number	Service areas
Amtrak	15%	62	800-USA-RAIL	U.S. and border points in Canada
Alaska Railroad Corp.	25%*	65	800-544-0552	Alaska
VIA Rail Canada	10%	60	800-561-3949	Canada

*Discount only available for Anchorage and Fairbanks service during off-season, mid-September to mid-May.

The new senior discounts are available on regular fares, special one-way fares, round-trip excursion fares, All-Aboard America fares and group fares. Standard holiday blackouts still apply. While senior discounts may be used with already discounted fares, they may not be used in conjunction with any other coupon or membership discount. In addition, Amtrak's senior discounts do not apply for travel on auto train or Metroliner service, sleeping accommodations or selected segments of through Amtrak/VIA Rail Canada routes operated by VIA Rail.

The Alaska Railroad, which serves Anchorage, Fairbanks, Whittier and Seward, offers a senior discount of 25 percent to those age 65 and older but only on its Anchorage and Fairbanks service during the off-season, from fall through spring. Alaska's main season is about 120 days, from mid-May to mid-September. Trains run daily in the summer but the service is reduced in the off-season. Example of savings: An adult fare from Anchorage to Fairbanks costs $135 in season; it's $75 off-season, or $56.25 for seniors. Reduced-service trains run on that route only on weekends in the off-season.

> *Take note!*
> ☞ **Book early on Amtrak.** The lowest round-trip coach fares often sell out quickly. Also, while Amtrak senior discounts are not applicable during holiday blackout periods, a "loophole" allows you to continue a trip on a holiday blackout date if you started within the required time.

In Canada, the national carrier is VIA Rail, which offers a 10 percent discount to seniors age 60 and older. The savings is available throughout the system on coach, first class and sleeper cars. There are no restrictions on travel dates or requirements for advance purchase in order to be eligible for the discount. The senior discount can be combined with Discount Day or seasonal fares for an even greater savings, up to 50 percent. But, when using these other discounts, senior passengers must adhere to applicable restrictions, including advance-purchase requirements and limited seats.

Europe

When you cross the Atlantic, you gain even better savings on trains in European countries, up to 50 percent off fares.

While most Americans wanting to save money think first of getting a Eurailpass, it's not always the best deal unless you plan extensive travel across several countries. If you plan only a couple of train trips in one or two countries, there are better ways to meet your needs and save money.

Senior discounts offer the greatest savings when you know you won't use a rail pass enough to warrant its cost. Also, senior discounts can be used on the less expensive second-class tickets. Second-class seats may not be quite as comfortable and the coaches may be more crowded, but if the trip is short, it's usually worth the savings.

While some countries require that you purchase a senior card to take advantage of the savings, most simply require proof of age, usually in the form of a passport, when you buy tickets. The qualifying age for senior rail discounts is 60, 65 or, in Norway, 67.

If you decide a rail pass is your best bet, be sure to ask if you're eligible for a discounted price. While Eurail offers no discount for seniors, some single-country passes do.

BritRail, which is not part of Eurail, offers a 10 percent discount on its rail passes if you're 60 or older. Passes vary in price according to the class of service — first or standard — and the length of travel time. For example, a 15-day first-class pass with senior discount sells for $479; a standard, or second-class, pass is $320. (Prices are subject to change each year.) The passes are good for travel in England, Scotland and Wales and may be purchased for periods of four days to one month. BritRail passes are available from most travel agents and must be purchased before traveling to Britain.

New from ScanRail is the ScanRail 55+ Pass, which offers a 13 percent discount for seniors over age 55. ScanRail passes are good for unlimited train travel in Denmark, Finland, Norway and Sweden.

Take note!

☞ **Protect European rail passes like cash.** If yours is lost or stolen while traveling, you will have to buy a replacement. However, you can buy insurance for $10 that will refund 100 percent of the unexpired time on the pass when lost — after you file the required paperwork when you return home.

Other Modes of Travel

While Greyhound Bus Lines offers a 10 percent discount off its full (or last-minute purchase) fares to seniors age 55 and beyond, its 21-day advance-

Rail Discounts in Europe

The rail systems in many European countries offer up to 50 percent savings to senior travelers. Austria, Finland, France and Germany require that you purchase a senior card, but others simply ask for proof of age, usually a passport.

Country	Discount	Minimum age	Card fee
Austria	50%	60/65*	$27
Denmark	30%-50%	65	None
Finland	50%	65	$9
France	50%	60	$29-$54
Germany	50%	60	$83-$165
Luxembourg	50%	65	None
Norway	50%	67	None
Portugal	30%	65	None

*Age 60 for women and age 65 for men.

purchase fares usually provide better savings. These fares are non-refundable, but can be transferred for a $5 fee. Greyhound used to offer three, seven- and fourteen-day advance-purchase fares as well, but recently revamped its fare structure to compete with the new breed of budget airlines. Example of savings: A round-trip ticket from Chicago to San Francisco purchased at full fare would cost $238; with the senior discount, that price would be $214. However, if you purchased the ticket 21 days in advance, the fare would be $178. For more information, contact Greyhound at (800) 231-2222.

CHAPTER 37

Senior City And State Discounts

City and state tourism offices offer a range of discounts from merchant coupons to city transit discounts and senior cards. But many tourism offices don't promote their discounts widely, so it's up to the consumer to ask what's available.

Before planning a trip, call state tourism offices for both general travel material and specific programs for seniors. Tourist offices for all states are listed in Chapter 13, "Getting Information."

City Transportation

Some major cities offer senior transit cards that entitle users to discounts on public transportation. Other cities only require that you show identification, such as a driver's license or a Medicare card, for a discount. For example, Washington, DC, Metrorail offers 50 percent off Metrorail travel for seniors 65 and beyond. Show identification and you receive a card free. For more information, call Metrorail, (202) 637-7000.

San Francisco has senior bus rates of 35 cents for those age 65 and beyond, compared to a normal bus fare of $1. You may need to show your driver's license to receive the discount, but many times transit employees don't ask for identification. San Francisco also offers a 75 percent discount on Bay Area Rapid Transit (BART) cards for seniors age 65 and beyond. Seniors pay $4 for the card, which allows $16 worth of travel. BART cards are available at banks, supermarkets, drugstores and BART offices. For more information, call BART, (415) 992-2278.

Guidebooks With Savings

Most state and many city tourism offices offer free travel guides, and many of them contain money-saving coupons. For example, the Discover Nevada Bonus Book, with coupons good at shops, hotels and restaurants, is available at most Nevada chambers of commerce and visitor welcome centers. The Ohio Pass guidebook, with more than $3,000 worth of coupons, can be ordered through the state tourism office.

Check with tourist offices in the states you plan to visit to see if they offer such money-saving vacation guides.

City Discount Cards

Some city tourism offices have their own senior discount cards, while others rely on independent companies to provide books of merchant discounts and coupons sold to the general public. For example, the Golden Washingtonian Club provides seniors age 60 and beyond with a directory of more than 1,700 businesses, merchants and service providers that offer various types of discounts. For more information, contact Family and Child Services of Washington, DC, 929 L St. N.W., Washington, DC 20001, (202) 289-1510, ext. 120.

Some major cities offer similar cards that are not age-related. For more information, see Ways to Save on Sightseeing at the end of Chapter 12, or call the convention and visitors bureau of the city you plan to visit.

Seasonal Savings

Many popular tourist locations offer discounts during certain seasons. Fall is the best time for seniors to check about special savings programs. Communities may promote an entire month, often September, as a senior discount time, while other places may target special weekends or festivals to attract seniors.

CHAPTER 38

Senior Travel Clubs And Cards

Senior travel cards and clubs not only can save you money but also provide a number of travel benefits, as well as connect you with other seniors with the same interests. Of the organizations surveyed, fees range from $5 to $95 a year, but some are free. Some clubs offer multiple-year or lifetime memberships.

Here's a look at some of the better-known organizations that offer travel savings.

American Association of Retired Persons (AARP), AARP National Headquarters, 601 E St. N.W., Washington, DC 20049, (202) 434-2277. Fee: $8 annually, $20 for three years and $45 for 10 years. Membership in this organization, with the resulting AARP card, earns the widest array of discounts at the earliest age. Members need be only 50 to join. Many hotels and car-rental agencies that give senior discounts at age 55-65 waive that age restriction with an AARP card. The card also earns discounts on motoring clubs and tours. Members receive a bimonthly magazine.

Canadian Association of Retired Persons (CARP), 27 Queen St. E., Suite 1304, Toronto, Ontario, Canada M5C 2M6, (416) 363-8748. Fee: $10 a year, $25 for three years; membership also covers spouses. The Canadian equivalent to AARP provides travel discounts on lodging and car rentals as well as discounts on health insurance to those age 50 and beyond. Members receive a bimonthly tabloid magazine.

Disney Magic Years Club, P.O. Box 4709, Anaheim, CA 92803, (714) 520-2524. Fee: $35 for five years. Seniors age 55 and beyond enjoy benefits and discounts throughout Walt Disney World and Disneyland, plus discounts on Big Red Boat cruises and National Car Rental.

Evergreen TravelClub, 404 N. Galena Ave., Dixon, IL 61021, (800) 374-9392. Fees: $40 per year for individuals, $50 for couples. This is an international bed-and-breakfast club for seniors 50 and beyond. Members make arrangements to stay in the homes of other members who are hosts, choosing from a list of Evergreen lodgings in the United States and abroad. Club members don't have to be hosts. Those who aren't pay a gratuity of $18 for one person, $24 per

---

Take note!

☞ **Ask for your discount.** A credit-card envelope stamped with the words "This card holder qualifies for senior discount" reminds seniors to ask for their discount. To order two envelopes for $1, send a check and self-addressed, stamped envelope to Credit Card Envelope, P.O. Box 812010, Wellesley, MA 02181-0012.

Ski Discounts

The following is a list of major ski areas that offer discounted lift tickets to older skiers. To obtain the discount, skiers merely show a valid form of identification that includes their date of birth, such as a driver's license. Many ski areas also extend discounts to members of ski clubs at a younger age with proof of membership (see this chapter for two such clubs). Prices shown are for a one-day ticket during regular season. Multiday tickets also are discounted.

Ski resort	Senior ski price (age)	Regular ski price
Aspen, Buttermilk and Snowmass, CO	$36 (65-69) free (70 and up)	$52
Breckenridge, CO	$23 (60-69) free (70 and up)	$43
Camelback, Tannerville, PA	$25 (65 and up)	$33-$39*
Jackson Hole, WY	$21-$24[†] (65 and up)	$42-$45[†]
Northstar-at-Tahoe, CA	$22 (60-69) $5 (70 and up)	$43
Okemo Mountain, VT	$27-$29[§] (65 and up)	$43-$46[§]
Park City, UT	$23.50 (65-69) free (70 and up)	$47
Purgatory, CO	$20 (62-69) free (70 and up)	$39
Steamboat Springs, CO	$25 (65-69) free (70 and up)	$44
Sun Valley, ID	$29 (65 and up)	$49
Telluride, CO	$25 (65-69) free (70 and up)	$45
Terry Peak, SD	$20 (65 and older)	$29
Waterville Valley, NH	$24-$28* (65-69) free weekdays (70 and up)	$37-$43*
Winter Park, CO	$18 (62-69) free (70 and up)	$42

* Rates are higher on weekends and holidays.
[†] Lower prices are for chairlifts only; higher prices include tram also.
[§] Rates are higher on weekends.

couple per day; members who agree to be hosts pay $10 for one person, $15 per couple per day when they travel.

Golden Age Passport, Golden Access Passport and Golden Eagle Pass, U.S. Department of the Interior, National Park Service, Room 1013, P.O. Box 37127, Washington, DC 20013, (202) 208-4747. Fees: The Golden Age Passport is $10, the Golden Eagle Pass is $25 and the Golden Access Passport is free. All three admit holders to America's national parks and other federal lands. The Golden Age Passport provides free lifetime entrance for U.S. citizens age 62 and beyond and any accompanying passengers in the car. The Golden Age Passport also entitles seniors to a 50 percent discount on federal use fees for such activities as camping and boating. The Golden Access Passport, which is free to blind or permanently disabled citizens, has the same privileges as the Golden Age Passport. The Golden Eagle Pass admits holders ages 17-61 but does not provide discounts on camping fees. The Golden Age and Golden Access passports can be obtained at any national park area that charges an entrance fee. A driver's license or birth certificate is required for a Golden Age Passport, and Golden Access Passport applicants must have a letter from their doctor stating their disability or proof of benefits received under federal law. The Golden Eagle Pass may be purchased from the National Park Service or at any national park that charges an entrance fee.

While Canada has no senior parks card, national parks in Canada waive admission fees for seniors age 60 and beyond with proof of age, usually a driver's license.

Mature Outlook, P.O. Box 10448, Des Moines, IA, 50306-0448, (800) 336-6330. Fee: $9.95 annually. Part of the Sears network, this club for those 50 and beyond provides discounts on Sears merchandise (including optical) and on Hertz, Avis, National and Budget car rentals. Members also get a 50 percent discount at certain hotels, as well as dining discounts. Members receive an identification card and a bimonthly magazine updating new discounts and specials.

Montgomery Ward Y.E.S. Discount Club (Years of Extra Savings), 200 N. Martingale Road, Schaumburg, IL 60173, (800) 421-5396. Fee: $2.99 a month or $34.99 a year. A division of Montgomery Ward, this club for seniors age 55 and beyond provides members with rebates on travel booked through its travel services department, as well as discounts on Montgomery Ward's merchandise and auto service. Members receive a bimonthly magazine.

Over the Hill Gang International, 3310 Cedar Heights Drive, Colorado Springs, CO 80904, (719) 685-4656. Fee: $37-$395 for individuals, $60-$660

Take note!

☞ **High-altitude illness.** If you're not used to high elevations, your first few days at a mountain ski resort may result in high-altitude sickness, with symptoms of nausea, headache, fatigue and shortness of breath. To lessen these side effects, exercise in moderation the first few days, drink more water, reduce your alcohol intake and eat food high in carbohydrates, such as grains and pasta.

for couples, depending on type of membership (can choose to be a chapter or at-large member for one year, three years or life). Ski organization for seniors age 50 and beyond with 13 local chapters from coast to coast and Canada and members in 13 countries. Membership earns discounts on lift tickets, equipment rental and lodgings at more than 80 resorts and on rental cars, as well as discounted group rates on ski trips for members. Other escorted trips offer rafting, biking, hiking and golf. Members receive a quarterly newsletter, trip catalog and directory of benefits.

70+Ski Club, 104 Eastside Drive, Ballston Lake, NY 12019, (518) 399-5458. Fee: $5 lifetime membership. Restricted to seniors age 70 or older. Must provide proof of age. Founder Lloyd Lambert, who is also the contact for the club, has been skiing since 1915. The club boasts 12,000 members worldwide, including former President Gerald Ford. Members receive a list of 200 ski resorts and lifts with free or highly discounted rates for members, an identifying patch and card as well as a biannual newsletter.

Take note!
☛ **Wear sunglasses.** Ultraviolet rays are stronger at high altitudes, so wear good sunglasses that filter out harmful rays. And, don't forget your sunscreen, even on overcast days.

The Golf Card, P.O. Box 7021, Englewood, CO 80155, (800) 453-4260. Fee: $95 for one person or $145 for two people annually. This club was designed with the senior in mind, though there are no age restrictions. Members receive two complimentary rounds of golf or 50 percent off fees at more than 3,000 member golf courses throughout the world. Most of the courses offer the complimentary rounds, but only when you rent a golf cart. Some golf courses restrict card usage to Monday-Friday or other non-peak periods. Members receive an identification card, a list of member golf courses and bimonthly *Golf Traveler* magazine.

CHAPTER 39

Low-Cost Learning Vacations

On her first vacation after retirement, Bonnie Margolin didn't spend her time lying on a beach or shopping for souvenirs. Instead, she learned about computers, studied geology and listened to lectures on pioneer history.

Margolin chose a learning vacation, an increasingly popular type of getaway among senior travelers. Two organizations, Elderhostel and Interhostel, specialize in providing these inexpensive enrichment vacations for travelers 50 and beyond.

For only a few hundred dollars, you could spend a week taking an in-depth look at famous shipwrecks, learning to fly-cast or studying the culture of a faraway land. Best of all, you'll be with other seniors who share your interests and passion for knowledge.

Elderhostel

Since its founding in 1975, more than 250,000 people have participated in Elderhostel's continuing-education programs, now at 1,900 locations in the United States and 50 other countries.

You needn't be a high school or college grad to attend. However, there is one important stipulation — you must be at least 55.

Those who've reached that magical age find an incredible potpourri of college-level courses, numbering in the thousands. A sampling: oceanography, astronomy, archaeology, architecture, the language of music, Dickens' London, the art of maple sugaring, calligraphy and such current topics as nutrition and world terrorism.

There are no exams, no homework, no speeches to prepare, but there is plenty of classroom discussion, often led by college professors.

"Elderhosteling is my kind of vacation — economical and intellectually stimulating," says Margolin. "Plus, there's an essential bonus. Fellow hostelers are vital, caring people fascinated by the world. No rocking chairs for this silver-haired group!"

Elderhostel was founded at the University of New Hampshire by educator Marty Knowlton and his friend David Bianco.

Marty, who was then in his 50s, had just spent four years backpacking in Europe and staying in youth hostels. He was impressed by how Europe's network of modest accommodations nurtured an adventuresome spirit in youth. He was impressed by the positive impact a live-in setting had on older Scandinavians attending classes.

The Elderhostel name (coined by Bianco) came before the two friends had figured out what Elderhostel would encompass. Within two weeks, however, the idea was born — education for older Americans for the sheer enjoyment of it.

Many Elderhostel programs are on university campuses, taking advantage of classrooms and dormitories. Others may be at conference centers, ranches, state and national parks or in rural villages.

Accommodations are simple — in dorms, cabins or modest hotels and motels. Sometimes rooms are more upscale, perhaps at a resort or even in a three-star hotel or chateau. Most participants must share accommodations; single rooms are the exception.

"We senior hostelers, like youth hostelers, have to be willing to take the bad with the good," says Margolin, who has participated in a number of Elderhostel programs. "I've slept in sleeping bags and on cots. I've also stayed in lovely college dorms and a beautiful old hacienda. Teachers range from crackerjacks to occasional yawns, meals from princely smorgasbords to ho-hum. Whatever, you get a lot of wallop for your dollar."

Elderhostel costs are intentionally modest. The typical charge for the standard six-night program in the United States is $350, in Canada, $370. The fee includes registration, accommodations, all meals (from Sunday dinner through Saturday breakfast), five days of classes featuring three diverse courses and extracurricular activities. Participants pay their own way to the site. Groups vary in size from 15 to 40.

Programs abroad last two to four weeks and cost $1,100 to $5,000, depending on length and location. Fees include airfare, room and board, classes, transportation within the country and sightseeing excursions.

For most Elderhostelers, it's the course content that lures them more than creature comforts, setting or location. Rosalyne and Harold Gottlieb of Wedgewood, NJ, have strong interests in the arts, history and religion. She's 65 and he's 72. They've Elderhosteled as far west as California and across the Atlantic to Great Britain in pursuit of such topics as the psychology of Judaism, the impact of arts on religion, medieval pilgrims, Mark Twain, Gilbert & Sullivan's "HMS Pinafore," and history and culture of the Shenandoah Valley.

> **Take note!**
> ☞ **Fit for action.** Elderhostel participants should be in good health and able to keep up with physically active programs. Trips may involve a good deal of walking, climbing stairs, getting on and off trains and buses, carrying baggage and sometimes climbing hilly or uneven terrain.

Harold Gottlieb says, "Lots of cross-pollination goes on. You learn from each other as well as from the professors."

Some participants, such as Charles Leung, choose programs for their locations. Leung is 69, a retired businessman and world traveler who lives in San Francisco. He isn't particular about what he studies but likes to get a close-up look at places he's never visited, particularly in the United States.

"As a hosteler, I've seen glaciers in Alaska, Bryce Canyon at sunset and fall colors in New York state," Leung says. "I've also rafted with a bunch of hostelers on the Colorado River from Moab, UT, to Lake Powell, NV."

Some avid hostelers, such as Wilma and Fran Wiser of Fort Atkinson, WI, base decisions on how far they have to drive to the program site.

"We don't like to put in more than one night on the road," she says. The Wisers are in their late 60s and veterans of a dozen programs. They've traveled to nine states to study such subjects as mountain music, botany, weather and creative writing.

"We love the informality and camaraderie," Fran Wiser adds.

Interhostel

Interhostel is different from Elderhostel in two respects: The age requirement is 50, and all its programs are overseas.

Interhostel, headquartered at the University of New Hampshire, owes much of its philosophical heritage to Elderhostel. It began in 1980 to offer foreign programs, which Elderhostel didn't do at the time.

Most Interhostel programs are two weeks. The institute currently has more than 60 programs scheduled worldwide. Costs are $2,000-$3,500 and include airfare, room and board, studies, sightseeing and transportation within a country.

Among Interhostel boosters is William Zitowsky, 68, a former federal government employee. At last count, he had taken 21 of their trips to 12 countries — England, Scotland, France, Germany, Italy, China, Sweden, Norway, Portugal, Spain, Holland and Costa Rica.

When asked why so many trips, he jokes, "To get out of New York City" and adds, "Actually, the real reason is the organization isn't commercial. With Interhostel, you're treated like a guest — not a tourist — in the host country. You get to meet families and perhaps even go to their homes for dinner. And the group is always congenial. No snobs. We Interhostelers aren't running overseas just to say we've been in such-and-such country. No, we're there to learn."

Like Elderhostelers, Interhostelers have classes in the morning and sightseeing excursions in the afternoon. However, instead of taking a minicourse on different subjects, Interhostelers attend a series of lectures, all focused specifically on the locale they're visiting. For example, in Vienna, lectures include the history of Austria and Vienna, the Hapsburgs, Freud, famous Austrian composers and the role of Austria since 1945. In Christchurch, lectures include New Zealand's turbulent geological history, flora and fauna, Maori and Pakeha (European) inhabitants, and recent economic and social changes.

A University of New Hampshire representative accompanies each group (maximum 40), and in the host country, programs are in conjunction with a university. Lodgings vary, but usually are in residence halls with shared baths or in modest hotels, which may not have private baths. Participants normally share accommodations. Most rooms are doubles, but single rooms are available for an extra fee in some programs.

Mollie Ampel is a seasoned hosteler: She's taken eight trips with Interhostel and 15 with Elderhostel, five of which were abroad. She's 71, a widow, lives in a New York studio apartment and hates to shop, which, she claims, is one reason she loves Interhostel and Elderhostel.

"Before discovering hosteling, I'd taken other group tours. You see nine countries in 22 days, 400 churches and in between you shop. No more. I don't need dust collectors.

"When I travel, I'm curious about culture, politics, history, social reform, educational systems, health care, and I want to exchange ideas with local people," Ampel says.

When it comes to the courses themselves, Ampel has one word — incredible.

"For instance," she says, "on my Interhostel trip to the Netherlands, our professor from The Hague University was determined we learn as much as possible. Evenings, on his own, he'd come and show us slides or films before we went sightseeing the next afternoon. And where else but on a trip like this could you ever spend two days studying a flower industry? It was mind-boggling. Did you know Holland exports $5 billion worth of flowers annually?"

As for sharing a room or a bathroom, Ampel says, "I enjoy it. Sometimes it's a real adventure. Once in Greece, 10 of us ladies found ourselves coping with showers that overran and toilets that took three people to pump up before they'd flush. We just laughed and had a grand old time. When you hostel, you become buddies right away."

Many people, at any age, might consider such traveling strenuous. Not her.

"On the contrary," says Ampel, who finally has learned to sleep in airplanes, "they are exhilarating!"

Resources

Elderhostel publishes 10 catalogs of trips annually; programs run year-round. Participants must be age 55 although spouses can be any age; a companion must be at least 50. If dietary supplements are required, participants must bring their own. With the exception of seeing-eye dogs, pets are not permitted on Elderhostel campuses.

A limited amount of assistance is available for those who cannot afford Elderhostel programs. These "hostelships" (scholarships) are not travel grants. They're normally used "close to home" and are valid for programs only in the United States and Canada.

For more information, contact Elderhostel, 75 Federal St., Third Floor, Boston, MA 02110, (617) 426-7788.

Interhostel publishes three catalogs a year (spring, summer, fall/winter); programs are year-round. Participants must be age 50; a companion age 40 and beyond is allowed. Interhostel cannot accommodate special diets. A University of New Hampshire representative travels with the group and acts as a spokesperson for the group with the host institution.

For information, contact Interhostel, University of New Hampshire, 6 Garrison Ave., Durham, NH 03824, (800) 733-9753.

CHAPTER 40

Extended-Stay Vacations

For travelers age 50 and beyond who like to explore on their own and get to know an area well, extended-stay vacations are an ideal option, giving added value while also stretching the budget.

Several companies offer extended-stay vacations, which allow travelers to base themselves in apartments or hotels for periods as long as three months and explore the surrounding region, usually on their own timetables. European countries are the primary destinations.

Such vacations give travelers a feel of living in a place, rather than merely passing through as a tourist.

On their three-week stay in Switzerland, Bob and Roberta Burnett of Mystic, CT, saw village life close-up. At 5 o'clock one morning, they were awakened by the sound of cowbells.

"We looked out at a herd of cows led by a dog and a little boy, with his father following behind," Roberta recalled. "They were going to pastures up the mountain for the summer. Every day they had to bring the milk down. Sometimes we'd see a can lashed to the back of a moped, or two cans sticking out the back windows of a Volkswagen bug."

The Burnetts are seasoned travelers who don't want to zip past cathedrals and scenic wonders or shuttle to a new hotel in a different city every day or two.

"A lot of people who go to Switzerland want the furs and diamonds of St. Moritz, or the cathedrals and museums of the big cities," Bob said. "But we wanted to be with the Swiss, in the country."

They signed up for an Untour arranged by a company called Idyll. They lived in a two-bedroom apartment in a chalet in Hohfluh, a village in the Bernese Oberland, and used it as a base for independent sightseeing.

Freedom to Explore

The Burnetts are like many mature travelers who prefer to stay in the same place awhile. They've taken the once-over-lightly tours. Now they want the freedom to make each day as leisurely or frenetic as they please. Other mature travelers choose longer stays in warm, relatively inexpensive resorts as an escape from Northern winters. They do occasional sightseeing but spend most days socializing with other residents of their hotel or apartment building as well as local people.

To cater to these types of senior travelers, tour operators have developed extended-stay vacations, which provide the basics such as transportation and accommodations but allow independent exploring.

Extended stays began as a way to fill empty resort hotel and apartment rooms during the off-season by heavily discounting the rates. Resort properties on Spain's Costa del Sol have used this technique for years during the fall, winter and spring, and the region remains a popular extended-stay destination.

Long-stay tours aren't restricted to the off-season, though. Many European programs are offered in the summer.

Packages usually include airfare and airport transfers, plus the services of a local host. Companies normally use regularly scheduled airlines but may turn to charters in rare cases to get customers to a destination more conveniently or inexpensively.

The package may include some meals; otherwise, you're on your own. In apartments, the package usually includes maid service once or twice weekly and a starter food pack. A rail or public transportation pass or a car rental may be part of the deal.

Most companies have a staff representative on site to assist travelers. There may be a range of group activities: parties, games, films and lectures, and language and cooking lessons. Some companies include orientation tours, but other excursions — whether the traveler plans them independently or joins trips offered by the tour operator — cost extra.

Types of Stays

Extended-stay holidays can be separated loosely into the following categories:

Stays in apartments and hotel complexes in resorts or cities: A minimum stay of one or two weeks is required. Major destinations are Spain, Portugal and Switzerland. There also are programs in several other countries in Western Europe and some cities in Western and Eastern Europe.

One week or more in two or three locations: It's possible to mix a two-week program in Switzerland, for instance, with a two-week stay in Italy. Some trips offer one week in each of three cities, such as Vienna, Austria; Budapest, Hungary, and Prague, Czechoslovakia.

Stays in individually owned accommodations: Idyll specializes in this option, offering family-owned apartments or cottages in towns and villages. The company, which blends pleasure and educational travel, first matches people as closely as possible with the type of accommodations and setting they want. In Switzerland, for example, lodging may be in an alpine village, close to one of the lakes or near a city. Travelers receive background materials, calendars of events and Untour sightseeing guides before they go.

Upon arrival, travelers are met and assisted by an Idyll staff member, who

Take note!
☞ **Ask for personal contacts.** Sometimes it's hard to choose one apartment or hotel over another in a major resort area, even after studying brochures and talking with the company. Ask the tour operator to put you in touch with customers who have stayed at places you're considering.

orients them to everything from the use of transportation systems and timetables to cultural differences. In Switzerland, vacationers receive a Swiss Pass for the train-bus-ferry system. Those who are going to villages board a train together, then disembark separately at their destinations, where each is met by a host family.

Idyll usually includes two sightseeing get-togethers during each stay, plus a final party. Other than that, Idyll travelers are on their own in planning their days, though a company representative is available should problems or questions arise.

What to Consider

Consider these points before choosing a program:

● Decide what you want from extended stays. Look at the different types of stays and determine which you prefer — being in a resort complex with group activities or staying independently at a site.

● Choose what type of location you prefer. Some resort hotels and apartments are a distance from a city or town. Others are part of a resort community. Apartments may be in cities or villages rarely visited by other Americans. If you enjoy golf, tennis, swimming or other sports, find a resort where such facilities are available at little or no additional cost.

● Ask about transportation. Is there a shuttle or local transportation to the nearest town, a close Underground station in London, or buses and trains to the places you most want to sightsee? If not, you may consider renting a car. The tour operator can help arrange rentals, sometimes at special rates.

● Consider a hotel vs. apartment. If you're combining several destinations, a hotel may be your choice. But if you're staying several weeks in one spot, an apartment provides living space, plus the convenience of a kitchen. Check square footage and ask to see a floor plan.

● Plan sightseeing. Read guidebooks and know what sights you want to see. If you will feel more secure sightseeing on group excursions than independently, choose a company or spot where tours are readily available.

● Check out food costs. Ask about local food costs, the availability of items you need and what's included in any starter pack. If coffee, for example, is extremely expensive, you may want to take some with you. Make sure markets are easily accessible. Food costs will be higher in cities or resorts than in villages. Even if your tour includes some meals, budget extra for individual dining out.

● Determine if there's a local host on site. Such contacts are valuable in planning itineraries and solving problems. If you like group activities and camaraderie, find out what kinds of special get-togethers or activities are planned. If you don't want to participate in many group events, however, you usually won't be pressured to join.

Getting Information

Here are some tour operators offering extended-stay programs. Prices will vary according to the destination and departure date. Costs are subject to change, as are the destinations.

Grand Circle Travel, 347 Congress St., Boston, MA 02210, (800) 221-2610. Programs in Spain, Portugal, Turkey, Greece, Italy, Switzerland, Austria, England, Scotland, Wales and Ireland, in the cities of London and Paris, and in Mexico. Some programs are two to three weeks, while others can be stretched to 26 weeks. Costs cover airfare, available from varying gateways; transfers between airport and lodging; accommodations in hotels or efficiency apartments; breakfast daily and some dinners; planned activities; and assistance of a local staffer. Prices range from $995 to $3,500 per person, double occupancy.

Idyll, Ltd., P.O. Box 405, Media, PA 19063, (610) 565-5242. "Untour" programs in Switzerland, Austria, Germany, France, Italy, Belgium and the Netherlands, and combination trips to Vienna, Austria; Budapest, Hungary; and Prague, Czechoslovakia. Most trips are two weeks and can be extended an additional two weeks at reduced rates; the three-city tour is three weeks. Costs cover airfare from the New York area or Boston; transfers between airport and lodging; accommodations in apartments; two sightseeing excursions; one social; and assistance of a local staffer. Some tours include rail passes, and the three-city tour includes transportation between the sites. Rates are about $1,450 to $1,900 per person, double occupancy, or lower if four people share accommodations. The largest center of operation is Switzerland, where Idyll has 100 apartments.

Home at First, P.O. Box 193, Springfield, PA 19064, (800) 5CELTIC. Programs in Scotland, Ireland, Wales, the Cotswolds part of England and in London; also bed-and-breakfast driving trips in New Zealand. British Isles trips are one week to two months; New Zealand trips are 14 or 21 days. Costs cover airfare from the New York area, Boston or Philadelphia (or the West Coast for New Zealand); accommodations (country cottage or city apartment); a car rental, except in London where vacationers get a rail pass; and assistance of a local staffer. Rates are $1,500 to $3,000 per person, double occupancy, for the British Isles and $2,500 to $3,000 per person, double occupancy, for New Zealand.

Saga International Holidays, 222 Berkeley St., Boston, MA 02116, (800) 343-0273. All-inclusive resort holidays in Turkey, Italy, France, Spain and Portugal. Trips are in the off-season, late fall into early spring, and last two weeks but can be extended. Costs cover airfare from varying gateways; transfers between airport and lodging; accommodations in hotels; all meals, including wine; sightseeing; social activities; and assistance of a local staffer. Prices from the New York area are $1,399 to $1,799 per person, double occupancy. On some departures, single supplements are waived.

Sun Holidays, 7280 W. Palmetto Park Road, Boca Raton, FL 33433, (800) 243-2057. Specializes in Spain and Portugal, with a wide range of hotel rooms and studio, one- and two-bedroom apartments available. Trips last one week to three months, and costs cover airfare from New York or Miami; transfers between airport and lodging; accommodations; social activities; and assistance of a local staffer. Rates are $699 to $1,299 per person, double occupancy, for one week, depending on the hotel chosen; extra weeks cost $199 per person.

CONSUMER TITLES CURRENTLY AVA

Magazines

VAC   *Vacations* (new vacation ideas and money-saving tips), 4 quarterly issues for $9.95

TFB   *Travel 50 & Beyond* (the only travel magazine for the 50+ crowd), 4 quarterly issues for $9.95

WTR   *Where to Retire* (helps you find the ideal setting for your new life), 4 quarterly issues for $9.95

Books

DTH   Discount Travel Handbook (everything you need to save money on every trip you take), $14.95

BPR   America's Best Places to Retire (the only guide you need to today's top retirement towns), $14.95

WTF   Where to Retire in Florida (America's most complete guide to retirement areas in the Sunshine State), $13.95

RMA   Retirement Migration in America (the size, trends and economic impact of 4 decades of retirement relocation), $39.95

WHE   Where to Retire (America's best and most affordable places), $14.95

CME   Choose Mexico (live well on $800 a month), $11.95

CCR   Choose Costa Rica (a guide to retirement and investment), $13.95

Special Reports — Travel

SR6   Discounts for Travelers 50 & Beyond, 48 pages, $3.95
SR9   Bargain Hunter's Europe, 48 pages, $3.95
SR10   America's 100 Best Undiscovered Vacation Spots, 48 pages, $3.95
SR11   Florida for Free, 32 pages, $3.95
SR12   America's Most Scenic Drives, 48 pages, $3.95
SR13   Great North American Rail Vacations, 32 pages, $3.95
SR14   Traveling Solo, 48 pages, $3.95
SR15   Guide to Traveling Healthy, 48 pages, $3.95
SR17   A Traveler's Guide to Outlet Malls, 48 pages, $3.95
CPC   Guide to Cruise Discounts, 36 pages, $3.95
CSR   Cruise Ships Rated, 38 pages, $3.95
CPR   Cruise Ports Rated, 52 pages, $3.95
CGF   Guide to Freighter Cruising, 32 pages, $3.95

Special Reports — Retirement Relocation

SR1   How to Plan and Execute a Successful Retirement Relocation, 48 pages, $3.95
SR2   America's Best Neighborhoods for Active Retirees, 64 pages, $3.95
SR3   Tax Heaven or Hell: Ranking 149 Cities and Towns by Tax Burden Placed on Retirees, 96 pages, $4.95
SR4   Should You Retire to a Manufactured Home? 32 pages, $3.95

ABLE AT VACATION PUBLICATIONS

Special Reports — Retirement Relocation (continued)

SR5	Retiring Outside the United States, 32 pages, $3.95
SR7	Guide to Lifelong Learning Opportunities, 48 pages, $3.95
SR8	America's Most Affordable Retirement Towns, 48 pages, $3.95
SR16	Should You Retire to a Continuing-Care Retirement Community? 32 pages, $3.95
SR18	Intangibles Taxes and Source Taxes, 10 pages, $3.95

Special Reports — Creative Retirement

RGH	50 Simple Steps to Good Health in Retirement, 32 pages, $3.95
RFS	30 Simple Steps to a Financially Secure Retirement, 32 pages, $3.95
RHR	50 Simple Steps to a Happy Retirement, 32 pages, $3.95

Special Reports — Personal Finance

MDP	How to Disaster-Proof Your Family's Fortune, 24 pages, $3.95
MFH	Put Your Financial House in Order, 24 pages, $3.95
MNE	Where to Put Your Nest Egg Now, 64 pages, $3.95
MSS	How to Get the Most Out of Your Social Security, 32 pages, $3.95
MTX	How to Slash Your Taxes Now, 32 pages, $3.95

ORDER FORM   Code   Price

Print code and price for each publication selected.   _____   _____

_____   _____

_____   _____

_____   _____

_____   _____

Subtotal _____

Add $2.25 total postage and handling if ordering any Special Report(s) **Postage** _____
Add $2.25 postage and handling for each book ordered **Postage** _____
Texas residents only add 8.25% sales tax **Tax** _____

Total Due _____

Name_____

Address_____

City_____ State_____ Zip_____

Include your payment and return this order form or a copy to: Vacation Publications, 1502 Augusta Drive, Suite 415, Houston, TX 77057. Please allow 4 to 6 weeks for delivery. **Canadian Delivery: Please add $6 U.S. for each magazine and $4 U.S. postage and handling for each book ordered.**

VACATION PUBLICATIONS

For faster service call (713) 974-6903 and order by credit card.